P9-DNA-979

Union Guy

Union Guy

CLAYTON W. FOUNTAIN

New York

THE VIKING PRESS · 1949

PUBLISHED BY THE VIKING PRESS IN FEBRUARY 1949
PUBLISHED ON THE SAME DAY IN THE DOMINION OF CANADA
BY THE MACMILLAN COMPANY OF CANADA LIMITED

PRINTED IN U. S. A. BY AMERICAN BOOK–STRATFORD PRESS, INC., N. Y.

Between the finite limitations of the five senses
and the endless yearnings of man for the beyond
the people hold to the humdrum bidding of work and food
while reaching out when it comes their way
for lights beyond the prison of the five senses,
for keepsakes lasting beyond any hunger or death.

—Carl Sandburg in *The People, Yes*

Dedicated to the memory of the late Eddie Levinson, UAW-CIO Publicity Director from 1938 to 1945, a labor journalist whose love of humanity was expressed in work that helped the author and thousands of other auto workers to see the lights beyond the prison.

Contents

	Foreword	xi
1.	A Yokel on the Loose	3
2.	Detroit Immigrant	15
3.	The Boom-Time Blues	25
4.	Free Enterprise Goes Haywire	34
5.	With My Eyes Wide Open	44
6.	"Arise, Ye Prisoners of Starvation"	56
7.	Politics with Passion	67
8.	A Renegade Is Born	83
9.	New Beginnings	95
10.	Force and Violence	107
11.	Revolution by Thesis	118
12.	"Starve the War . . ."	130
13.	Super-Dupers and Flip-Flops	139
14.	"Forward with Fountain in '42"	149
15.	The Gruesome Twosome	157
16.	A Look at the Books	172

17. Boardwalk Ballet: Act I 187
18. Comrades in Retreat 199
19. Boardwalk Ballet: Act II 201
20. Brotherhood versus Buckshot 216
21. "Give Me Liberty . . ." 226
Index 235

Foreword

This book is my story of the unionization of an American worker—and an American industry.

It does not represent the official viewpoint of my union, the UAW-CIO, or of any of its top leaders. It is simply my own tale of how I came to Detroit reaching for fat paychecks and got hit in the face with a depression; of how I joined a union in self-defense and was sucked into the Communist party; of how I walked out of the party because it violated my freedom, and then helped to clean a lot of Commies out of my union; and of how hard the people in my union are working to make democracy serve the welfare of their communities and their country.

It is intended to give the reader an inside view of the workings of a powerful labor organization, to help to inform him on the labor problems about which so many people shout so loudly and know so little.

I express heartfelt gratitude to Edith Fountain, Frank Winn, Nat Weinberg, Don Montgomery, Paul Sifton, Lewis Corey, Leonard Shatzkin, and Marshall Best for their help in making this book possible.

Dearborn, Michigan
November 1948

CLAYTON W. FOUNTAIN

Union Guy

1. A Yokel on the Loose

A substantial portion of the American populace has been convinced by the press that labor organizers spring full-grown, armed with horns, blackjacks, and brass knuckles, from the womb of some mythical and monstrous she-devil. There is a legend in the land picturing us as a mob of muscular cigar-smoking goons who grow fat and arrogant by snitching sweat-stained dues dollars out of the pockets of masses of browbeaten workers. I suspect that many parents frighten their offspring into obedience by warning them that the CIO porkchoppers will get them if they don't watch out. Even my own people in the backwoods of Northern Michigan give me this line when I go back home for a visit. They are hard put to it to dope out how a youngster from their own ranks, who was only a mediocre devil in his youth, has been transformed into one of the CIO rascals they hear so much about.

My American background is a matter of record—though I am not one to put importance in where a man was born, any more than I care what color his skin is or what church he attends. I was born on April 21, 1909, in a log cabin on the Lake Michigan shore of the Upper Peninsula of Michigan. Scott's Point was the name of the village hidden there in the wilds at that time. It was settled sometime in the 1870's when the Soo Line (short for Minneapolis, St. Paul & Sault Ste. Marie) railroad was built westward from historic Saint Ignace. Construction supplies were unloaded there from Great Lakes steamers and barges, to be hauled on wagons ten miles north to the right-of-way. At the point where the tote road intersected the railroad a settlement called Gould City had been built up as the local seat of government in Newton Township, Mackinac County.

At the time of my birth, Scott's Point was a quiet and peaceful place peopled by the hardy folk who took their livelihood from the blue waters of the lake in the form of whitefish and lake trout. No more than half a dozen gasoline launches, successors to the sturdy sailing schooners originally used for Great Lakes fishing, were moored at the dock jutting out into the lake on the lee side of the point.

The people living at Scott's Point accepted hard work and the hardships of wilderness living as inescapable facts of life. If wind and weather victimized them, they had no choice but to work and sweat all the harder to make up for their bad luck. The price they were paid for their fish shifted up and down with the conditions in the big cities that were their markets, just as the lake itself acted cruelly and kindly in turn, as the weather changed. They had to put up with low prices in the fish market in the same way that they bore the devastation of savage storms, believing the whims of free enterprise to be as inevitable as the gales sweeping across the lake.

During my childhood the citizenry in and around Scott's Point and Gould City operated a kind of primitive mixed economy that was common in the Great Lakes area at the time. Commercial fishing was the major source of ready cash for my particular family, but the folks had other ways of supplementing their livelihood. I can perhaps best explain the diversity of their labors by relating briefly how the family settled in Newton Township.

Andrew Fountain, my paternal grandfather, who was either a full-blooded Chippewa Indian or so close to it that you couldn't tell the difference, brought his French wife, Mary Ann, and his three sons and three daughters to Scott's Point from Mackinac Island. They came in a small sailing schooner laden with their nets, tools, and other worldly goods. My father, Edward Fountain, youngest of the three sons, was just a boy at the time the family took up a homestead of eighty acres. It was located three miles north of the beach and a half-mile east of the gravel road running from Scott's Point to Gould City.

Forty acres were cleared with much hard labor and a log house was built in the center of the clearing, with a barn behind it to house the livestock. After the family got settled, the following division of labor was worked out: In the spring, when the warming sun had melted the snow off the roads and the ice out of the harbor, all hands turned out to launch the boats. It was a festive and ceremonious rite, with all of the fishing families doing their launching on the same day. The boats were skidded down the beach by teams of horses hauling on ropes threaded through pulleys. It was customary to stage the launching on a Saturday. No matter how hard they worked all day, the folks had enough energy left to indulge in an old-time dance in the evening. A local wit called such rustic jamborees "kitchen sweats" because they were mostly put on in the kitchen of the village boardinghouse. Music was furnished by a fiddling French cobbler, who also built the barrels in which the fish was shipped to the cities. Their spirits quickened by snorts of whisky out of jugs fetched from Gould City, the younger fellows sometimes indulged in slugfests on the beach under the moonlight, contesting over the favors of a local beauty.

Once the boats were launched, the younger men, with few exceptions, manned them and labored at the work of harvesting the fish crop. They set the nets, lifted them, mended them, kept the boats in repair, dressed the fish, and packed tons of whitefish and trout in barrels between layers of salt. Later, in my time, ice was substituted for salt, as faster methods of transportation made it possible to ship fresh fish to the big cities. While all this was going on at the beach, the elder men and the women and children worked the land of the homesteads to produce the bulk of the food needed to satisfy pioneer appetites. In my family these workers were Andrew—my grandfather—his daughters and daughters-in-law and their children. They milked the cows which roamed the woods and fields and came home in the evening to their calves imprisoned in crude pole corrals. Each day that the fishermen lifted their nets and had fish to haul to the railroad depot in town (after ice had succeeded salt as a preservative) Andrew took his team of horses to the beach and performed this chore. The round trip was twenty miles. He timed his journey exactly to make the four o'clock train heading toward Milwaukee and Chicago.

At the end of the fishing season, some time in November, the boats were beached again and made secure against the winter. But there was no vacation for their crews in this slack season; they turned their sinews to the task of logging off the virgin timber that forested untracked miles northward from the lake shore. First they took the precious pine and hardwood on their own acres, hauling the logs on homemade bobsleighs to a railroad siding at Gould City. When their own acres were depleted of first-growth timber, they hired out for wages in the employ of jobbers and lumber corporations operating in the area. These timber companies swept through the highlands in a few years, gutting the acres of billions of feet of valuable lumber to satisfy the demands of fast-growing American cities. After denuding the rolling sand hills of pines, and the hardwood forests of their maples, beeches, and birches, the logging crews invaded the swamps to cut "short stuff." Out of these swamps poured a flood of eight-foot sticks of balsam, spruce, cedar, tamarack, and hemlock, to be transformed into pulp and paper.

It was in these logging camps that I first heard a plaintive protest from workingmen against the miserable conditions imposed on them by their bosses. One of the songs they sang while they worked voiced this protest. The important stanza of it went as follows:

Oley Olson is a jobber
Who will go to hell some day
For working men long hours
And cutting down their pay!

The name of the boss varied from camp to camp, but the theme of the complaint was always the same. Organized protest, however, was rare. Dissatisfied workmen usually asked for their time, packed their belongings, and hiked away on foot to seek better conditions.

It was also in and around these logging camps that I first came into contact with Europeans who had fled their homelands to find a richer life. There were many of them employed in a huge camp built by the Wisconsin Land & Lumber Company just a half-mile west of our farm, right at the side of the main road. The crew at this camp was made up almost entirely of Austrians, Poles, Czechs, Hungarians, Slovenians, Croatians, and a swarm of Finns, Swedes, and Norwegians. The natives described the Slavs as "Hunkies" and the Nordics as "Scandyhoovians," exercising the seemingly inevitable human inclination to discriminate against the unfamiliar.

The bulk of these liberty-seeking laborers could speak little or no English. I remember sharply how they trooped past our house, coming and going from the cutting operations, shouting back and forth to each other in their native tongues. Sometimes they sang soft, melancholy songs in minor keys, the words of which were meaningless to me, but the feeling unmistakable. The sad melodies gave one the feeling that these men were laden with loneliness in this cold, wild country thousands of miles from their native lands; a feeling that their hearts were heavy with longing for the loved ones they had left behind, hunger for the places they knew as home.

Thoughts of these immigrant timber workers came back to me many times later during my years in the auto factories of Detroit, where I became intimate with many Poles, Czechs, and Hungarians. Thinking of them makes me remember Archibald MacLeish's poem "Burying Ground by the Ties," in which he wrote this line about immigrant railroad workers: "There were none of us born to be buried in this earth. . . ." That line always seems to me to express the undertone of infinite loneliness in the songs I heard those lumberjacks sing years ago.

Edward Fountain, my father, of whom I have no recollections at all, died at the age of thirty-three when I was but four years old. He succumbed to tuberculosis—then called consumption—spending his last hours in the University of Michigan Hospital at Ann Arbor, Michigan. What I know best about my father is that he was a top-notch woodsman who spent countless happy hours hunting, trapping, and fishing in the territory now designated on the map as Mackinac State Forest. At the time of my birth he ran a small grocery store in the front end of his log cabin at Scott's Point. He also took up a homestead a short distance south of his father's farm.

Death cut short Edward's projected development of these acres in the wilderness. The property reverted to the state. Beyond these fragments of hearsay, I know little of my father's character and capacities except that he was an untrained fiddle player of considerable talent.

My maternal grandfather, Alex Sly, was a local politician of considerable stature. First elected to the Mackinac County Board of Supervisors at the age of thirty, Alex served his constituents in Newton Township in various capacities until his death at the age of seventy-eight. The highest office to which he was ever elected was that of Representative in the State Legislature of Michigan. He served two terms in this capacity and was defeated when he had the audacity to battle the timber barons, who poured money into his district to beat him in the Republican primary election.

Lily Sly Fountain, daughter of Alex, was mothering three youngsters, two sisters and myself, at the time of my father's death. Our family was split up shortly after they buried Edward on a sandy slope in the Newton Township cemetery. The log cabin at Scott's Point was abandoned and I was bundled off to live at Grandfather Andrew Fountain's farm. There I stayed for eleven years, until my grandfather became incurably ill and was carried away to a state hospital, where he died in 1925.

My scholastic experiences began at a little red schoolhouse—it was really red—beside the main road about halfway between our farm and Lake Michigan. Students walked to this school every day, weather permitting, carrying their lunches in tin pails. During those first years of schooling I mastered my lessons easily, and there were probably justifiable grounds for the accusation that I was something of a teacher's pet.

When the tragic time came to take my grandfather to the hospital, there were but three of us left at the homestead: old

Andrew himself, his eldest son Billy, who was my uncle and benefactor, and myself. For the last two troubled years of my residence there, my uncle and myself had our hands full caring for my grandfather. Finally, finding it impossible to manage any longer, we arranged to take him to the hospital, though he fought bitterly to the very end against leaving his acres.

We abandoned the farm then, and my uncle took me some forty miles west to Manistique, Michigan, the seat of Schoolcraft County. My uncle went back to his work as a fisherman at Cheboygan in the Lower Peninsula. He shared his wages with me, sending monthly allowances to pay my board and room and buy my books. I lived in Manistique with my Aunt Angeline, the oldest married sister of my deceased father, a hard-working woman who mothered me as if I had been one of her own children.

Manistique was full of fascination for a juvenile backwoods bumpkin. Its population of some five thousand boasted electric lights, running water, indoor privies, a movie theater, a harbor visited by Great Lakes steamers, and department stores overflowing with marvelous merchandise. Spellbound, I gawked at these entrancing wonders—until I discovered the even more alluring miracles of pool halls and gangs of young males feeling their oats in rowdy games under the street lights at night. As a newcomer, I was promptly challenged to prove my prowess in a wrestling match on the commons, where sand-lot ball games were staged each evening. A city lad was sicked onto me by his fellows while they clustered around us in a circle, waiting to see the invading redskin bite the dust. Though I had little heart for the match, there was no way to escape without showing cowardice, so I took him on. By more good luck than skill, I managed to throw him and pin him to the ground with a speed that surprised me as much as it did him. Thereafter I was accepted as one of the gang —to the despair of my aunt, who thought that I should spend more time on books and less on roughneck games.

The fact was that I did considerable reading—but the books I read did not impress my aunt as being very educational. Not an educated woman herself, she nevertheless felt that I could not improve my mind by poring over volumes written by Edgar Rice Burroughs, Zane Grey, and James Oliver Curwood. The one exception to this diet of blood and thunder was Jack London, whose works I devoured hungrily. This craving for printed matter, which I found time to indulge even while feasting my senses on Manistique's many wonders, had come upon me at an early age. At home on the farm, about the only thing I had had to read—in addition to the Sears Roebuck catalogue—was a weekly paper published in Saint Ignace. One fall a hunter whom one of my uncles was guiding stumbled over me as I lay on the floor engrossed in a chapter of *Tarzan and the Jewels of Opar*, which was running as a serial in the weekly paper.

"You like to read, don't you, son?" he said, beaming at me.

"Uh-huh," I mumbled, turning my eyes again to the deeds of the mighty Tarzan.

At Christmas time that year a box of books came to me from the home of the hunter. It was packed with used volumes, including tales of the exploits of Tom Swift, the Rover Boys, Frank on the Mississippi. I read these prizes over and over again in the following years.

Perhaps it was this passion for adventure novels that helped me to master easily even the more complicated scholastic tasks in the Manistique schools. In the Lakeside Grade School, where I went first, the prim and tiny maiden lady principal named Edna Tucker, whose cold blue eyes glittered through a pair of pince-nez clamped on her angular nose, was much impressed with my capacity for knowledge. I spent just half a semester in the sixth grade under her instructions. Then she graduated me to the Central School downtown, where all students went for their seventh and eighth grade years of schooling.

Edna Tucker, whose mania for discipline and devotion to lessons earned her the hard feelings of most of her pupils, was more than kind to me. The credentials she sent with me to the Central School carried the recommendation that I should skip the seventh grade entirely. She must have carried weight with the authorities, for I was placed in the lowest section of the eighth grade, which was divided into three groups, A, B, and C. The most brilliant students were located in 8A; the mediocre ones were in 8B; while the unruly brutes and the alleged dimwits were relegated to the lowest rank in 8C.

Looking back—for I did not notice it at the time—I am amazed at how closely this academic stratification followed the class lines of the social pattern of the town. The 8A group was graced by the presence of the sons and daughters of bankers, merchants, doctors, lawyers, and prominent dignitaries in the community. 8B contained the children of bank clerks, department store clerks, government employees, and others representative of families of typical middle-class standing in a small American town. 8C, of course, was filled with the ill-clad offspring of the proletarians who toiled in the limekiln, the tannery, the foundry, the paper mill, and the numerous lumber mills.

I was a natural for 8C. My uncle worked in the paper mill and my aunt did laundry and housecleaning work for the parents of the students in 8A. But I promptly proved that the barrier could be scaled by getting promoted—greatly to my own surprise—from 8C to 8A at the end of my first month in that seat of learning. My erstwhile classmates in 8C inclined to look down their noses at me for this betrayal of my class interests. But, since I lived in a working-class neighborhood where few 8A students were to be found, I managed with difficulty to maintain my social contacts with both groups. Needless to say, my industrious aunt was heartened by my step up the scholastic ladder.

In the autumn of 1924 I started attending Manistique High School. My marks continued to be good, though I cannot recall taking any exceptional interest in the subjects I studied, except, perhaps, my course in French. This subject was especially easy for me, since my father's people had spoken a patois variety of French all the time during my earlier childhood in the backwoods. I served as Verse Editor on the staff of the high school paper, a little four-page sheet called *The MHS Crier*. An occasional urge to compose doggerel that scanned and rhymed and was very corny must have been my only qualification for this honor. My good marks, it seems, were not due to any conscious effort to excel in school work. The subjects seemed easy to master, and I rushed through them in order to have more time for planning fishing trips, inventing football plays, and doing odd jobs to earn petty cash to spend in the pool parlors.

It was in high school that I was given a nickname which clung to me until I departed from Manistique in search of adventure. This impromptu christening took place when I went out for the freshman basketball team. The coach, a pleasant Scandinavian chap named Pete Lundeen, not recalling my name at the moment, took one look at the coppery color of my skin, and said: "Hey, Smoky, you play left guard." Manistique knew me as "Smoky" from then on.

Mentioning this earning of a nickname by reason of the color inherited from my Indian ancestors reminds me that this was my first bitter taste of racial discrimination. There were a number of us in that town with various strains of Indian blood in our veins. While we were not segregated, and we had the run of the town socially, there were definite indications that some people felt superior to us simply because they possessed white skins. This feeling of superiority was exhibited in the business of tacking nicknames onto people, if in no other way. I was known as "Smoky"; another lad was dubbed "Tarpoon," an idiomatic variation of tarpaper; still another was branded as "Cooney," reflecting a far-fetched connotation connecting him with the Negro race.

I can't help believing that this early experience kindled in my heart the fierce resentment I feel today against racial prejudice in all of its hateful and unreasonable forms. In my adult life the experience was never repeated, except during a brief period when I hoboed through the Southwest. Then I knew some tense moments involving encounters with racially arrogant railroad detectives who treated me scornfully as a Mexican, for whom their contempt was only a little less than that reserved for the unhappy Southern Negro. I have even had some whites argue fiercely with me that Indians should not be classified with Negroes in discussions of the stupidity of racial prejudice. My argument in these instances is that I am not white, and that, therefore, I cannot find it in me to believe the mental fantasies which some people dream up to support the notion that their white skins make them superior to people with dark skins.

But "Smoky" I was and stayed until the summer of 1927. At that time, while visiting relatives at Gould City, I suddenly decided to go to Escanaba, Michigan, and live with my mother. She was also visiting in Gould City when I arrived at this momentous decision, and her presence may have had a bearing on my flighty action. I was eighteen years old. At this age a fellow gets the feeling that, while he may not be legally mature, he has long pants on and is man enough to make some important decisions. My formal scholastic training ended at that point, for I never returned to win my cap and gown at Manistique High School.

Escanaba was the locality of my official initiation into the ranks of the working class. There I hired out as a grease-monkey in a garage, at an apprenticeship wage set by the boss, who took a dim view of the mechanical talents I assured him I had. Most of my time was spent greasing cars, washing them, and delivering them to owners who were frequently critical of my best efforts with sponge and chamois. But the mechanical "talents" kept popping to the front and finally got me into trouble. One night while the boss was away a customer came in with a crippled windshield wiper. I rattled off some shoptalk about the ways of windshield wipers, and the gentleman must have been impressed, for he returned to his hotel, saying he would call for his car in the morning. I assured him it would be ready, with the recalcitrant wiper in tip-top shape.

Full of confidence, although I had never seen the innards of a windshield wiper, I detached the gadget from its moorings and yanked its working parts out of the housing. In doing so, I hopelessly mutilated a gasket, but I told myself that it would be a small chore to manufacture another one. But somehow the contraption got the best of me. After tearing it down, I just could not get it back together. I gave up that night, went home to bed, and came back early next morning to try a fresh start before the boss arrived. When he did arrive, the wiper was still the top dog;

and right then and there occurred my first experience with the heartlessness of capitalism toward its victims. The boss fired me on the spot, and thus ended my initial venture into the hazards of the wage system.

I loafed for a couple of months and then took off for Toledo with two buddies to get a berth in a ship on the Great Lakes.

2. Detroit Immigrant

We made the trip to Toledo by rail, on borrowed capital, promising to repay the fare out of our first month's pay. My two pals were a year or so older than myself. One of them, the leader of the adventurous trio, had spent a year away from home working in Milwaukee and Chicago, and the other two of us regarded him with the respect due a man of such worldly experience. The jobs on the ship in Toledo had been arranged for us by the uncle of one of my pals, a wizened and strange little man who was the ship's steward. We three youngsters were to be his helpers in the galley. I do not recall the exact rank enjoyed by my two companions, but I was classified as a porter. My job turned out to be that of a kitchen flunky—similar to what we had called a "cookee" in the language of the lumber camps. I set tables, washed endless streams of dishes, pots and pans, and scrubbed floors—or, rather, in the language of the sea, swabbed them. Between sessions of wrestling with utensils in the galley, I was responsible for tidying up the cabins of the first and second mate. For all this I was to receive a wage of seventy-five dollars per month in addition to my board and room.

It was on this ship that I had my first of two experiences with a company union, but I was too green at the time to recognize the beast or to be rightfully outraged by its contaminating touch. We were all signed up, willing or not, in an outfit known as the Lake Carriers' Association, which was vaguely represented to us by the ship's officers as some sort of benevolent brotherhood. It never held meetings, nor did we ever know the identity of its officers. I presume that, if any of us had ever had the gumption or the wits to start organizing a union, we would have been swiftly advised that the Association was a good enough union for our purposes.

My sojourn on the sea, however, turned out to be neither lengthy nor lucrative. I never drew a full month's pay; in fact, I didn't even sail outside the harbor of Toledo. Our longest and most exciting cruise was a twenty-minute trip from one wharf to another. We kept our berths just about two weeks—long enough to go downtown one Saturday night to gawk at the carnal wonders of my first burlesque show. Then calamity exploded unexpectedly in our faces.

It seemed that the steward who had buttoned up our jobs and his own had been quietly losing his mind. The poor chap was seized with spells of depression; he talked to himself loudly about matters completely strange to his fellows; and he took to forgetting what he was doing and turning his attention elsewhere in the middle of vital tasks in the galley. Naturally, the captain had to let him go, and his three helpers were given the gate along with him. It was a custom on the lakes then for the steward to hire his own help, and, of course, the new steward was bringing his own flunkies.

We could have used a grievance procedure right then, if that Lake Carriers' Association had boasted any such useful feature, but it didn't. The lack of devices to protect the unfortunate workman from unjust firings is one of the distinguishing marks of the company union. But I was still too innocent—even after this second knockout punch tossed at me by capitalism—to comprehend that I was a victim of the rough working conditions on the lakes, which finally led to the organization of a militant seamen's union.

So, in my ignorance, I put the episode down as a turn of hard luck and focused my thoughts on the knotty problem of what to do next. I did not have enough cash to finance the trip back to the Upper Peninsula of Michigan, and I did not relish the prospect of writing home to beg for more capital. In desperation,

I hit upon the scheme of going to Detroit to crash the gates of the automobile factories. In that city, according to the stories I had heard from workers who had worked in the auto plants, fabulous wages were paid in the shops that turned out millions of cars every year. Besides, I had a sister living there who might be good for a touch or know somebody with influence enough to wangle me a job in one of the auto plants. A more compelling factor shaping my strategy was the fact that I had only a couple of bucks more than enough to pay my fare on the interurban electric train from Toledo to Detroit.

It was on a hazy evening in April 1928, and I was just nineteen years old, when I stepped off the interurban car on West Fort Street in the shadow of the towering Penobscot Building. Bag in hand, my eyes staring at the bright lights and the streams of noisy traffic, I made my way up Griswold Street to Capitol Park. There a kindly cop told me how I could catch a Grand River streetcar. The conductor on the car was also friendly. He promised to let me off at the number I asked him about.

When I arrived at the number—it was an upstairs apartment over a meat market—I was dismayed to find that no one answered the bell. I waited a while, brooding over what to do if no one showed up or if I had the wrong number, then walked a block to a restaurant and spent fifty cents of my last two dollars for a couple of pork chops.

Looking back, I am amused at the ironic symbolism of that first meal I devoured in the city of motors, for I am today described by the dues-payers who support me as a "porkchopper." This term, applied with impartial regularity to all auto worker unionists who contrive to get out of the shop and on the union's payroll, is a variation of the old IWW[1] title of "pie-card artist." We have "big porkchoppers," meaning the union's top officers, whose salaries are somewhat fatter than those of the ordinary organizers, sometimes referred to as "little porkchoppers." In the rough-and-tumble political battles within the union the term sometimes carries a connotation of contempt—but, on the other

[1] Industrial Workers of the World, one of the first American industrial unions, now defunct. It flourished prior to and during World War I.

hand, I have heard rank-and-file convention delegates orate at length in utter sincerity on behalf of a raise in pay for the "pork-choppers, who have done a damn good job for this union."

But that night in Detroit, as I chomped away on my pork chops, my mind had not even begun to travel the long road that was to lead me up to the position of porkchopper on the payroll of the UAW-CIO. I was worried about my finances, of course, but the sorry state of my bank roll did not impel me to blame my hardship on the economic conditions of the country. Being broke, it seemed to me, was a small matter of stumbling momentarily into a pitfall of ill fortune. Who knew what tomorrow would bring? Perhaps in two weeks I would be filling a vital spot on one of Mr. Henry Ford's assembly lines, and possessed of a fat paycheck that would enable me to spit in the eye of the demon hard luck.

As it turned out, my actual induction into the auto industry was delayed for three months. During that interval, at the beginning of which my sister and her friends did help me out financially, I went swiftly through an assortment of odd jobs.

A young policeman, who was married to a very good friend of my sister, got me my first Detroit job as a kind of combination dishwasher and assistant short-order cook. This post was in a tiny hot dog and hamburger joint on Fenkell Avenue, better known then as Five Mile Road, away out in Brightmoor, a suburb on the northwest fringe of the city. It was certainly no promotion from my berth on the ship in Toledo; in fact, it was a demotion, for the job paid less money and I had to find a place to room at my own expense. This was no place for a lad bent on getting on in the world, I told myself as I peeled potatoes or slapped mustard on smoking wieners.

In rapid succession thereafter I toiled as a grease-monkey on a used car lot, as a landscaper's aide, and as a truck driver for another landscaper. But as I flitted across the fields of free enterprise, leaping from one green pasture to another, the dream of a job in an auto plant was always uppermost in my mind. I spent hours questioning the men in blue denim shirts, with lunch boxes under their arms, whom I met in hashhouses and pool halls, about where to get a job. The city was always full of rumors about which shop was hiring what classifications.

One worker would tell me, "They was hiring punch-press operators yesterday at Chrysler's." Another would say that he had heard that "Ford took on a mess of grinders last week." Still another would advise me: "If you go out to Dodge's early tomorrow morning, you'll get on as an export boxer, sure enough." Tirelessly, in odd hours when I was off duty from the various boring jobs that provided me with meals and beds, I rode the streetcars and buses out to the employment offices of auto plants, eager to have a personnel man give me the nod.

One morning in August I eased my way into the employment office at the Packard plant, and Lady Luck smiled at me at long last. When my place in the line of applicants came up to the man behind the desk, he glanced at me and said in a mechanical tone, "What can you do?"

"Oh, I can run punch presses, drill presses, lathes, and grinders," I lied earnestly in what I hoped was a convincing voice.

"What kind of punch presses can you operate?" he came back at me, his eyes boring into mine with a glare asserting his certainty that I was lying.

"Any kind at all—Toledos, Blisses, Hamiltons," I responded with forced confidence. I had learned the names of the machines from the men I queried about jobs, memorizing them for just such an occasion.

"Okay, step over there and the clerk will write you up," he said, motioning me out of the line and turning his glare on the next eager job seeker.

Happily, but with my nerves tense and trembling, I answered the questions fired at me by a bored clerk who filled out my employment record. He classified me as a press operator, told me my wages would be fifty cents an hour and bonus, and that I would work the night shift in LH Department starting at six that evening. I was whisked through a quick but basic physical examination, for the auto industry liked its young workers to be in good condition; otherwise they could not keep up with the pace of the mass-production machines. Then I was given a temporary badge and instructed to report back for the night shift. As I left the plant to hurry back to my rooming house and tell of my good fortune, a surge of fellowship impelled me to pause and tell the fellows standing in line that they were hiring press operators inside.

It occurs to me now that I had been able to go to the Packard plant that morning because I had been fired from my job of driving a truck for a landscaper the week before. The boss had decided to reduce the working force—and that meant me. Since I was the only employee, he laid me off with the usual regrets, and took to driving the truck himself. Thus, at the time of my induction into the auto industry, I was not only jobless but penniless as well. In fact, I had financed the excursion to Packard's with carfare borrowed from my landlady.

Happily, I returned to tell this generous friend of my good fortune. She assured me that she would extend my credit until I had my first payday, and urged me to try to get some sleep before going back to the plant that evening. I tried hard to follow her advice, but it was no go. Each time I closed my eyes, visions of hundred-dollar paychecks danced in front of them. Daydreams full of new suits and Saturday nights with a pocketful of dough to spend in the speakeasies floated through my mind. I was just too excited to sleep.

That afternoon, armed with a borrowed lunch box and more borrowed carfare, I set off at four-thirty on my way to make my debut as a machine-tender in the throbbing heart of the mass-production world. Shoulders high and chest stuck out, with the justified pride of a nineteen-year-old yokel making the grade in a big city, I joined the ranks of the auto workers. While eight hectic years were yet to pass before I became conscious enough of my proletarian environment to join the ranks of the insurgent CIO movement, my actual experience as an auto worker began that night in August 1928. Overflowing with ignorance and ambition, I took my place in the army of machine-tenders destined to smash tradition a decade later with their sit-down strikes.

After ringing in my time-card, I stood around with a small group of other recruits waiting to be assigned to a job. The stamping department at Packard's was housed in a long, low one-story building containing row upon row of clattering, thumping machines. There were tiny presses no higher than a man's head, which blanked out and formed small parts; and there were enormous toggle presses that nearly touched the roof, which formed such parts as fenders, cowls, and quarter-panels with a single crunching stroke of the gigantic dies. Smoke swirled between the machines from operations where such deep-drawn parts as headlight shells were heated on gas flames to anneal the metal for easier stretching under the pressure of the dies. Electric trucks scurried back and forth, laden with parts; and overhead cranes juggled huge dies and heavy bundles of sheet steel.

My first assignment was that of helper on a square shear. Apparently my line about my skill as a press operator had not registered with enough force to get me that classification right away. Undoubtedly the employment office was accustomed to dealing with applicants who lied about their skill. At any rate the job given to me that first night required no other qualifications than the traditional "strong back and weak mind" necessary for most unskilled occupations in industry.

A square shear is a sort of hungry mechanical guillotine which consumes unlimited quantities of sheet steel during a shift. On occasion it bites off the fingers and hands of workers who are so unlucky or careless as to thrust their members into its jaws at the wrong moment. But it is one of the least dangerous machines in an auto plant, due to the limited area of hazard under its blade.

The job-setter entrusted with the task of breaking me in took me over to where a middle-aged Pole was cutting sheets of steel into two equal pieces on a square shear. He showed me how to stand behind the machine and take the end of a sheet of steel, pull it up snug against a gauge and hold it there while the operator on the other side stepped on the treadle that caused the blade to descend. At the conclusion of the cut, I piled the sheets up to be hauled away on an electric high-lift truck. This was my introduction to the monotony of most mass-production operations in a big factory. I don't know how many sheets of steel I slid off the bed of that shear onto the pile at my right that night.

Pull the sheet up against the gauge, hold it there for the cut, take it away and put it on the pile—and repeat, over and over and over again. My cotton gloves were cut to shreds by the sharp edges of the sheets long before the night was over; I reinforced them with old discarded ones retrieved from the rubbish cans. But even then I cut my hands in several places; however, I was too proud to go to the first-aid station. They were just small cuts and did not bleed much.

Long before morning I felt the dragging weight of fatigue that comes on during a twelve-hour shift—especially a night shift. Accustomed to sleeping nights—or at least the latter portion of them, after I had come in from tomcatting—I felt my eyes getting heavier and heavier along about two in the morning. I had to fight to keep them open.

"Go sleep a few minutes in the crapper," the operator told me the next time we had a break to adjust the gauges for a differently sized cut. "Then wash your face in cold water; you'll feel better."

I took his advice and learned my first trick as a night shift worker in the auto industry. Sitting on a stool in the can, elbows on knees and my face in my hands, I dozed off for about ten minutes in spite of the terrific clamor of the huge presses nearby. But I had made the mistake of taking my nap just before the plant protection watchman came through on his hourly round to snoop for workers smoking, loafing, or sleeping in the toilet. I awoke to the pressure of his heavy hand shaking my shoulder.

"Better get back on the job, bud," he said. This first brush with a company cop was mild, but it kindled a prejudice against them that grew with the years, culminating when two of them threw me out of the Chevrolet plant in 1937, as I shall relate in a later chapter. That night I just nodded obediently, washed my face in cold water, and went back, feeling somewhat better, to pile up more hundreds of sheets of steel.

I thought six o'clock would never come—and before it did, at five-thirty, the straw boss came by and told us to work overtime until seven-thirty, the starting time of the day shift. The extra time meant more cash on payday, of course, but by that time I was far too groggy to be spending my dollars before I had earned them. It was just another hour and a half of torture. I no longer dreamed of new suits and excursions to speakeasies; all I could think of was that wonderful soft bed waiting for me at the rooming house. When the shift finally ended and I did get home to bed, my dreams were full of scenes in which I went on piling sheet steel, and I awoke in the early afternoon still dazed and groggy.

The stamina of youth carried me through those first weeks of working twelve hours and more a night, and I was promoted to more interesting jobs. From helper on a square shear I graduated to operator and gloried in my own prideful moments of breaking in new helpers. Then I became a helper on a big Bliss press that formed headlight shells. On this job I simply leaned against the back of the press and pulled the shells out of the die after they were formed and tossed them into a truck. Then the operator took off one night, and I was entrusted with the task of running the press all by myself. After about a month on the job I had a press of my own and was setting my own dies. In six weeks' time I had become so proficient that I was operating a multiple-die press, with four helpers putting radiator shells in the dies and taking them out while I proudly stood at the controls timing the up-and-down motions of the ram.

The work was hard, the hours were long, and the pay was not too bad—I averaged between forty and fifty dollars a week—but the romance of working in an auto plant soon began to wear off. I began to think of getting into another business, one that could provide excitement and adventure in addition to substantial paychecks. Somehow I hit upon the notion of becoming an aviator. Commercial aviation schools were going strong in Detroit at that time. Acting upon my impulse, I started attending one of these, building new dreams of a glorious and swaggering career as a pilot. But half-way through the course I caught a bad cold, stayed home from work for three days, and, when I went back to the plant, found my card pulled from the rack because I had been too dumb to call in and report the reason for my absence. So ended my job at Packard's and my career as a pilot, all in one stroke of ill fortune.

Again the lack of a grievance procedure had caused my downfall in an industry in which the bosses had all the say, with no way open for workers to appeal their rulings. But I still had a long way to go before I would understand the necessity of organizing unions to protect workers from such injustices. During the period between my hiring in August and my firing in November I heard no discussion of unionism at the Packard plant, and probably would have paid small heed if someone had tried to interest me in such a profound problem. There were heated debates concerning the respective merits of Hoover and Al Smith, I recall, but I was too young to vote and had no time for politics anyway.

Full of confidence from the experience gained at Packard's, I started looking for another job.

3. The Boom-Time Blues

In November 1928 Detroit was riding merrily along on the boom destined to blow up in the face of the nation a year later. Herbert Hoover was elected President to continue the works of Harding and Coolidge, whose administrations had given business a free hand to begin the job of putting two chickens in every pot. It was not long before millions of Americans were wondering where to get a pot, let alone chickens to put in it, but the voters who backed Mr. Hoover were blissfully unaware of the impending dark days when he was to peer vainly around corners in quest of elusive prosperity.

It was during this lull before the economic storm of the great depression that I made the acquaintance of a lad whom I shall call Andy, who was to have a profound influence on my life. At that time I was chasing around Detroit with the son of my benevolent landlady, making merry in the blind pigs frequented by workers during the days of prohibition. It was on a Saturday night junket to a blind pig that I met Andy. We promptly became fast friends, although we had little in common except the youthful energy we spent in tearing around at night. He was short, quick to act, aggressive, and more than a little belligerent, while I was tall, seemingly stoical, and timid.

This friendship started off a chain of events which, at the time, seemed to lead nowhere in particular, but which eventually built up to the beginnings of my activity in the labor movement. To begin with, Andy took me out on a blind date with two very young waitresses named Dorothy and Lee, who worked in a hamburger stand known as Daddy Jack's Place out on Telegraph Road. He had a 1927 Ford roadster—some class in those days—in which we took the gals out to movies and dances. Stricken by the romantic zeal that often smothers the judgment of youths of nineteen, I got the notion of getting married to Lee, who was just sixteen herself. Of course, we were just foolish kids, as I now understand. But at the time it seemed the only thing in the world to do. However, despite the powerful pressure of my romantic urge, I had to have a job before I could get married. So, once again—this time driven by one of the most potent motivations known to the human race—I stepped up my efforts to get back into an auto plant. It didn't take me long.

My second venture as an auto worker was in the Briggs body plant away out on the east side of Detroit. This plant is called the Briggs Mack Avenue plant. I got my job there by a strange whim of circumstance.

While working at Packard's I had made arrangements to buy a suit of clothes from a guy I knew who had lost his job as a policeman and was selling men's garments while keeping on the lookout for more suitable work. The sale took place in a poolroom. I chose a fabric, he took my measurements, and then he took me financially, for he left with half the price of the suit, and I did not see him again for a long time. Four months later, in January 1929, I ran into this same chap in a blind pig. He seemed to be flush, so I put the bite on him for a refund of my down payment on the suit, explaining that I was out of work and very hard up for ready cash.

He apologized and made some excuse to cover up his failure to deliver the suit, then asked me if I wanted a job. It turned out that he was a plant protection guard at the Briggs Mack plant. He assured me that, if I would look him up at the employment office, he would get me in easily. The next day I was Johnny-on-the-spot to hold him to his promise. He met me at the gate, took me into the employment office, and I was quickly assigned to an assembly line on the third floor of the plant that built Ford backs and seat cushions. Here I made the acquaintance of the piecework system, sometimes politely called incentive pay, which is supposed to reward wage workers with the fruits of individual initiative in a competitive society. All production workers were paid under the piecework system in the Briggs plant at that time.

I was given the classification of "hog-ringer," which sounds like something to do with pigs on a farm. Actually, the tool I used was a hog-ringer, the same kind used on farms to squeeze wire rings into the snouts of pigs to discourage the porkers from rooting up the sod. In a body plant the rings are used to fasten the fabric of backs and seat cushions to the wire springs inside these parts.

The backs and cushions were fabricated on a conveyor which consisted of a long, endless, heavy canvas belt running past the workers at waist-high level. The first worker on the line threw the springs on the belt along with a wooden frame. The next two workers, one on each side of the line, fastened the springs to the frame with short nails. Another worker placed a cotton pad on the springs, covered it with a piece of stout unbleached sheeting and turned the job upside down with a heave of his powerful arms. Then we hog-ringers did our stuff.

There were two of us on each side of the line; one team worked on backs, the other on cushions. As the cushions moved past us, we grabbed the sheeting at one corner, pulled it through a coil in the springs and fastened it there with a single hog-ring. These corners had to be shaped just so, or the inspectors would send them back for repairs, and somebody would catch hell from the straw boss if there were too many such rejects. With the cushion still moving past us, we fastened the sheeting to the coils all along the edge, and then finished off by making another corner. The cushions and backs came down the line alternately; when one of us finished a job, he had to step back and duck around his neighbor to get at the next job. The corners on the backs had to be shaped a certain way, somewhat in the fashion of sheets tucked at the corner of a bed.

Our particular line handled backs and cushions for one of the Ford models that was very much in demand. It was a typical mass-production operation. Next to the hog-ringers was a crew of girls who stitched the fabric of the cushion cover to the springs with heavy needles by looping stout twine to a steel wire running down the center of the cushion. The job was tough, and we had to work fast, but we fellows always found time to fuss around with these gals, asking them for dates or reaching down the line to give one of them a pinch or a pat. Most of the gals were buxom Polish lasses—they had to have muscle to stand the gaff—who endured our sportiveness with tolerant good nature. They cracked back at us with ready wits, belittling our boasted amatory powers and advising us to take our passions to the Hamtramck[1] brothels.

The Briggs plant was notorious at that time as a sweatshop, a place that paid low wages and worked the folks in the plant until their fannies were dragging. Working conditions were lousy in all the auto plants, but Briggs was one of the worst. Only four years after I worked there the Briggs plants were involved in the strike of 1933, one of the first in the auto industry, which was largely engineered by a few Communists. Even as early as 1929 there were rumblings of discontent among the workers.

Our major gripe was the piecework system. I don't recall exactly what our piece rate per cushion was at the time, but we made something like about $6.50 or $7.00 a day. According to the theory of incentive pay, the harder and faster you worked, and the more cushions you turned out, the more pay you received. The employer, however, reserved the right to change the rules. We would start out with a new rate, arbitrarily set by the company time-study man, and work like hell for a couple of weeks, boosting our pay a little each day. Then, bingo, the timekeeper would come along one morning and tell us that we had another new rate, a penny or two per cushion less than it had been the day before.

One day when this happened we got sore and rebelled. After lunch the whistle blew and the line started up, but not a single worker on our conveyor lifted a hand. We all sat around on cushions waiting to see what would happen.

In a few minutes the place was crawling with big shots. They

[1] A municipality surrounded by the city of Detroit and largely populated by Polish industrial workers.

stormed and raved and threatened, but our gang stood pat. We just sat on the cushions and let them rant and blow. When they got too abusive, we talked back and told them to go to hell. We told them that the Briggs plant was run by a bunch of rats who did nothing but scheme how to sweat more production out of workers and that we didn't care a damn how many of us they fired; we just weren't going to make any more cushions or backs at the new low rate.

We didn't belong to a union and we had no conception of organization. There were no leaders chosen by us to deal with the angry bosses; we all pitched into the verbal free-for-all with no epithets barred. Some of the workers threatened to take the bosses outside and beat hell out of them—in fact, they had a damn good notion to do it right then and there inside the plant.

Finally, after about forty-five minutes of confusion, the bosses relented. They agreed to reinstate the previous piecework rate. With this assurance, we went back to work. Looking back, I can see that, in a small and disorganized fashion, we tasted the power of the sit-down strike on that far-away day in the Briggs plant in 1929. Though I was ignorant of its significance at the time, that little "quickie" of ours was an omen of the historic days for labor that were not too many years away. By 1933 there was sufficient discontent among the Briggs workers to ignite a plant-wide strike, and the passage of another four years found the Briggs workers marching with their fellows from the other auto plants in the victorious uprising of 1937. But I personally had a long way to go before taking my place in the ranks of the insurgent auto workers.

In April 1929, one week before I was twenty years old, and against the advice of most of my few intimates in Detroit, I got married to the sixteen-year-old waitress named Lee Taylor. We celebrated the event with two quarts of prohibition gin in a little wooden house owned by her father, who rented it to us for twenty-five dollars a month. This wedding seems to me now to have typified the era of the boom-time blues, when American capitalism, out on a spree and heading for a bust and a big hangover, was figuratively starting to look for a lamppost to cling to.

I think I was a typical young American worker caught in the

web of merry madness in which all America threshed about during the years just before the depression. After working hard for a long shift in the factory, I sought relaxation in movies, dances, and bouts with bottles of prohibition liquor. We tore around at night in automobiles, speeding from one blind pig to another, banging away on ukuleles and singing such tunes as "Me and the Man in the Moon" at the top of our voices. Perhaps this period was a mixture of a hangover from World War I, the frustrations of prohibition, and the "easy come, easy go" economic attitudes of pre-depression America. At any rate, I have the feeling now that it was something about the mood of America at that time which impelled me to get married at the youthful age of twenty years.

Three months after the wedding, with the characteristic irresponsibility of youth, I decided that it was all a mistake, and that Detroit lacked in opportunities; so I set off on another jaunt, leaving my wife to shift for herself. Andy and I set out in his 1927 Ford Model T roadster for California.

We got as far as Kansas City and went broke. The Ford roadster ate up our funds by burning out connecting rods every two or three hundred miles—we finally sold it in order to keep on eating. Then I got a job running a punch press in a small shop that manufactured beauty compacts. For the same kind of work that had paid me as much as fifty dollars a week at Packard's in Detroit, I got fifteen dollars a week in Kansas City. But hard luck came to my rescue. One night the punch press clipped off the first joint of the second finger on my right hand—and the boss paid me off with a cash award of $150. It was the most money I had ever had in my hands at one time. We got a suite in a hotel and pitched a magnificent drunk with apricot brandy. When the hangover had receded, we quit our jobs and divided up what cash I had left. Andy decided to go back to Detroit. I took off for Galveston, Texas, on a Kansas City Southern freight train with a chap named George Haynes. My new friend had been to sea a couple of times; he was to get us berths on a ship in Galveston. We were going to see the world from a porthole.

Again my plans went haywire. I could not get a job on a ship in Galveston, because I did not have a birth certificate and could not get a passport. We drifted eastward from Galveston to New Orleans, spending a few days in the clink on charges of vagrancy in Beaumont and Orange on the way. In New Orleans we lived on the docks for a couple of weeks, eating bananas and coconuts and bumming meals off the ships.

On a rainy night in October we caught an Illinois Central freight going north. I planned then to ride the boxcars all the way back home to the Upper Peninsula of Michigan. Somewhere between Jackson, Mississippi, and Memphis, Tennessee, George and I got separated—I think it was at the little town of Laurel, Mississippi. I jumped off a freight in the dark, and I never saw George again. Perhaps the railroad dicks caught him, or perhaps he was fed up with my company and just stayed on that boxcar. I have often wondered what happened to him.

The next morning I made my way into Memphis, Tennessee, by myself. Wise in the ways of hoboing by now, I asked my way to the Salvation Army, intending to bum a breakfast. I got a job as well as a breakfast. My duty was to assist the driver of a truck who hauled waste paper from the Memphis Ford assembly plant to the Salvation Army warehouse. One day the driver went on a binge and didn't come back, and I was promoted to his job. Then I went on a binge, in January 1930, and got picked up by the cops and sent to the Shelby County Workhouse for a ten-day stretch. There I got a taste of the Southern penal system. We were taken out in trucks to work on the roads—and we worked in chains. Our shackles were riveted onto our ankles each morning and cut off at night. Some of the guards carried whips, some carried clubs—and all carried guns.

When I finished my sentence, I went back to the Salvation Army, before taking to the road again, to get some clothes that I had accumulated. In a hamburger joint across the street from the "Sally," as we called the place, I met a tall Southerner named Bill Davis. He hired me to drive a tractor on the plantation where he served as overseer. I spent the balance of the winter and part of the spring of 1930 with Davis in Millington, Tennessee, working cotton and corn land with a tractor. This was my first contact with sharecroppers. There may have been a faint stirring of social rebellion in me at this time. It burned me up to see how the owners of the land kept the sharecroppers in debt to them all the time. It burned me up even more to see how the whites lorded it over the Negroes and kicked them around just for the hell of it. I remember one big jolly Negro named Clint Cobb, who carried me to the house on his broad back when I sprained my ankle in the field. He was as gentle and kind as any human could be. Later I loaned him money to buy a new plow, and I shall never forget the amazed joy on his face when I agreed to help him out.

Early in the spring of 1930 I returned to Detroit on a bus, all unaware that prosperity had skidded into the ditch of a depression while I was away. I had not read the papers in Tennessee, and a radio was an unheard of luxury among the sharecroppers with whom I lived and worked, so I was almost totally ignorant of the hard times that had hit the industrial centers of the nation. It took several months for the depression to catch up with me economically, since I had the good fortune to get a job almost as soon as I landed back in Detroit.

My wife's father, George Taylor, who had many years of seniority as a truck driver with the Public Lighting Commission, managed to get me a job. Frank Murphy, who later served as Governor of Michigan and was appointed an Associate Justice of the United States Supreme Court, was then Mayor of Detroit. His administration tried to relieve unemployment by completing public works projects. I went to work as a laborer on one of the projects engaged in servicing the Detroit street lighting system.

There have been many gripes about the lot of a ditchdigger, but I can honestly say that I enjoyed working as a laborer for the Detroit Public Lighting Commission. I earned something like twenty-seven dollars a week, which was enough to enable my wife and myself to live fairly well. The job required me to work eight hours a day and four hours on Saturday. Perhaps the best feature of the job was the absence of the speed-up mania that I had learned to hate in the auto plants. We put in a fair day's work and that was all that was expected of us. The bosses did not hound us all through the shift to throw more dirt out of the ditches, tunnels, and foundation holes in which we worked. We could smoke on the job and stop a few minutes to gas with our fellow workmen when we felt like it. When the weather was good there was something positively satisfying about the scent of the broken earth and the physical effort involved in working in and around it. On payday we even took off for twenty minutes to get our checks cashed and have a quick beer in a nearby blind pig, and no one raised hell about it. I met men on that job, especially a few Italians, who had a philosophical aversion to earning their living in any way other than by outside construction work. They would not think of going into a factory, holding that outside work is much better for a man's body and soul. I learned while working on this job that there is much to this philosophy—for I enjoyed working in the sun and wind.

In February 1931 my wife bore me a daughter whom we named Dolores Jean. Two weeks after her arrival the depression caught up with us. The funds appropriated by the city administration to finance the project I was working on ran out; the foreman came around and passed out lay-off slips to all but a handful of the oldest workers on the crew.

Two and a half years were to pass before I again got my hands on a regular paycheck.

4. Free Enterprise Goes Haywire

Unemployed again, but now with a wife and an infant daughter to provide for, I was promptly inducted by necessity into that hapless legion of men who haunted the welfare offices in Detroit during the depression. Unable to pay rent, we doubled up with my wife's aunt and uncle in a tiny three-room shack. The house was one of many built by workers with their own hands, clustered into a working-class community known as Elmoor. Most of the buildings had water, but few of them had bathrooms or basements. They had outdoor privies in the back yards similar to those we had always used up north on the farm—the only difference being that the metropolitan models were equipped with back editions of the *Detroit News*, the *Detroit Times*, and the *Detroit Free Press* instead of the customary mail order catalogues.

There were seven of us, four adults and three children, crowded into a building that was certainly no bigger than a two-car garage. It had one bedroom, a living room, and a tiny kitchen. At night we packed ourselves away into one three-quarter bed, a crib, and a folding bed. The place was heated with a large coal-burning stove, and we cooked with a kerosene range. When it was time to cook a meal or do a washing, the men had to go outside to get out from under the feet of the women.

My wife's uncle was a native Michigander like myself, who worked in good times as a painter. I don't think he ever belonged to a union or thought much about organized labor as such, but he had plenty to say about the hardship of the depression. He used to turn on the radio and listen closely to Jerry Buckley, a news commentator who was sympathetic with the thousands of unemployed workers roaming the streets. Buckley was later murdered by gangsters who were hooked up in some way with a political scandal under the administration preceding Frank Murphy's regime as Mayor.

After Buckley was killed we fell into the habit of listening to Father Coughlin, whose Sunday afternoon broadcasts were beginning to attract widespread comment and attention among the unemployed. When we went to the welfare station to get our weekly pittance, the men hanging around on the park benches in the waiting rooms would hash over the Royal Oak priest's latest blast at the bankers. Having learned later how Hitler employed the technique of demagogy to ride to power in Germany, I can remember that the conversations in those relief offices revealed a smoldering desire to follow a leader—any leader who promised to promote security—in order to escape the misery of the depression.

At first we had to ride buses and streetcars, spending precious pennies for carfare, to get our relief checks: most of the few relief offices were located in the central part of the city. Later, branches were opened in the outlying districts, close enough for us to walk to them. As the bitter months dragged on and prosperity stayed so well hidden around Mr. Hoover's corner that no one seemed capable of luring it out, the resentment of the workers flamed higher and higher. By the winter of 1932 thousands of us had given up hunting for jobs. In a few places bands of desperate men raided grocery stores at night and carried supplies of food home to their families. I was never personally involved in any of these expeditions, but I knew some men who were, and nearly all of my jobless acquaintances applauded the looting of the stores.

On March 7, 1932, the Communists organized the hunger march of the unemployed to the gates of the Ford River Rouge plant. Four men were killed by machine guns. Harry Bennett, head of the Ford Service Department—a polite title for what was then a very efficient and ruthless goon squad—was beaned with a flying brick. Early the next day, March 8, my son Ronald was delivered by a city physician who resented having to drive out to where we lived through a severe snowstorm. I read about the Ford hunger riot in the papers that day as I welcomed the arrival of the addition to my family—aside from the usual reasons—because his presence would force the welfare to increase the size of my relief check. With a family of four to feed, I was entitled to $4.90 per week—about as much as I now get clipped for a drink and a steak when I dine in a hotel.

That summer the depression hit bottom for our family group when my father-in-law was laid off from his job as a city truck driver in spite of his ten years of seniority. So he joined us on our weekly trips to the welfare office. But we were not satisfied with our allowances, and so we figured out a way to supplement our incomes. One night when we were driving home from a fishing trip in my father-in-law's battered 1928 Chevrolet, we passed a farmer's field of ripe corn. We parked the car in a dark spot, invaded the field, and loaded our arms with heavy roasting ears. Next day we feasted on corn and fish.

Then it dawned on us that we could go back and get more of the corn and maybe peddle it from house to house. We quickly put the idea into action. Two or three nights a week we drove into the country and raided some unfortunate farmer's corn field. We scattered our raids around, never going back to the same neighborhood twice in a row. Then we peddled the stuff from house to house for fifteen cents per dozen ears. Down the street we went, glibly misrepresenting our wares. "Fresh sweet corn," we shouted at the top of our voices. It was only field corn, but what did we care; we did not peddle the same streets again.

After a few such ventures, we had a scanty supply of capital to invest in a stock of fruits and vegetables. We quit stealing corn then and, like all good honest capitalists, bought produce as low as possible and sold it for all that the traffic would bear. I don't particularly want to defend those corn-stealing raids, which were made under stress and in the heat of youth; but after digesting many books on political economics I am not so sure that we violated the accepted practices of capitalism. Many a private enterprise has been founded on property filched from others.

Circumstances forced me to commit another act, which I confess was morally wrong, in that very tough summer of 1932. Early in the morning, in a car, along with one or two unemployed buddies, we invaded Rosedale Park, a nearby residential district inhabited by some of Detroit's swankiest aristocratic families, to swipe milk from their porches. We justified this pilfering with the old Robin Hood theory that it was okay to steal from the rich to help the poor. Anyway, we tempered our raids with a perverse sense of fairness. We never stole all of anyone's milk. Cruising along slowly, we passed up the porches with only one or two quarts. But the houses supplied with three or more quarts were the ones we tapped. We always left our victims one quart for their breakfast. And we never touched the coffee cream at all.

In the fall of 1932 I was old enough to vote, being then twenty-three and never having cast a ballot before. I voted a straight Democratic ticket along with the millions of other hungry Americans driven by the old American feeling that "it was time for a change." Rarely have I missed an election since that desperate day when a worried people swept Franklin D. Roosevelt into office.

By the spring of 1933 the future had begun to look just a little brighter. The papers were full of the promises of the NRA, and word began to get around that some of the shops were hiring a few men. There was an immediate rush for the employment offices; workers who had given up all hope of ever getting a job again began to get up in the middle of the night to travel miles across the city and stand in long lines of job seekers.

Up until July my search for a job was fruitless. Week after week I went to the plants and stood in the long lines of expectant men who filed through the employment offices. I went to the Chrysler plants, the Briggs plant, the Packard plant, and many others, but it was no use. The lines were so long sometimes that hundreds of men were in them hours before the gates opened. When the weather was bad we built fires to keep warm. Those who had food enough in the house to spare brought lunches. Often we slept on the ground to hold our precious places in the line. There were card games and long discussions of our troubles. Each day just enough men were hired to keep hopes alive in the hearts of those who did not make it.

One evening we had a visit at home from a distant relative of my wife who was a foreman in the maintenance department at the Chevrolet gear and axle plant, one of the largest divisions of General Motors in Detroit. I told him of my vain attempts to get a job.

"I think I can help you out," he said.

"What can you do?" I asked, not daring to hope that he really could do anything helpful.

"They're putting on a third shift out at the shop, and I know they'll be hiring quite a few men—maybe I can get you in."

"Are they hiring punch press operators?" I asked more hopefully.

"Yes, I'm pretty sure they are," he replied. Then he took a pad of factory passes from his vest pocket, scribbled some words on one, and gave it to me. "You show this to the watchman at the employment office gate, and he'll let you in," he assured me.

Next morning, clinging to that blessed bit of paper, I made my appearance at the Chevrolet plant. Where all my efforts had failed before, the magic pull of the piece of paper did the trick. That memorable day was July 12, 1933, when GM hired me as a press operator on the third shift at Chevrolet Gear and Axle. I have over fifteen years of seniority there, having accumulated the last six years under a clause in the union contract permitting workers to accumulate seniority while on a leave of absence for union activity.

That night, carrying a paper-wrapped lunch under my arm, I rang in my card at 9:45 P.M. to begin the shift that ran from 10:00 P.M. to 6:00 A.M. This shift was something new, started in compliance with the NRA. Previously, the Chevrolet workers had been on two twelve-hour shifts. My starting rate was fifty cents per hour. This gave me a gross pay of $3.75 per shift, or $18.75 for a five-day week. The same jobs in 1948 paid better than $1.50 per hour. But in 1933 that $3.75 per shift—almost as much as the welfare had been giving me per week—looked like a gold mine.

Before that first shift was over, however, I thought that I was going to get canned, because I ran into trouble right away. Instead of getting a punch press to operate, I was put on a rotary resistance welder, which was very hard to run. I was assigned to the brake shoe job, and there were plenty of punch presses on that job, but for some reason the straw boss, a tiny, hard-boiled individual with a game leg, insisted on making me operate that rotary welder.

A resistance welder is a mechanical contrivance which presses two pieces of steel together between dies of tempered copper, and at the same time switches a strong current of electricity through the steel causing it to become incandescent and fuse together. On that 1933 model Chevrolet, and for two successive models, the brake shoes were welded twice this way before they were finished. The welder the boss insisted I must master was one of those devilish devices that has a fixed speed of operation. There are many such gadgets in the auto industry, including the famous assembly lines.

This particular machine was equipped with a revolving turntable containing eight copper dies. In the center of the turntable was bolted an unfinished brake drum full of steel stampings the size of a half-dollar. These were called reinforcements; they were stamped out on a punch press which raised five little pimples on one side. The operator stood on a platform that raised him up until the turntable was just a little above waist level. At his left was a metal truck full of brake shoes to be welded; at his right was a long metal chute down which he threw the welded shoes to the next operation, a powerful punch press set up with a coining die.

You pushed the starting button and the table began to revolve. With your right hand you picked up a reinforcement and put it into a depression in the die coming at you from the right, which it fitted very snugly. By then your left hand was supposed to have grabbed a brake shoe from the truck at your left to be placed in the fixture on top of the reinforcement. Then your right hand picked up the finished shoe out of the next fixture coming from the right; you tossed this welded shoe down the chute at your right. This completed one cycle of the operation, and you started all over again. As the shoes placed carefully on top of the reinforcements moved away from you to the left, the turntable carried them under the upper die at the back of the machine, which moved up and down in synchrony with the revolving table. Each time the shoe to be welded was exactly under the upper die, the table paused a moment, the head pressed down, sparks flew as the weld was made, then the head lifted and the table turned another notch.

This gadget was timed to turn out eight hundred welded shoes per hour. To make his production, a skillful operator had to keep it going almost constantly. This required a degree of dexterity which a beginner believed it impossible to attain—except for the cold fact that the old operator could do it. To master it, you had, in effect, to perform that old stunt of rubbing your belly and patting your head at the same time; that is, you had to learn to do one thing with one hand while doing something else with the other. The way the machine was timed, you just could not keep one hand idle while the other worked. When the dies were old and worn, the shoes stuck to them after they were welded, and that added to the complication. It was then necessary to make another motion, banging one shoe with another to loosen it.

The dies were bad that night, and the shoes stuck to them. I remember that the straw boss stood glaring at me as I tried frantically to keep up with the machine.

"Don't peck at them like a baby," he said scornfully as I tried to loosen the shoes from the dies. "Hit them like a man, like this." He pushed me aside and ran the table around three or four times without missing a lick. Sweating and fearful, I watched him, and then had another go at it. After one round, I began to fall behind.

He badgered me continuously until about three o'clock in the morning, trying to get me to master that welder. It was no go. The damned thing was too much for me. Finally, he gave it up as a bad job and put me on the punch press that blanked out the reinforcements. I sighed with relief when he didn't fire me, as I had been sure he would. In later months, when I had become more confident, I did learn to run that welder and worked on it many times until the operation was abolished in 1936.

With a few paydays under my belt, I moved my family into a small furnished house on Biltmore Street, still in the little community of Elmoor. Later we saved up enough cash to buy some second-hand furniture and make down payments on a gas stove and washing machine. We then moved into a slightly nicer place on Ferguson Street, a block away. This time we obtained the luxury of a bathroom, but we still had stove heat and no basement.

For the next three years I lived the life of an average Detroit auto worker in that time. My kids had the usual run of childhood illnesses and accidents, and I ran up the customary doctor's bills.

We had no hospitalization or health insurance of any kind in General Motors in those days. By scrimping and stinting I saved up enough money to make a down payment on a 1931 Ford. I took my wife out to beer gardens when we had the cash to spare for such a luxury. We went on picnics and participated in family reunions. Sometimes I went to a ball game. But I never felt secure.

The annual layoff during the model change was always a menace to the security of the workers. Along about June or July it started. The bosses would pick the men off a few at a time, telling them to stay home until they were notified to come back. There was no rhyme or reason in the selection of the fortunate ones chosen to continue working. The foreman had the say. If he happened to like you, or if you sucked around him and did him favors—or if you were one of the bastards who worked like hell and turned out more than production—you might be picked to work a few weeks longer than the next guy. Some few lucky fellows were transferred to the maintenance or materials departments, which meant that they worked right through the period of the inventory layoff and model change. But most of the men were laid off outright, and there was no unemployment compensation to tide them over until they were rehired.

It was customary for auto workers to go broke during this layoff. Sometimes you could get a job in another plant, maybe a feeder plant, where they made parts. These plants were busy during the layoff in the big shops, building up an inventory of parts for the new model.

One summer I tried my hand at selling vacuum cleaners during the layoff. A high-powered and glib gent representing the vacuum cleaner company rushed a gang of us through a class designed to make us into super-salesmen. Each morning we opened the class with songs—parodies of popular tunes—extolling the virtues of our cleaner. We were taught a number of sly tricks used to belittle the products of competitors. As a last resort, to crack the resistance of dubious housewives, we were taught the stunt of emptying the contents of a vacuum cleaner dust bag on the floor and threatening to drop the baby into it. When the outraged mother protested, we were supposed to say: "But madam, I took all this dirt out of your rug; your baby has been playing in it for days." For all this schooling in the wiles of free-enterprise marketing, I flopped as a salesman. In three weeks of ringing doorbells and giving housewives the song and dance, I managed to sell only one machine.

General Motors in those days operated a kind of private welfare system that many workers had to depend on to get groceries enough to get by during the layoffs. It worked like this: when you were broke and still unable to get back into the plant, you went to the personnel office and applied for help. If you proved your need, the company gave you a book of coupons that could be exchanged for groceries at a chain store. These coupons were a kind of scrip, in denominations running from a dollar down to a dime. The company charged these against your name on its books; and when you went back to work, they deducted five or ten dollars a week from your pay until they had it all back.

Any way you looked at it the layoffs were tough. In 1935 I had to sell my 1931 Ford in order to keep on paying the rent, while getting my groceries with the Chevrolet coupons. The year before that, I had my electricity turned off because I couldn't pay the Edison bill.

In October and November we began to trickle back into the plants. Again, the bosses had the full say as to who was rehired first. Years of service with the company meant nothing. Every day the lunchroom upstairs over the front end of Plant Two at Chevrolet Gear and Axle was crowded with workers for an hour before the shift started. The foremen would come upstairs and walk down the aisles picking out those they wanted on the job. Apple-polishers, suckers, and job-killers got the nod first in most instances. I must note here that all the foremen were not given to practicing this system of favoritism. There were some who felt that years of service were important, and who tried to work out a kind of unofficial seniority system in their departments. But, generally speaking, the laid-off worker had no assurance of any kind that he would be called back at any specific time. He had to be there when he was wanted, in most instances, or someone else got the nod. Sometimes, when the job was hot, workers were notified by mail to report for work.

Before the NRA was held to be unconstitutional, General Motors took action to beat its workers to the punch under the famous Section 7-A, which gave workers the right to organize unions. I think it was late in 1933 that we Chevrolet workers were given cards making us members in the Chevrolet Employees' Association. This was my second contact with a company union, but again I was too ignorant to know what it was all about. Company-dominated elections were held to choose representatives of the workers, who were supposed to take up grievances for us. As is usual in a company union, the Works Council never got around to discussing anything but broken windows and safety hazards. When some unruly committeeman had the temerity to mention wages or seniority, the company representatives promptly sidetracked the discussions into less dangerous channels. The Chevrolet Employees' Association was a joke, but perhaps it served its purpose, which was to make the workers believe that they had an organization to represent them collectively in their dealings with management. I think it was at this time that I heard my first discussions of unionism. Some of the old-timers, mostly former coal miners, who knew the meaning of unionism, explained the iniquities of a company union to the greener workers like myself. But I was still not much impressed.

I recall that in 1933 there was a strike of some tool and die makers in Flint. They sent pickets to march in front of the Chevrolet plant in Detroit, asking the skilled workers there to join them in their fight for union recognition. I must confess with shame that I crossed that picket line, not knowing that I was committing a cardinal sin. If confession is good for the soul, I make this admission now with my head bowed in penitence, hoping that my ten years of devotion to organized labor since 1937 have somehow expiated this sinful act committed in the ignorance of my youth.

Anyhow, I sweated and struggled through these final years of blindness and drifted into the summer of 1936, when events occurred which changed the entire pattern of my life.

5. With My Eyes Wide Open

I think my initiation into the world of ideas and labor activity really started in April 1936, when I was twenty-seven years old, during a discussion with my trusted friend Andy.

"Why don't you read some good books?" he asked me one evening when we were sitting around chewing the fat. I knew he had literary leanings, but they had rarely cropped up in our long association because most of our time together was spent drinking and tearing around at night. He had done a lot of reading and some exploratory writing, but I had never felt impelled to join him in his esthetic adventures.

"What should I read?" I responded in complete innocence.

"You could start on some Sherwood Anderson, or Hemingway, or Keats and Browning," he suggested. "Maybe later you could have a go at some philosophy."

"What good will that do me?" I asked, puzzled.

"Well," he said, "it seems kind of useless to spend all our time drinking and dancing—we ought to broaden out and try to make a place in the world for ourselves."

Just what power moved me to take his advice is something I shall never know. Anyway, I started going to the library and bringing home volumes he recommended. Reading them was hard work at first; after a period of effort it came easier, and I began to get interested. Several months later, I was struggling with the works of Kant and Nietzsche, getting little out of their profundities except a greater mystification over the workings of the human mind.

Poetry, however, really caught my fancy and fired my imagination. I waded excitedly through numerous books of poems. Soon I was quoting long passages of Omar Khayyám, to the puzzlement of my drinking companions.

The next step in my intellectual emancipation was even tougher. Acting on Andy's advice again, I started playing around with words, putting them together in atrocious rhymes. Inspired by a sudden vision of a literary career, I purchased a portable typewriter on the installment plan. The ownership of this marvelous tool moved me to compose the following jingle, which a generous columnist, Elmer C. Adams of the *Detroit News*, published in his column:

Lines to a New Typewriter

The weeks crept by on leaden feet,
  I waited for today,
Now that you're here, I find I haven't
  Anything to say.

With your aid, I had hoped I might
  Accomplish my desire
To kindle lines of poetry
  And set the world on fire.

But never mind, my little pal—
  I'll let you be my world,
Together we can marvel
  At the verses you've unfurled.

And if my digits disobey
  My mind's obtuse reflexes,
I'll cover up the errors
  With your ever-handy X's.

While I wrestled mightily with the rules of syntax and composition in giving birth to such masterpieces as the above, it dawned on me that I would have been wiser in my youth to pay more heed to my lessons. Painfully, with the aid of a second-hand textbook on grammar, I repaired the flaws in my grasp of language, filling them in with hours of study and practice. I even carried the book to the shop with me and pored through it before the shift started and at lunch time. This sudden devotion to letters was very amusing to most of my fellow workers; however, I stuck to it in spite of their joking criticisms. By the end of the summer, I began to feel just a little proud of knowing when and how to surround a parenthetical expression with commas or dashes. Out of this belated cramming grew a super-sensitive concern with the formalities of punctuation that still lingers with me. Often, when reading, I stumble and fall in a rage over a comma inserted where I am convinced a semicolon should be.

It was on an afternoon in October of that year, while I was still a victim of the annual inventory layoff, that an acquaintance drove by and suggested going to the Olympia Stadium to hear a speech by Earl Browder, the Communist candidate for President in the 1936 election. Neither of us knew much about politics of any kind, let alone the complications of the Communist philosophy. I am not certain what reasons motivated me to go to the Browder rally that night, but it seemed like a good idea at the time. Perhaps there was brewing within me that insurgent swell of sympathy with so-called radical doctrines that washed into the lives of many Americans in the years following the depression.

The Olympia in Detroit is a massive arena ordinarily used for hockey games, prize fights, and circuses. That night the Commies, then riding the crest of a depression-born popularity, staged a circus of their own that had a strong appeal for me. At least ten thousand people filled the main floor of the arena and overflowed into the lower sections of the stands. The usual language groups of Europeans were there, with signs designating them as Polish Communists, Hungarian Communists, and so forth. There was a heavy sprinkling of Negroes in the crowd. At one end of the arena a big platform was bedecked with a slogan reading: "Communism Is Twentieth Century Americanism." Over this banner hung huge pictures of Lenin and Stalin on each side of a gigantic hammer and sickle. Members of the Young Communist League circulated through the crowd soliciting funds to help the Spanish Loyalists.

Browder blasted away at the capitalists and their evil works for almost two hours. Hewing to the line of the "united front," he denounced the German and Italian governments for their intervention in Spain, and was equally critical of America, England, and France for their failure to help the Loyalists. He recalled the privations of the depression and predicted an early doom for the capitalist system. Thunderous applause greeted his warm praise of the Soviet Union. Several times in his speech he called the attention of Detroit workers to the efforts of the infant CIO to organize mass production workers into one big union. It was important, he repeated over and over again, for the workers in the auto industry to join forces with this move to organize labor unions among workers in the basic manufacturing industries of America. He foresaw the building of an American people's front movement with powerful labor unions as its base.

Then the cheering throng, charged with emotionalism, rose to sing the stirring strains of the "Internationale," its echoes ringing from the steel girders overhead. I stood on my feet, too, filled with the strange passion that drives the followers of revolutionary political movements.

I bought some literature after the meeting. One of the pieces was a current copy of the *New Masses,* which I read from cover to cover. Its contents sounded good to me. I do not recall the exact process of reasoning that made me into a Communist sympathizer. Part of it was probably my naturally rebellious spirit. A deeper motive, I am sure, was the belief beat into me by recent experience that depressions were man-made and unnecessary, my growing conviction that people ought to work for the establishment of a program to prevent depressions. The Communists were the first group I had found who claimed to have an answer to economic disaster. They proposed to kick the ruling capitalist class out of power and put the working class in charge of economic affairs. They said their program would lead America and the world to abundance and security. I had heard no other program that sounded as positive as the Communist line, so I fell for it. It is likely that I was gullible and ignorant; but I refuse to shoulder the whole blame for having been taken in by the Communists. American industrial and political leaders were at least partially at fault for my victimization by a totalitarian philosophy. I feel that they had the power and the opportunity to prevent the depression that turned me against capitalism—but they failed to live up to their responsibility.

Browder's speech was not strong enough to win my vote in 1936. I voted for FDR again, along with the millions who turned out to put him in office for his second term. And in November, shortly after the election, the United Automobile Workers of America, newly affiliated with the CIO, carried its message to the gates of the Chevrolet Gear and Axle plant. It found me ready and eager to turn my small talents and larger energies to the task of organizing the working people in the auto industry into a strong labor union.

The October 1936 edition of the *United Automobile Worker*, official organ of the fast-growing auto union, carried a five-column banner headline which read: "CIO Enters Auto Drive." Above this headline, just below the title of the paper, was a small line saying: "Affiliated with the American Federation of Labor." In November the identification with the AFL was stricken out and replaced by a line reading: "Member of the Committee for Industrial Organization." This same November edition carried a two-line five-column banner head in caps, reporting: "Auto Drive Smashes on to Great Gains."

This November edition was distributed at the gates of the Chevrolet Gear and Axle plant on a cold gray afternoon as the day shift came rushing out of the shop to go home. Many workers, fearful of spies in their ranks, ignored the men passing out the papers. I took one and carried it home, where I read it carefully. It told of the growing membership of the union in Flint, Michigan, in Anderson, Indiana, and in Racine, Wisconsin. On the front page was a personal message from John L. Lewis, President of the United Mine Workers of America and Chairman of the CIO, saying: "I believe that each and every man working in the automobile industry will welcome and will aid the United Automobile Workers of America."

That night, studying this labor journal, I made what was probably the most serious decision of my life. I decided to go to the union headquarters and volunteer to assist in the drive to organize the auto industry. I knew that this decision meant danger to myself and my family. It held the possibility of getting fired and blacklisted, so that I could never work in the industry again if the organization drive failed. It meant personal danger from the goons and spies employed by the auto companies to resist unionism. Nevertheless, I decided in favor of the union. And I made the decision all by myself. My wife, a girl of twenty-three, was not the type of person to be interested in such deviations from the routine life of an average auto worker. She looked upon my messing around with books and writing as more or less of a nuisance; she just did not care about such matters. I knew it would only kick up extra trouble to share with her my determination to join the ranks of organized labor. If I got into trouble and lost my job, I would cross that bridge when I came to it.

On a Saturday afternoon I ventured timidly into the headquarters of the union in the Hofmann Building in downtown Detroit. I told a girl receptionist that I wanted to see the editor of the union paper. She advised me that the editor was not in, but that I could talk to Frank Winn, the union's Public Relations Director. Frank was then twenty-five years old, a big slow-talking Texan who had quit a job as a newspaper reporter to devote his life to the labor movement. Later he again became Public Relations Director of the UAW-CIO after a decade of ups and downs in the factional struggles for control of the union.

I began our talk by telling him of my interest in writing.

"I thought maybe I could write some stuff for the union paper," I said shyly.

"What have you written?" he asked me.

"Oh, just a few poems and letters to the editor—stuff like that," I said modestly. "But," I added quickly, "I've been reading your paper, and I think I could do some pieces that would help, because I've been around the industry since 1928."

I showed him a sample of my work. It was a piece I had written about my views on the sit-down strikes, which I intended to submit as an article to the *New Republic*. He said he thought it was a good job, but that GM would fire me if it was published. All in all, he was very cautious throughout our meeting. Years later he told me—to my immense amusement—that there had been the possibility of my being a company spy. Of course, he had a right to be suspicious, for the employers had agents working in strategic spots inside the union at that time. It was entirely possible that I was acting in that capacity—and I may have aroused Winn's suspicion because I wanted to get an inside track right from the start.

Then he asked me if I belonged to the union. I had to admit that I didn't—but explained that until then no one had ever asked me to join.

"That would be a good way to get started—by joining the union first," he suggested in his slow drawl, with a twinkle in his eyes.

"Okay, how do I get in?" I asked.

He called in an organizer, who signed me up on the spot. I paid three dollars, which included a two-dollar initiation fee and one month's dues. During the confusion that followed, my application was lost and I had to sign up all over again, so that the initiation date on my card in Local 235, the Chevrolet Gear and Axle local, is February 20, 1937. I have been in continuous good standing in the UAW-CIO from that date on. Since that November afternoon when Frank Winn helped to open my eyes, I have not only written many pieces for union papers, but actually handled the technical work of editing and making up the *United Auto Worker*, official UAW-CIO paper, for two years.

When I left union headquarters that day I carried a pocketful of application cards to distribute among my fellow workers in the Chevrolet plant. In the meantime, big events began to happen in Flint and elsewhere. Although the union was not recognized in Flint, the heart of the GM system, it was making its greatest gains there among the unorganized workers. In some places—Atlanta, Georgia; Kansas City and St. Louis, Missouri; Toledo and Norwood, Ohio; Janesville, Wisconsin—the workers were fairly well organized and the union recognized unofficially by management. General Motors' policy of resisting the union, however, was carried out in all its plants, including the Chevrolet plant in Detroit. Organizational progress was much slower in my plant than in Flint and other places where the sit-down strikes erupted.

GM strategy followed two lines of attack, direct action and psychological action. The direct action took the form of organization of squads of goons, who manufactured blackjacks and bludgeons in the plant on company time—for the purpose, as they put it, of resisting "the invasion by CIO Communists." The corporation also reinforced its crew of plant protection police, hiring the biggest and toughest men it could find to don the company uniforms and patrol the plants.

The psychological action worked two ways. First, the company announced payment of a Christmas bonus. This was an obvious bribe, an effort at the last hour to convince the workers that the company wanted to do right by them, to prove that they did not need a union. Employers seem never to realize that workers see through this gag at a glance; they catch on quickly that, if the boss is scared into granting a bonus or a raise by the mere threat of unionization, the pay-off is bound to be fatter when the union does get going in the plant. In Chevrolet, where we did not even have a skeleton organization, many of us saw through this bonus stunt on the eve of the sit-down strikes.

The other angle of psychology played by GM involved a whispering campaign by spies and company pets. Some of these whispering agents were probably paid provocateurs; others were ordinary workers duped by the company line. They circulated among the machines, before the Flint strike started and for its duration, denouncing the union and praising the company. There was a false note about this maneuver that the workers sensed at once. I cannot explain it in any other way than by saying that we thought it very unusual for any worker, even a company stooge, to be so free to leave his job for such a long time. The foremen had always been on our necks from the start of the shift to its end, yammering at us to get out more production. Now they looked the other way while the stooges floated around, leaving their machines idle, to whisper against the union. It just didn't make sense to us for GM so suddenly to relax its demand for uninterrupted production.

Our lack of organization at Chevrolet was pathetic. Out of the thousand or more workers on the Plant Two day shift I did not know another person who carried a card in the union. Frustrated, I seethed inside, aching for a chance to strike back at the company. The whispering agents were busier than ever. Goons swaggered about caressing their blackjacks, bragging about what they would do to "any Communist son-of-a-bitch who tried to start a sit-down strike in here." There I was, alone in that uproar of anti-union activity, feverish with desire to do something for the cause, but helpless and isolated as a babe in the woods.

Then the company stooges began circulating a petition stating that the Chevrolet Gear and Axle workers were opposed to the union, that they deplored the un-American sit-down strikes. This happened late in January, and I was too green to figure out that it was a trick to spot the pro-union workers. Overjoyed at my first chance to get in a lick for the union, I bluntly refused to sign the petition. It was a small enough gesture but it made me feel better. Not only did I refuse to sign the damn thing; but I was careful to note that three other workers on the brake shoe job also refused. At the first opportunity I contacted these three men and offered them union application cards. Two of them took the cards and quickly hid them in their pockets; the third was afraid and refused.

On February 1 General Motors struck back at me. Right after the shift started in the morning, my foreman came to my punch press, where I was operating a brake shoe trimming die, and stood there a minute before speaking.

"Petrie wants to see you out in the aisle," he said. Petrie was one of the assistant superintendents of the building.

"What's he want?" I asked above the clatter of the machines, my heart beginning to hammer. I had a feeling that this was it.

"He didn't say what he wants; you better get out there and find out for yourself," the foreman answered, trying to make his voice sound casual.

I left the press and strode bravely out to the aisle, putting on a courageous front for the benefit of the other workers, who watched out of the corners of their eyes. Petrie was waiting in the aisle, flanked on one side by a big, red-faced plant policeman.

"Callahan wants you in the office—come on," he said, without giving me a chance to say a word.

We started down the aisle, Petrie on one side of me and the big uniformed guard on the other side. They didn't put their hands on me, but they kind of squeezed up against me with their shoulders, pushing me along toward the front end of the plant on Holbrook Avenue. I didn't get the pitch of this rushing act at first. Later I realized that they were fearful that I had enough followers to pull off a sit-down in protest against my being fired. Strikes had started that way in other plants. They were giving me no chance to contact workers on the way out.

In the front office Callahan, the chunky superintendent of the Plant Two day shift, looked grimly at me across his desk and handed me a discharge slip.

"I've got to let you go, Fountain," he said.

"What's the matter, isn't my work good enough?" I asked. Glancing quickly at the dismissal slip I noted that there was a check mark opposite the word "fair" in a column indicating a worker's performance as good, fair or bad. In another column headed "cooperation with others" I was checked off as "poor."

"Your work's okay, but the men on the job refuse to work with you," he said, dropping his eyes away from mine.

"Which men refuse to work with me?" I inquired insistently, raising my voice a little.

"That's not important," he grunted. Then he told the guard to take my badge.

The big goon snatched the badge off my chest with both vigor and relish, tearing my shirt a little in the act. I did not resist. I could see that two more guards were just outside the door, and I knew that the three of them were itching for an excuse to give me a going over.

"Take him to the personnel building," Callahan told the guard. He began to fuss around with his papers, indicating that I was washed up so far as he was concerned.

In the personnel building Bill Smith, big boss of the plant guards, made me sit on a chair while he gave me what he thought was a third degree.

"Do you belong to the union?" he demanded, peering at me with an inquisitorial gleam in his eyes.

"You're damned right," I shot back at him.

"How long have you been in it?"

"Long enough to know that you're not going to get away with firing me," I retorted firmly.

"How many others in Plant Two belong to the union?" he asked, leaning forward eagerly to catch my answer.

"Oh, about three hundred, I guess," I lied casually.

"Did you sign them all up?" he wanted to know.

"Hell no; there's half a dozen of us in there organizing—you haven't got spies enough to catch us all," I boasted untruthfully. I guess he began to get the drift then, for he dropped that line of questioning.

"Aren't you afraid the Communists will take this country over if the CIO gets into these plants?" he asked in utter sincerity.

"I don't know much about that," I said, "but you might as well get used to the idea that there is going to be a union here, and that I'm coming back before this fight is over."

"Do you really believe that?" he said, impressed a little by the determination in my voice.

"It's a sure thing," I told him. "You can bet your last dollar that those guys in Flint are going to hang on until GM puts back every last guy you've given the works to like you are doing to me today."

"It's too bad you had to go and get messed up in this," Smith said as our chat came to an end. "You had a good record here, and now you've gone and spoiled it."

He was right; I did have a good work record. In 1935 I had even served as a job-setter for a while. I had also doped out a safety device for some punch press dies and had helped my foreman design a fixture for repairing brake shoes rejected due to a faulty radius. On another occasion I had written some verses for a safety campaign, and management had posted them on the bulletin boards in the shop. But that made no difference to the GM brass in Wall Street. Maybe that was why the management did not want to look me in the eye when I was given the gate. They may have been ashamed of their part in carrying out the GM anti-union policy.

But there I was, canned out of the plant for union activity—and on my daughter's birthday, too.

6. "Arise, Ye Prisoners of Starvation"

I did not go home all that day of February 1, 1937—putting off the ordeal of facing my wife and telling her that I was fired for union activity. Instead, I went down to the Hofmann Building, looked up Frank Winn to tell him of my hard luck.

"What happened to the piece you sent to the *New Republic?*" Winn asked right away when I saw him that day.

"It got published as a letter to the editor—and they paid me four dollars for it," I bragged with what pride I could summon.

"Did you get fired?" he asked.

"Yeah, that's what I came down to see you about," I replied glumly.

He had me make a formal deposition and get it notarized, for the purpose of filing a claim for back pay under the National Labor Relations Act. Newspapermen clustered around me, questioning me about the details of my firing. I told them my story as simply as I could. The afternoon editions carried a few lines about my discharge deep in the latest rehash of the Flint strike. I clipped it for a souvenir.

Years later that newspaper clipping was tossed into a War Labor Board hearing on GM contract negotiations in a manner that gave me great satisfaction. The company was then asking the WLB panel to kick the maintenance-of-membership clause out of its agreement with the union. Such a clause permits workers to quit being union members within a certain period. But, if they do not drop out within that particular period of time, they must remain members for the duration of the agreement, or be discharged by the employer. GM, trying to get rid of such a clause, which had been previously required by the WLB, argued that it wanted to protect the individual rights of its workers. Company spokesmen pleaded passionately before the panel that it was grossly unjust to fire a worker simply because he did not belong to the union and was, therefore, out of step with his fellow workers.

As one point in rebuttal, Walter Reuther, acting in his capacity as director of the union's General Motors Department, submitted in evidence the newspaper clipping reporting how GM had fired me in 1937 "because, the company said, his fellow workers refused to work with him."

"Where was the corporation's concern for the individual rights of this man in 1937?" Reuther demanded, while I sat there gloating in my hour of glory.

Late in the afternoon of that eventful day when I was fired I returned to the plant to catch a ride home with the driver of the car in which I rode to work every day. It was necessary to let him know that I would not be going in the next day. By a strange coincidence a crew of organizers, most of them volunteers from the Dodge main plant a few blocks away, came out that afternoon to distribute handbills at the Chevrolet gates.

I saw these men take up their posts in front of the plant and pull the leaflets out from under their coats. They began to give the union message to second shift workers going into the buildings. They had hardly started when a gang of uniformed guards rushed out of Plant Three and jumped them with flying fists. Outnumbered, the union men scattered and fled. While all this was happening, I leaned against the fence trying to drum up enough guts to get into the skirmish on the side of the union men. But it was all over in a jiffy. Then one of the guards recognized me and came over to where I was standing.

"Wasn't you fired this morning?" he growled at me.

"Yes," I mumbled discreetly.

"Well, what in hell you hanging around here for now?"

"I'm just waiting to get a ride home with my driver," I said, my muscles tensed to duck if he should make a pass at me.

"Get the hell over to the parking lot and wait there, then," he shouted, giving me a push.

Seeing nothing to be gained by making an issue of it, I shuffled off toward the parking lot. On the way home my driver and two fellow passengers sympathized with me. But none of them was sympathetic to the point of taking the application cards I offered. Months later, when there was no danger of getting fired, they all became good union members.

When I got home there was a good warm fire burning in the big heating stove in the dining room of the little frame house I had rented on Lindsay Street. Dinner was ready and waiting. There was a modest birthday cake, decorated with six pink candles, for my daughter Dolores. Looking at the cake, I decided to stall off the bad news until after eating. So I put on a good front until the festivities were over. My little girl opened her gifts with the wide-eyed excitement that six-year-old kids feel on their birthdays.

"How many days are you going to work this week?" Lee asked me in her usual conversational tone. This was, and still is, a routine question asked by the wives of auto workers. The size of the paycheck depends on how many days are worked during each pay period, and budgets are planned to meet the limits of the work week.

"I'm not working any more this week," I answered. I looked down at my empty plate.

"How come?" she asked.

"I got fired this morning," I said bluntly, bent on getting it over in a hurry.

"Fired!" There was shock and terror in her voice.

"Yeah, they canned me for union activity," I said. "But I'll get back when the strike is settled; the union says that the guys in Flint will not go back unless all the fired guys are rehired," I went on hurriedly.

For a few minutes Lee didn't say or do anything. She just sat there across the table from me, her face strained with emotion, while the two youngsters chattered away all unaware that our little world had been smashed by a policy issued from GM headquarters in Wall Street. Then tears began to run silently down her face. She got up without a word and began putting dishes into the sink.

"That's what your old union gets for you," she mumbled through her tears a few minutes later. "How are we going to pay the rent? What about the doctor's bills? I suppose we'll have to go back on the welfare," she said bitterly.

I went into the front room and picked up a newspaper. It was no use arguing with her. This was the beginning of a split in the family ranks that never healed. She refused to accept the union as a part of our life, resisting it until we separated for good in 1938. She was a capable housekeeper and a devoted mother, but union activity just wasn't in her scheme of life.

Next morning I put in an early appearance at a downtown welfare station. It was crowded with strikers and workers laid off because of strikes—by then the rebellion of the auto workers was catching on in other plants. When my interview was finished, and I had been told to come back on a certain day for a check, I circulated around the room passing out union application cards and making little speeches in favor of the CIO. The response was gratifying; I used up all the cards I had with me.

Ten days later the strike was settled, on February 11. In a memorandum written by William S. Knudsen, then president of GM, to Governor Frank Murphy, the UAW-CIO was recognized as the exclusive bargaining agency in the plants that had been on strike for a period of six months. In plants that had not struck, the union was recognized as bargaining agent for its members. A condition of the return to work was the opening of negotiations on all matters in dispute on February 16. The terms of this settlement were threshed out in a Detroit hotel, with John L. Lewis participating from a room where he was confined to bed with a bad cold. In the subsequent bargaining sessions, GM came through with concessions that started the union on its way. A grievance procedure was established, with union committeemen to represent the workers. A seniority system was worked out. The agreement specified that wages, hours of work, and speed-ups were subject to collective bargaining. It was a far from perfect agreement, but it cleared up the main issue in dispute: The GM workers, acting through an organization governed by themselves, were going to have a voice in the determination of economic policies and plant regulations affecting their lives.

It took until March 9 for the union to get around to getting me back to work. There were sixty-two workers besides myself who had been thrown out of Chevrolet Gear and Axle for union activity. Some had been beaten up by plant guards and confused workers. One young welder had his head gashed open with an iron bar when he fought with the men who threw him out of Plant Three. One by one we were called to an interview with Joe Harbaugh, assistant plant manager.

I can't forget the little speech he made when my turn came to visit him.

"The corporation hopes that there are no hard feelings over our difficulties," he said. "After all, you know, emotions ran high and many of us may have engaged in regrettable actions. Nothing like this has ever happened in General Motors before, and difficulties are bound to arise in the course of adjusting our policies to this new situation, these new conditions." He went on in this manner for several minutes before he got around to giving me a pass admitting me to the employment office the next morning.

I strutted boldly into Plant Two next day at the beginning of the day shift, with my chest sticking out a mile or more. My Chevrolet badge, shaped like a miniature 1926 model Chevvy radiator shell, was pinned again to the left breast pocket of my blue denim shirt. Beside it—making my fellow workers bug their eyes out—was a UAW-CIO March 1937 dues button. This tiny trinket, about the size of a two-bit piece, made of tin and covered with gaudy celluloid, was my badge of honor. Pinned there on my shirt beside the Chevrolet emblem, it gloated louder than words over the downfall of a proud and mighty corporation. The boys clustered around me before the shift started. They fingered the button curiously, fired questions at me, pressed me for details about the union's program. A new order had begun at

Chevrolet Gear and Axle; conditions were never to be the same again. Before lunch time, two more buttons appeared on the brake shoe job and three on the adjacent wheel job. Every time I went to the can I was besieged with demands for application cards. And Petrie came around personally to tell me that I would get a raise which had gone through while I was out of the plant.

Building a local union from scratch in an unorganized industry is a big job. But out of the ranks of the Chevrolet workers there appeared men eager to work at this task. Some were ex-members of the IWW or the United Mine Workers; these, aided by their experience, fell naturally into the role of leaders. Some were quiet, soft-spoken men, with better educations than you suspected, driven into the shops by a tough turn of fate in their lives. A few were the loud-mouthed, bullying type, their guts full of hate kindled by harsh treatment suffered for years in an open shop. Some just had stars in their eyes and a deep, burning love for their fellow men. In the meetings called to proceed with the work of organization, these men began to get up on their feet and talk. Out of their lips, often in crude, ill-constructed sentences, poured a flood of words expressing devotion to the simple principles of honesty and decency. For most of them it was the first chance to voice their thoughts of what kind of a life they believed workers should live. Clumsily, as an infant learns to walk, they began to reach out for the lights beyond the prison.

Our charter from the International Union designated us as Local 235. Assigned to get the local under way was a fellow in his early thirties named Elmer Dowell, who turned out to be a brother-in-law of Homer Martin, the union's International President. With Dowell's aid we elected a bargaining committee and local officers. Our first local president was a Polish veteran of World War I named Joseph Sawicki. I ran for the office of financial secretary against a Polish boy named Joe Opoka, and was defeated by a few votes. Undaunted by this setback, I took the appointment of steward on my brake shoe job, although this office was not recognized by the corporation under the agreement. My duties were to sign up new members, collect dues, and help the committeeman for my district to process his grievances.

Meanwhile, I continued to fuss around with books and writing, and thus fell into the post of Educational Director of the local union.

Under the union's constitution, I was actually only the chairman of the Education Committee. The title of Educational Director was my own idea; it seemed to indicate more prestige than a mere committee chairmanship. Besides, it helped to compensate for the fact that the job carried no financial reward for services rendered. I had to do my work on my own time, outside of working hours, except on rare occasions when the local paid my lost time and expenses while I attended a class or conference called by higher union leaders.

There must have been a majority of men with stars in their eyes on the committee that drafted the first UAW-CIO constitution, under which we got our local unions into motion in those early days of our history. Education of the union membership was stipulated as a mandatory union activity in one of the articles of that constitution. It was also mandatory that five cents out of each dues dollar be spent for educational purposes. Two and a half cents was to be spent at the international level, and the other two and a half at the local union level. As chairman of the Education Committee in my local union I was responsible for planning the expenditure of this fund. With a dues-paying membership of some eight thousand, the fund amounted to about two hundred dollars per month.

Being responsible for direction of educational activities in Local 235 made me a natural target for the Communists, who were making hay while the morning sun of unionism shone bright in the automobile factories. The party follows a studied policy of trying to win converts among new key people in the labor movement. It is especially keen on getting as members those unionists with ideas and talents who gravitate to the educational and publicity tasks. One bright and energetic party member working as an educational director or editor in a strong local union is worth a dozen members occupied with the lesser duties of settling grievances or negotiating contracts. Such a spot gives the party member an outlet through which to pour a steady stream of Communist propaganda.

For this reason, I was high on the list of new up-and-coming unionists on whom the party focused its wiles in Detroit early in 1937. I reacted quickly and favorably. The party line, then hitched tightly to the "united front" and the "defense of democracy," sounded good to me. I was twenty-eight years old, full of fire and fury, all hot to speed up the work of rooting greed and injustice out of the affairs of man. The party's description of its program, as it appeared to a young man eager to purge the world of poverty, hunger, and war, made good sense. As I studied the program, which was outlined in tracts showered on me by the recruiters, it appeared to me to be founded firmly on the intent to end exploitation of man by man. This was to be accomplished by a revolution—peaceful if possible but violent if necessary—which would dump the capitalists out of power and place the working class in control of the economic system. The workers would then guide the affairs of society in accordance with the principles of justice and brotherhood. Material resources would be used to satisfy the needs of the people as a whole, not to make profit for a few greedy employers. As a natural result of this humane administration of the economy, unemployment, depression, and war would be abolished. Thus, under the Communist party program, mankind would advance swiftly toward a "higher stage of civilization." This was the seemingly logical pattern of reasoning that I found so alluring in the basic literature of the party.

It was purely accidental, I believe, that the Communist party got to me first. Ripe to be plucked by a political party pledged to change things for the better, I might have fallen for the doctrine of the Socialists, the Trotskyites, or the Lovestoneites. It was largely a matter of first come, first to win the new convert to the true faith. And the Communists beat their competitors to the punch.

One afternoon in May 1937 I followed two Negro comrades up a dark stairway to a cramped little apartment in Paradise Valley, the East Side Detroit slum where thousands of dark-skinned Americans are packed into rotten buildings infested with rats and vermin. There, in an atmosphere heavy with conspiratorial secrecy and the odor of fried catfish, I was questioned seriously by the comrades. They measured my fitness for party membership by my answers to their questions.

Did I know that a party member had to forsake all other loyalties and cleave only to the ideological breast of the Communist organization? Did I realize that the members of the party were sometimes subjected to abuse and ridicule, and required the utmost courage to stand firm by the party line? Did I understand that party members were often called upon to perform assignments involving physical danger and hardship? Did I comprehend, above all, that the directions of the party were supreme, to be followed unswervingly and never, never questioned? All these and a score of other questions were fired at me by the comrades chosen to test my responses.

Finally they must have been convinced that I possessed the makings of a good Communist. I was signed up and given the pseudonym of Curtis Fowler. I was pledged to obey the party's orders, to promote its line in all my waking hours, to stand by it through thick and thin, for richer, for poorer, until death should us part. I was initiated into the structure of the party, shown how it was broken down into districts, sections, and units. East Side Detroit was a section, part of the Detroit district, with a cluttered-up headquarters on East Canfield Street near Hastings. Without understanding the subtlety of the arrangement, I was pleasantly surprised that a blonde female member of the Young Communist League showed up frequently to help with my initiation. My first formal assignment was the building of a strong party unit at Chevrolet Gear and Axle inside Local 235.

Full of revolutionary idealism, I threw myself into my new role as a front line soldier in the ranks of the "vanguard of the working class." The party placed me in contact with another comrade in Local 235. Together we began the work of peddling the party line and organizing a party unit in our plant.

It did not take me long to master the rudiments of Communist philosophy. My grasp of some of the angles of "dialectical materialism" is revealed in the following quotations from one of my numerous letters to the editor, published in the *Detroit News* that summer:

> With the invention of private property, individual enterprise, and the consequent possibility of accumulating material wealth, came the class division of society. And, by the same tokens, came the necessity for a weapon, the State, to protect the minority owning class from the majority class that owned nothing.
>
> The State became, then, a force supposedly over and above society, for the common good of society; but actually it was only an organized force used to settle, by violence if necessary, conflicts between the "haves" and the "have nots."
>
> Every nation in the world today is dominated by a class. Russia is ruled by the majority class, the proletariat; all others are ruled, in various degrees, by the capitalist class.
>
> The capitalist class ruled America with an iron hand until the Roosevelt New Deal appeared. State power was directed by the bankers and industrialists; they used it to dominate society. Democracy existed, it is true, but only because it served the ruling class well during America's period of industrial expansion—an expansion that today results in the immense gap between market prices and public purchasing power—the major contradiction in the capitalist system.

Diatribes like the sample above poured from my typewriter as a result of reading large doses of Lenin and Engels. For some odd reason, the letter box editor of the conservative *Detroit News* seemed to favor my shrill trumpeting of the party line. He printed dozens of my letters. As a result of this printing of my pieces in the *News*, I became rather widely known about town, especially in labor circles, in a relatively short time. This reputation survived my brief honeymoon with communism. Although I have not written a letter to the *News* for eight years, I still run into people who say, "Oh, you're the guy that used to write all those letters in the *Detroit News* letter box."

Building the party at Chevrolet, however, involved more than cussing out the capitalists in print. It required endless hours of meetings with likely prospects and explaining to them the urgent need for members who would accept party discipline. Some militant and intelligent workers were willing to go to party mass meetings, to contribute funds, and to back the party line in union meetings, but balked at the final step of signing up. Each recruit was won over only by lengthy and painful exercise of the art of oral persuasion. By the summer of 1938 there were twenty-six Communists in the Chevrolet unit. Their names are not important in this document because nearly all of them fell away from the party in later years. In fact, from what I know of political affairs inside Local 235 today, I cannot say for sure that there is a single member of the Communist party now occupying a position of leadership there. The turnover in its membership has always been a sore spot with the party; the number of people who join it in any given year, only to desert it two or three years later, probably exceeds the number of those who remain members.

7. Politics with Passion

Factional feuding plagued the UAW-CIO from its birth until the November convention in 1947. Homer Martin, the former Baptist preacher who was elected President of the union at the 1936 South Bend convention, fought with his opponents in a battle that raged until he was ousted in 1939—and after that the struggle continued. The trouble was due in part to the fact that the Communists were permitted to grab a foothold in the union during the early days. John L. Lewis, then chairman of the CIO, was as much to blame as anyone for its infiltration by the Commies.

A confirmed anti-Communist himself, Lewis took a risk by putting capable Commies in key spots as organizers during the initial organizational drives of the CIO. Convinced of his capacity to run the CIO with the same kind of one-man control he wielded in the United Mine Workers, Lewis reckoned that he could exploit the organizing talents of the Communists and still keep the situation in hand. It turned out that he very much overestimated his own power and underestimated the zeal of the Commies in their quest for power. The magnitude of his error was still apparent during 1947 and 1948 in the fight between pro-Communists and anti-Communists within the CIO.

In the spring of 1937 I was drawn swiftly into the raging conflict between the pro-Martin and anti-Martin forces, particularly after I had joined the Communist party. It is difficult now to say just how much of that fight was due to a clash of ideologies and how much was caused by a natural desire of young men for leadership in a youthful and dynamic organization. Certainly both of these factors were deeply involved in the "Homer Martin fight," as we called it, which ran over a period of nearly two years. My personal experience in the battle reflects the presence of both factors, as I look back on it now.

I was elected a delegate to the 1937 convention of the UAW-CIO, which was held in Milwaukee in the middle of August. Local 235 was credited with thirteen delegates; out of those elected, two of us were Communists pledged to the Unity Caucus, the other eleven being committed to Homer Martin's Progressive Caucus.

On the surface, there did not seem to be a great deal of difference between the two factions. The Unity Caucus was led by Wyndham Mortimer, Ed Hall, Bob Travis, and the Reuther brothers, Walter, Victor, and Roy. Mortimer was a CP-liner from the White Motor plant in Cleveland; Travis, another CP-liner, was from the Chevrolet Transmission plant in Toledo; Hall was a leader from Seaman Body in Milwaukee. The Reuther brothers all came out of Detroit plants; Walter from GM Ternstedt, Victor from Kelsey-Hayes Wheel, and Roy from Chevrolet Drop Forge. The Unity Caucus favored re-election of Martin as president. But they wanted to elect four vice-presidents instead of the three favored by the Progressive Caucus. Their candidates for vice-presidents were Mortimer and Hall, plus Richard T. Frankensteen from the Dodge Main plant and R. J. Thomas from the Chrysler Jefferson plant, both of Detroit. This meant dropping one incumbent vice-president, Walter Wells of Detroit. The Unity Caucus was in favor of re-electing Secretary-Treasurer George F. Addes of Toledo.

The Progressive Caucus proposed re-election of Martin and Addes to their respective posts, and endorsed Frankensteen and Wells and Russell Merrill of Indiana for vice-presidents.

Beneath this overlapping of favored contestants for top offices boiled a controversy over wildcat strikes and the role of the Communist party in the union's affairs. Martin was apparently against wildcat strikes. He criticized those leaders in the union who were inclined to call quickie strikes for purposes of winning minor disputes over grievances and, incidentally, building up their political prestige in the shop. Somehow, most of his criticisms applied particularly to the Communists. But Martin himself used wildcat strikes when such tactics served his political purposes. Non-Communist opponents of Martin, such as the Reuther brothers, also disapproved of wildcat strikes, but they opposed harsh crackdowns on workers participating in such stoppages when the employers were to blame.

In the Unity Caucus, Wyndham Mortimer and Bob Travis usually followed the Communist line. I never saw them at a party meeting, but William Weinstone, chief of the Detroit CP district, and Bill Gebert, party commissar assigned to the auto union, praised them up to us often. The Reuther brothers, on the other hand, were commonly identified as Socialists. Their reason for opposing Homer Martin's policies was that they felt he was sliding back toward the conservative philosophy of the AFL. They disapproved strongly of Martin's tendency to have contracts negotiated with employers by top union officers alone, with little or no participation by the rank-and-file representatives of the local unions. They were fearful of a concentration of control and power in the hands of a few top union executives. Moreover, they believed that Martin was a poor bargainer and a worse administrator. The future of the union was menaced, they felt, by Martin's drive to purge all his opposition, Communist and non-Communist alike.

Not feeling strong enough to defeat Martin, the Unity Caucus strategists sought to dilute his power by electing their vice-presidential and Executive Board candidates. In my local union, the Unity Caucus didn't make much of a showing. Walter Reuther, who was a member of the International Executive Board of the union, came to the local meeting at which we had a battle over voting on instructions to the convention delegates. The hall was jammed with sweating, excited workers; all the seats were filled and even the aisles were packed. Reuther could not even get up to the platform.

I climbed up on top of a steam radiator and waved my hand to try to catch the attention of the local's President, Joe Sawicki.

"Mr. Chairman, Mr. Chairman," I yelled at the top of my

voice, over and over. A few of my supporters began shouting at Sawicki to give me the floor. Finally he recognized me.

"Mr. Chairman and fellow workers," I shouted. "I don't think we should instruct the delegates to the convention without hearing from a member of the International Executive Board who is here in the hall right now. I am a delegate to that convention and I believe I have a right to hear what this Board member, Brother Walter Reuther, has to say."

At the mention of Reuther's name a few Unity Caucus followers began to cheer, while the Martinites booed loudly. Sawicki rapped his gavel for order.

"Mr. Chairman," I shouted again to make myself heard over the confusion, "I move that we give Brother Reuther the floor to explain the issues of the convention to this meeting."

Elmer Dowell leaned over and whispered in Sawicki's ear.

"You're out of order, Brother Fountain," Sawicki suddenly yelled, banging his gavel and giving the floor to someone else.

Reuther pushed his way up to the platform and argued with Sawicki and Dowell, but it was no use; they wouldn't give him the floor. I left the meeting and went with him to another meeting being held by Bohn Aluminum Local 208. The chairman of this meeting was Fred Williams, who, I knew, was a Communist comrade. Reuther had no trouble in getting the floor there—because Williams also ranked high in the Unity Caucus. Williams is still a prominent Communist, and Local 208 usually elects delegates who are solidly anti-Reuther.

While the pre-convention jockeying was still going on in the locals, Merlin Bishop, Educational Director of the International Union, sent out a call for a summer-school session to be held at a camp near Brighton, Michigan. Local unions were urged to send members of their education committees to this school for training in economics, labor history, parliamentary procedure, and other appropriate fields.

It took a lot of fast talking on my part, but I persuaded the local union Executive Board to send me to that school, with all expenses and lost time paid out of the local treasury. Loaded down with my typewriter and a bundle of Communist literature, I set out for the school with a carload of workers from other shops.

The school ran pretty smoothly, despite the fact that a lot of the students were Communists. We Commies attended the classes diligently, especially the economics course. In this class we missed no opportunity to spout the party line. One of the workers who was active with me in party work at the school was Ralph Urban of Packard Local 190. He went overseas with the Air Corps during the war and, on his return, was elected president of Local 190, a post he still holds.

After classes, when the evening's recreation program was ended, the students engaged in bull sessions. At these gabfests, we Commies really went to town with the propaganda. Late at night we held our own secret caucuses to plan strategy for the next day and the next night, to make sure that our forces were fully utilized in the best interest of the party.

Late that summer, at a reunion of the summer school students, it was decided to set up an alumni organization. By that time we Commies were so well organized among the students that we captured the alumni group lock, stock, and barrel. I was elected president of the group. Urban was named secretary.

A special train was chartered by the union to transport hundreds of delegates from the larger Detroit local unions to the Milwaukee Convention, which opened Monday, August 23, 1937. The train was equipped with one or more cars in which beer was served; and scores of delegates carried bottles of stouter beverages to fortify them during the long ride. By the time the train reached the smoky outskirts of Chicago, where the steel mills stretch along the shore of Lake Michigan for miles, many of us were careening up and down the aisles singing "Solidarity Forever" and "We Shall Not Be Moved" at the tops of our voices. Once, in an excess of revolutionary zeal, I began to lead a group in singing the "Internationale," but a couple of big shots of the Unity Caucus came along and hushed me up.

The opening ceremonies and speeches were taken care of on the first day of the convention. On Tuesday the delegates got down to business by pitching into a furious fight over the report of the Credentials Committee. This committee was split two to one over a dispute as to the seating of several delegates; ten members of the committee favored Homer Martin and the Progressive Caucus, and the other five upheld the views of the Unity Caucus.

Fisher Body Plant One, in Flint, scene of the historic sit-down strike and the "Battle of the Running Bulls," was the biggest bone of contention in the divided report of this committee. There fifteen delegates, each with one vote, had been elected, on the basis of the number of votes allotted to the plant in the convention call. Later it was decided that the plant was entitled to twenty-three votes instead of fifteen. By one of those quirks of fate and the democratic process, it happened that the first fifteen delegates elected were mostly Homer Martin supporters, while the next eight candidates on the ballot were largely backers of the Unity Caucus. Supported by his majority on the International Executive Board, Martin ruled that the additional eight votes were to be prorated among the original fifteen delegates, and were not to be given to the next eight candidates on the ballot. The candidates disputed this; they were on hand in Milwaukee to fight for their rights. But the Martin majority on the Credentials Committee backed the Board's decision. This led to an open fight on the floor, with George Edwards, of West Side Local 174—who is today President of the Detroit Common Council—leading the five-member minority of the Credentials Committee. Stuart Strachan, another shop leader from Local 174, was the pro-Martin chairman of the Committee.

Martin showed his hand throughout the convention by ruling consistently in favor of his Progressive Caucus. In connection with this particular dispute he at first permitted the minority of the Credentials Committee to be heard, and seemingly agreed to defer final allocation of the disputed votes until the Committee had held further hearings and reported back to the convention. Thereafter he worked with the majority of the Committee to keep the report off the floor until after the Michigan members of the Executive Board had been elected. The disputed eight votes would have resulted in placing another Unity Caucus adherent on the Board in place of a Martin man. When the time came to hold the regional elections, the Unity Caucus leaders fought hard to have the Credentials Committee report for action by the convention before the Michigan Board members were elected by Michigan delegates to the convention. But Martin ruled that the fifteen delegates from Fisher One could cast the entire twenty-three votes.

On the final day of the convention, the Credentials Committee finally made its report, at which point the confusion and frustration on the floor approached the proportions of a riot. The Unity Caucus leaders repeated their appeals to the delegates to grant the eight delegates from Fisher One their right to vote. The motion was to concur in the majority report, which denied a vote to these eight delegates. When the question was at last put to a voice vote Martin ruled that the "Ayes" had it. At this point the verbatim proceedings reveal better than my words how Martin conducted the convention.

President Martin: I would like to say this, I made a decision as chairman, and may I say to you that there is a machine, an electrically equipped machine in this building that registers the vote "Aye" and "Nay."

(There was renewed confusion and shouts.)

President Martin: Just a minute—let me tell you.

A Delegate: Take the vote over, will you do that?

Another Delegate: Go home, sorehead.

President Martin: Let me tell you this machine registered the vote here, and the operator here can tell you that that machine scientifically decides this question. The answer of this machine was 16 to 12 in favor of the decision.

Delegate Ditzel . . . : Point of Information. Are we going to register a vote according to a machine which will tell which side can yell the loudest?

President Martin: That is the only way to decide an "Aye" and "Nay" vote.

(Confusion renewed.)

The remarks inside the parentheses were inserted by the reporter taking down the proceedings, and they do small justice to the degree of noise, bitterness, and bafflement that prevailed in the convention at that moment. Delegates stood on tables shouting for a roll-call vote, so that the issue could be decided by the actual votes of the delegates instead of by the volume of their voices. But Martin firmly refused the loud demands for a roll call.

Finally George Addes, Secretary-Treasurer, who more or less held himself aloof from both caucuses, made a speech for unity, asking the delegates to accept Martin's decision. Then Walter Reuther, probably realizing the futility of a further fight, accepted the decision under protest, for the sake of getting the dissatisfaction of the Unity Caucus into the record.

Martin suffered only one real setback during the entire convention. That happened when his majority on the Constitution Committee tried to sneak through a clause that would give small local unions a big advantage over large local unions in the next convention. Since the majority of the powerful new locals in Michigan were largely in the Unity Caucus, this plot was designed to give the Martinites an automatic edge in the election of delegates for the succeeding convention.

This proposition was just too raw for the convention to swallow. Walter Reuther got the floor and pointed out the undemocratic character of the scheme with an illustrative example of what would happen if the majority report were adopted. He explained that this maneuver would give one hundred small locals, each with not more than a hundred members, an aggregate of one hundred votes in the next convention, while one large local, with a membership of ten thousand workers, would be entitled to only twenty-three votes.

When the vote was taken, Martin's proposal was defeated by a substantial majority. The minority recommendation, giving all local unions an equal voting strength of one vote for each hundred members or major fraction thereof, was adopted instead.

The fight over election of top officers was not resolved until John L. Lewis himself came into the convention and compelled the factions to agree to a kind of armed truce. Under the Lewis compromise, Martin and Addes were unanimously re-elected as President and Secretary-Treasurer, and Wyndham Mortimer, Ed Hall, Walter Wells, Dick Frankensteen, and R. J. Thomas were all elected as vice-presidents without rank. In the balloting for regional Executive Board members, the Unity Caucus was able to win only five out of sixteen places.

Martin was thus assured of control of the new Executive Board. I think this summary of the 1937 UAW-CIO convention shows plainly that the anti-Martin faction, which the Communists bored into but could not control, had legitimate grounds for wanting to be rid of Martin. His conduct in the convention indicates the lust for power that impelled him to stray ever farther from the democratic principles of industrial unionism.

My personal role in the convention was too small to occupy much space in this chronicle. I attended a number of Communist party caucuses, at which Weinstone and Gebert, the commissars in charge of CP affairs in the auto union, gave out orders for the conduct of party members on the floor. As a member of the Education Committee, I echoed the party line devoutly. I made only one speech, on the seventh day of the conclave, when I questioned the right of the Constitution Committee to report out a clause dealing with education before the Education Committee had made its report. In the regional voting, I bolted, with another comrade, from the unit rule governing my delegation, to cast my votes for the Unity Caucus slate.

Back home from the convention, I plunged myself furiously into party activities. In Local 235, working through our growing unit of comrades, we lost no opportunity to heckle the Martin followers who controlled the local executive board. We held party caucuses before and after all union meetings. Sometimes I was called into skull sessions with the higher-ups of the party to get the line fresh from the commissars. I introduced resolutions on the floor of local union meetings to aid the Spanish Loyalist government and to boycott the purchase of silk from Japan. I led the Communist forces in efforts to affiliate the local union to the National Negro Congress and the Civil Rights Federation, both Communist front organizations.

When our opponents objected to the injection of such matters into local union meetings, we wore them down in a number of ways. For one thing, we had superior speakers. Our boys not only attended all the union educational classes they were eligible to participate in but also took lessons in speaking from party experts. We were also trained in the fine points of parliamentary trickery. Sometimes our knowledge of parliamentary procedure was enough in itself to impress the unschooled workers at union meetings—they backed our proposals with the conviction that such learned fellow workers must know what was right for the local. On other occasions we raised points of order, points of information, divisions of the house, objections to consideration of the question, amendments to the amendment, and appeals from the decision of the chair in endless and swift succession. After two or three hours of shouting and confused exchanges of parliamentary thrusts with our less skilled opponents, many of the union members left the meeting in sheer disgust and weariness.

The comrades and their cohorts stayed on in such disrupted meetings until the voting odds were in their favor; then the party line resolutions and motions to contribute funds to CP front outfits passed the meeting with machine-like precision. This is one of the traditional tactics by which the party gets its way in organizational situations where it does not have a majority. Once it gains control of an organization, it uses all these tactics in reverse, so to speak, and denies the opposition its democratic rights. Packed committees, stolen elections, physical violence, and any other convenient dictatorial tactic—such as holding union meetings and elections miles away from the shops—are employed by the party to maintain control of locals in their power. In many CIO councils these tactics are used on a much larger scale. The Detroit and Wayne County Industrial Union Council, for instance, was so completely dominated by the Communist party that top CIO officials had to move in to rescue it from the clutches of the comrades. It was captured by the Communists with exactly the same tactics that I was schooled to use in Local 235 back in 1937 and 1938.

Opportunities for Communist agitation were enlarged the following winter by the recession that hit Detroit and sent many workers trudging back to the relief offices. In Chevrolet Gear and Axle we worked only two days a week nearly all that winter. At an hourly rate of one dollar, my pay for two eight-hour days amounted to sixteen dollars minus deductions for insurance and social security. This did not leave me enough to pay the rent, the grocery bill, and incidental expenses. I met this problem by giving the grocer whatever I could spare and letting the bill run on up. Later, when work picked up again, it took me six months to pay the grocer off.

With five days a week free, I devoted myself to assignments given to me by the party. A Renters and Consumers League was organized to fight against evictions and efforts of landlords to collect back rent owed by desperate workers. The party sponsored this outfit and assumed control of it from the start. A chap named Mort Furay was named as director, and I worked under him in a tiny office set up in the Hofmann Building to direct our agitation among disgruntled tenants. Furay later became an organizer and regional director for the United Public Workers of America, one of the unions with a "paper" membership which the Commies use to throw their weight around inside the CIO.

In apartment buildings where one or more comrades were present to fan the flames of discontent it was simple to organize the tenants around such an issue as an increase in rent or an eviction. A comrade in such a situation would report such an increase or eviction notice to us, and we would grind out a mimeographed leaflet calling a meeting in the building. After one or two such meetings a tenants' committee would be elected—usually with a comrade as chairman or secretary—and a picket line thrown in front of the building to advertise the protest. Such skirmishes with the landlords produced little in the way of direct benefits for the suffering tenants. Sometimes a landlord would bow to the weight of numbers and agree to negotiate on rent scales, but such victories were rare.

It mattered little to the party, though, that the uproars we fomented in such situations seldom paid off in measurable cash returns to the tenants who served as troops under our commissars. In fact, I have become convinced by my experience with the Communists that they prefer to lose most of their day-to-day battles with the capitalists. A battle lost to an employer, to a landlord, or to a hostile government executive gives the party its best opportunity to beat the drums for the "final conflict" to overthrow capitalism. Under such conditions, party stalwarts emphasize the inability to make progress under capitalism and stress their theory that it is necessary to build the Communist movement in order to win the final victory. Anyway, our struggles with the landlords in Detroit that winter paid off with new converts and recruits for the party. So long as the rent strikes and eviction riots provided an atmosphere of confusion and conflict in which to build up Communist membership, the commissars were happy.

It was on the occasion of an eviction riot led by myself and another comrade that I was tossed into jail in February 1938—covering myself with glory in the true spirit of a front line fighter for communism. The incident started when a member of Local 157 came running into the Local 157 hall on Sproat Street to announce breathlessly that an eviction was taking place at 686 Stimson Avenue. We had a crew of unemployed unionists on hand for just such emergencies—with a sprinkling of party members for ideological guidance.

Out of the union hall we ran, and covered the few blocks to the scene of the eviction in a few minutes. When we arrived a pair of constables were directing a moving crew in the work of depositing the final sticks of rickety furniture on the sidewalk. A crowd had already begun to gather; it was swelled by the arrival of our "flying squad."

Here was a situation tailor-made for Communist leadership. As the constables departed, their worked finished, I mounted a chair and began to address the assembled "prisoners of starvation" with revolutionary fervor. The episode took place in the heart of the Detroit downtown slum area and my audience looked really seedy and bedraggled enough to fill the role of "prisoners of starvation." The victim was a widow with three children. Her tears moved me to a crescendo of eloquence portraying the plight of the poor under capitalist oppression.

"Fellow citizens," I shouted to the throng, "are we going to stand here idle and see this poor woman thrown out in the cold to suffer? What kind of a social order is it that takes the roof from over the head of these three kids in February, when the temperature is below freezing? Here is a classic example of the brutality of the employers and bankers and landlords, whose hearts are colder than the north wind blowing down Third Street." I waved my hand in a dramatic gesture, my language taking on the imagery in which my Indian ancestors may have voiced their complaints against the greed of the encroaching pale-faces.

"Yes, the law is on the side of the landlord; that is the way capitalism works; the law is always on the side of the rich and privileged," I told the crowd. "But there is another law more powerful than the laws of capitalism; it is the law of justice and common decency—and I say that the law of decency demands that we put this family back into that house, so they will not have to sleep in the street tonight. What do you say?"

At this point the comrade who had accompanied me to the scene of the eviction spoke up in his role as my stooge, apparently as just another member of the crowd. "This brother is right," he shouted. "We can't let this family stay out in the cold. Come on, let's put this stuff back in the house." With these words, he grabbed a table lamp and ran up the steps with it.

The crowd, moved by this demonstration of militant leadership, laid willing hands on the poor woman's shabby possessions and carried them back into the house swiftly and efficiently. Just as the last of the stuff was carried in, a scout car loaded with police came dashing up the street. Most of the crowd scattered and escaped, but three other fellows and myself were trapped in the house. The cops hauled us off to the Canfield Station. There we spent the night, waiting for a union attorney to spring us the next morning. Two of us were Communists; and such was our zeal that we did not even waste the time spent in jail—we used it trying to convert the other two prisoners to the cause. Later, when we were tried by jury in Recorder's Court on a charge of inciting to riot, a sympathetic group of jurors found us not guilty despite ample evidence presented by the prosecutor to show that we had started the row.

Communists were not the only participants in those battles against the recession of 1938. The UAW-CIO itself carried on a large-scale welfare program which was far more effective than the noisy protests conducted by the comrades. It was as Director of the union's Welfare Department that George Edwards began the career of public service later climaxed by his election to the Detroit Common Council.

On April 2, 1938, I again fell into the clutches of the law, this time as a result of my participation in a bloody riot at the gates of the Federal Screw plant. The workers in this plant, organized in West Side Local 174, were on strike over a wage dispute. Mayor Richard Reading, who was later convicted and jailed for grafting, sent scores of mounted police to escort a few scabs out of the plant on the day of the riot. UAW-CIO top leaders had mobilized the full power of the union's Detroit membership to back up the strikers. It was a legitimate strike, provoked by the refusal of management to deal with the union in good faith. This attitude on the part of the company, coupled with police attacks on the picket lines, played directly into the hands of CP commissars eager to exploit flare-ups of violence.

By this time I had been promoted up the scale of party offices to Detroit correspondent of the *Midwest Daily Record*, the Communist paper started in Chicago in 1937 under the editorship of Louis F. Budenz. In that capacity I wrote a signed story, which the *Record* displayed in a five-column spread, under the title "I Saw Police Terror."

According to my story, I was simply watching the fighting, in which dozens of workers were having their heads split open by police clubs, when a burly detective seized me and hurried me into a police wagon. The cops told the prosecutor a different story. They said I was one of a crew so depraved, so scornful of law and order, that it stooped to the crime of shooting marbles at police horses with slingshots made of heavy wire and strips of inner tubes. Of course, I indignantly denied this charge. It was beneath the dignity of a correspondent of a daily paper—in spite of the fact that he received no stipend for his journalistic labors—to indulge in such resourceful methods.

Happily, the prosecutor, who was friendly to labor, found a technical flaw in the manner in which the police had obtained a warrant for our prosecution. I got off again with only one night in jail and raced to the Renters and Consumers League office, where I banged out my story for the *Record.*

In summing up these highlights of the period when advancement of communism was the most vital factor in my life—and I have tried to indicate the degree of zeal and devotion that motivates most Communists—I feel required to justify the chapter heading, "Politics with Passion."

The kind of passion I have in mind is that fanatic brand of devotion which grips the minds of people with such force that they are transformed into unquestioning slaves of an idea. Down the ages of human experience, people gripped by the impulse to give their all to a cause have turned largely to religion as a channel for expressing their devoutness. Every theological doctrine has had its faithful servants who ask no questions, raise no doubts, who are always on hand to perform the most difficult missions and tasks for the cause. I do not make this point in a spirit of criticism, for I believe that religion has worked much good in the world; but only to show that religion has been the cause which has most frequently attracted the services of instinctive zealots. In those instances in which religious zeal has overstepped its boundary and has persecuted and tortured unbelievers its excesses have been carried out by the unquestioning zealots staffing the ranks of the faithful.

Today, I am convinced, the Communist movement, directed from Moscow, has taken on the character of a kind of political religion. It offers zealots a star to which they can hitch their wagons—their passion to serve as willing slaves of a cause. It provides emotional nourishment for those who are so disgusted with the sorry state of the world that they are ready to use any means to fight poverty, depression, and war. With Russia as a base, it has taken on the solidity, bulk, and momentum that give it a strong appeal to rebels who want to be identified with a going concern powerful enough to trumpet its capacity for success.

Much of communism's strength in the world today derives

from the support of workers, party members, and fellow travelers who are loyal to the original objectives of Marxism without realizing the degree of control exercised over the party by the Soviet government. During my time as a Communist, I think I fell into that category. Communism to me did not mean Russia. It meant a cause which I believed to be devoted to humanitarian and liberal objectives. I was convinced, when I was a party member, that the Communist movement was rooted in unswerving devotion to freedom of speech, freedom of the press, free representative government, racial equality, decency, and truth. Believing this, I was willing to accept the word of party leaders that the Soviet government was committed to these principles and working for their realization on a world-wide scale.

Since I firmly believed that the party was devoted to noble objectives, and that all opposition to communism was inspired by reactionaries who wanted the working people to remain slaves of the capitalist system, I fell readily into the carefully nurtured theory that the party could do no wrong. Like a puppet on a string, I echoed the chant of "Red-baiter, Red-baiter," at anyone who voiced a criticism of the party. It seemed perfectly reasonable to me then that our objectives were so worthy as to make any criticism of the party a denial of basic human rights.

It was not until the long arm of Soviet power reached across land and sea to interfere with my personal freedom—as I shall presently relate—that I began to comprehend that the survival of the Russian state had taken precedence over the professed noble objectives of Marxism.

8. A Renegade Is Born

Late in April 1938 the factional struggle inside the UAW-CIO was complicated by a double cross that split the Unity Caucus wide open. The maneuver that divided the anti-Martin coalition into two sub-caucuses was engineered by the Communists at the first Michigan State CIO convention, held at Lansing, Michigan. As a result of this stratagem—pulled out of a hat by the Commies in one of their overnight revisions of policy, commonly known as flip-flops—the Reuther brothers took off on an independent course of their own, in opposition to both the Martinites and the Commies.

I was a delegate to that convention from my local union. Our delegation was divided again, this time almost evenly pro-Martin and anti-Martin. Two of us were Communists, three were fellow travelers, five were pro-Martin, and two were indifferent.

The convention was called under the auspices of the National CIO to set up a functioning CIO council for the state of Michigan. Delegates were elected by all CIO unions in Michigan on a basis of representation worked out in advance by top CIO officers. Under the organization pattern proposed, these delegates were to adopt a constitution and a program and elect officers. The officers were to be a state president, a state secretary-treasurer, and a dozen vice-presidents, all of whom were to comprise the State Executive Board. Two major projects were specified for the council: first, to direct the work of a staff of organizers assigned to complete the organization of workers under the jurisdiction of the CIO and to service the smaller locals in negotiations with employers; and, second, to coordinate the political action and legislative work of the CIO at the state level. These functions were to be financed by payment of a per capita tax of one cent per month per member from the treasuries of all locals affiliated with the council.

There was no contest for the office of state president. With the heavy hand of John L. Lewis guiding the parleys by remote control, a compromise was worked out, in the American political tradition, behind closed hotel-room doors. Adolph Germer, a battle-scarred veteran from the ranks of the United Mine Workers, then serving as CIO Regional Director for the Michigan area, was chosen by agreement of all factions to fill the position of president. But the representatives sent to Lansing by Lewis could not get the various groups to agree on a compromise to fill the important job of secretary-treasurer. It was in connection with the contest over this job that the Commies pulled off the double cross that shattered the ranks of the Unity Caucus.

The Martin faction put up Richard T. Leonard, president of the UAW-CIO DeSoto Local 227, as their candidate for the job of secretary-treasurer. Leonard was a run-of-the-mill local union leader, with a long record of union activity, who had started his labor career in an AFL local at the old Hupp Motor plant. Neither brilliant nor stupid, interested mainly in the routine wages-and-hours chores of unionism, Leonard was regarded as a non-political choice who would follow the guidance of Martin's brain trust.

In opposition to Leonard, the Unity Caucus at first agreed to put up young Victor G. Reuther of West Side Local 174 in Detroit. Vic Reuther was very much the opposite of Leonard. While both candidates sprang from families steeped in the precepts of unionism, Vic Reuther was a scholar, a thinker, and a powerful orator, overflowing with determination to rid the world of poverty, hatred, and war.

All through the convention the campaign for the secretary-treasurership was conducted around the merits of these two candidates. Then, on the eve of the election, the Commies pulled their double cross. I remember vividly how we comrades were hastily rounded up and called into a caucus to have the party strategy spelled out to us. William Weinstone and Bill Gebert were the commissars in command. All the party-line UAW-CIO leaders from Michigan were there. Thirty or forty comrades of lesser rank, like myself, sat around listening while the powers of the party gave us the line. Out of nowhere they came up with instructions to desert Vic Reuther and turn on the heat for Dick Leonard.

The reasoning behind this switch arose from the developing trend toward abandonment of the United Front program formulated by the 1935 meeting of the Communist International. Party bosses were becoming more and more troubled by the devotion of the Reuther brothers and of other influential non-Communists in the anti-Martin coalition to democracy for democracy's sake. Unable to control the anti-Martin coalition and run it strictly in the interests of Russia—because the Reuthers and others insisted on plugging away in the interests of the workers and the American people—the Commies decided to break up the caucus. This is a typical Communist tactic employed in situations where the comrades decide it is no longer strategic to work inside a group they cannot control rigidly. It is used tirelessly and effectively by Communist agents from the level of tiny local unions on up to the United Nations.

Leonard won the election, and the Martinites secured control of the Executive Board of the new Michigan State CIO Council by a comfortable majority. But the Martin faction never admitted that it owed the Communists anything for helping to elect Dick Leonard. Martin kept battling away for the possession of dictatorial power against both fragments of what had been the Unity Caucus, right on up to the time that John L. Lewis gave him the cold shoulder and placed his blessing on Martin's enemies.

On June 15, acting under what he interpreted as power properly granted to him by the union's constitution, Martin suspended Secretary-Treasurer George F. Addes and Vice-Presidents Richard T. Frankensteen, Wyndham Mortimer, Ed Hall, and Walter Wells. One vice-president, R. J. Thomas, who was later picked by top CIO leaders to become president, escaped the ax in this first Martin purge. This marked the beginning of a brief period of dual unionism that carried the factional fight down into the shop levels of the union and was characterized by flurries of violence. Two of the suspended officers, Frankensteen and Wells, had previously been among Martin's stoutest backers. Their desertion from his camp indicated a growing realization among the union's leadership that Martin's power in the union was slipping badly.

With a scant majority of the remaining members of the Executive Board still backing him, Martin, on July 5, shoved through a resolution expelling George F. Addes from the union. Addes, together with the other four suspended officers, had written a letter to the local unions urging them to withhold their per capita taxes from the Martin-controlled International Office.

The battle dragged through the hot months of the summer. Martin staged a so-called trial, trying the suspended officers under his personal interpretation of the union's constitution. Meanwhile, local leaders from both factions journeyed to and from Washington, asking the mighty John L. Lewis to intervene in their behalf. These appeals to the parent CIO body were more than just political maneuvers; they indicated a growing desire in the lower ranks of affiliated CIO unions for more guidance and responsibility at the top level of leadership. By then the character of the national CIO structure had become more clearly defined. New, strong unions, organized on an industry-wide basis, had been built in the steel, rubber, oil, and other mass-production industries. These were united with the auto workers and with the old clothing, garment, and textile unions in the CIO, which was now formally known as the Congress of Industrial Organizations. This title had been chosen in order to retain the CIO initials, formerly used to abbreviate the Committee for Industrial Organization. All affiliated CIO unions were autonomous, of course; but the appeal of both UAW-CIO factions to Lewis displayed a belief that the parent federation could and should encourage stability and peace in the member unions. Late in August Lewis came out with a peace proposal that was mailed to all local unions with the request that they urge the Executive Board to accept it. In the September 3 issue of the *United Automobile Worker* Martin denounced the Lewis peace proposal. Two weeks later another issue of the official paper announced that a truce had been reached through the intervention of Philip Murray and Sidney Hillman, CIO vice-presidents. This truce provided for resolution of the differences by a joint committee made up of Murray, Hillman, Martin, and R. J. Thomas. It provided further that Murray and Hillman were to arbitrate the case of the suspended officers. Early in October they were reinstated. On the surface there was an appearance of unity, and we threw our strength into a furious campaign to re-elect Frank Murphy as Governor of Michigan.

I was called out of the shop on a leave of absence to direct the CIO phase of the election battle of 1938 in my home territory, the Seventeenth Congressional District of Michigan. We pooled forces with the Democrats and worked long hours ringing doorbells, passing out literature, and holding meetings to advance the cause of Governor Murphy. Except for the presidential campaigns of President Roosevelt, that 1938 campaign for Frank Murphy aroused more enthusiasm than I have witnessed in any other political drive. People came out to meetings; precinct workers slaved to win votes for the man who enjoyed the greatest labor support any Governor of Michigan had ever had. The people of Michigan really went for Frank Murphy in a big way. It was in the course of this campaign that I began to stray from the Communist line.

Clarence Hathaway, then editor of the *Daily Worker*, came to Detroit on the eve of the 1938 election to make a speech for the party. In the course of his remarks he stated that the Communists were working just as hard as they knew how to insure the victory of Governor Frank Murphy. The daily papers promptly snatched up this endorsement and transformed it into a kiss of death. Coupled with a blast by the Dies Committee in Washington, insinuating that Murphy was tolerant—if not enamored—of the Reds, the Hathaway contribution to the campaign may well have done the trick for the Republicans that year in Michigan.

The Hathaway stunt raised serious doubts in my mind about the effectiveness of Communist tactics. At first I kept these doubts to myself. It seemed to me that Hathaway—and the party—had hurt the Murphy campaign by coming out openly with an endorsement of the Governor. There were many thousands of people in Michigan who did not know, as I believed I did, that the Communist party was an instrument of decency and freedom. Many people, "misled by the capitalistic daily press," thought communism was committed to free love, dictatorship, and destruction of the American home. As I reasoned it out to myself, Hathaway's endorsement must undoubtedly have frightened many such people into voting for the Republican candidate. On the other hand, if the party had held its tongue and plugged away secretly in the wards and precincts, Murphy might have been re-elected by a safe majority.

As I turned this question over in my mind, a more profound contradiction arose to plague me and push me farther down the dangerous road of doubt. If I was not sufficiently sold on the party to justify the Hathaway endorsement of Frank Murphy, then there was something seriously wrong with my political convictions.

In my troubled mind, the fermenting doubts worked themselves out into a feeling that the party ought to make up its mind to be totally conspiratorial or totally open and aboveboard—that it could not operate successfully as a will-o'-the-wisp. I felt that I could justify either a tactic of total conspiracy or a tactic of complete openness, but I inclined strongly toward the idea of being open and aboveboard. After all, if one was loyal to an idea that embodied brotherhood, equality, freedom, and decency—and communism was supposed to represent all these noble things—what did one have to hide? It was true that the enemies of the cause had incited such hatred of communism in some localities as to put the lives of admitted comrades in danger. But if the entire party all over the world were to raise its voice loudly and proclaim its devotion to freedom, equality, brotherhood, and peace, and back up its proclamation with militant action, would not the masses rally to it in sufficient force to protect it from reactionary terror?

The more I mulled over this problem the more I drifted toward the conviction that a party pledged to the things that I thought communism stood for had no reason to be conspiratorial in America. Why, the whole tradition of American democracy was steeped in a sturdy appreciation of the basic right of people to rebel against oppression! As a nation we were young; we had a revolution and a civil war under our belt, both fought unquestionably for human freedom. We had freedom of speech, freedom of the press, freedom of assembly, freedom of religion, and the forms of free parliamentary government. These precious rights had been won for us by the blood our ancestors had shed in open revolution against a dictatorial king. Why should anyone who wanted to add economic freedom for the poor to these other basic democratic rights have to hide his convictions?

I began to discuss these doubts with other comrades. One night at a union party, fortified with several applications of the auto worker's cure for fatigue—a shot and a beer—I grew overly eloquent in my suggestions that the party ought to Americanize itself. I expounded my developing theory at length. In America, I argued, with her revolutionary background, there was no need for a truly radical party to operate secretly. The ideas we stood for were essentially the same as those espoused by Adams, Jefferson, Paine, Madison, and other leaders of the American Revolution. The trouble was that, in the course of a century and a half, a few rich plutocrats had grabbed too many controls and were steering us back into the same jam our ancestors had rebelled against. All we had to do was to identify ourselves with this revolutionary heritage and we, too, could win popular backing for an assault on the citadels of privilege. In my alcoholic enthusiasm, I think, I even went so far as to suggest that the party might change its name to something more in keeping with the American tradition.

"What does it matter what we call ourselves?" I shouted. "The important thing is to prove by our actions that we stand for freedom, equality, justice, human brotherhood, and peace—and that we are out to get those things for the American people."

"But we are an international organization," one comrade protested. "We have to shape all our policies within the framework of the international revolutionary situation."

"International or not," I countered with an eloquent hiccup, "I still say we can use the American revolutionary tradition to get things done here for the workers, no matter what happens in the rest of the world."

A few days later I was called into party headquarters and lectured severely for my waywardness. Billy Allan, one of the top commissars in Detroit, was assigned the task of guiding me away from the path of sin and heresy. He ascribed my doubts to an unnecessary consumption of alcohol. "You just stay away from the bottle and you'll be all right," he said.

For the time being, I was not too much concerned with having been called in and told to mend my ways. I still felt that the party was democratic enough to permit me to advocate its Americanization—that is, I believed that freedom of speech and freedom of thought existed within the party. That was where I made a mistake. And I made an even greater mistake in assuming that the party might even have a sense of humor.

Thinking to do the party a favor, I wrote the following letter to the Editor of the *Detroit News*:

To the Editor:

Between the Dies Committee quiz and the UAW factional fight, the Reds are getting plenty of publicity these troubled days. The question seems to be who is, and who is not, a real Communist—or who has deserted the revolution and the dictatorship of the proletariat?

Earl Browder, national secretary of the Communist party, in his pamphlet, *The Democratic Front*, says: "The main objective of labor must be to secure at all costs the defeat of the candidates of reaction and Fascism. . . . Labor must strive in every way for the unification of all democratic forces behind a single progressive candidate for each office. The Communist Party of the USA is based upon the fundamental program of the revolutionary reorganization of our country. . . . Because the majority of the American people are not convinced of the necessity of this socialist reorganization . . . and because today the main enemy is Fascism, the Communist Party finds it necessary to dedicate all its forces to realizing the program of the Democratic Front."

Jay Lovestone, head of the Independent Communist Labor League, in his pamphlet, *People's Front Illusion,* declares: "In short, in practice, the People's Front policy entails not merely a postponement of the struggle but even the abandonment of the agitation for the proletarian dictatorship for an indefinite period. The very emergence of the Fascist movement proves that only a proletarian dictatorship can today guarantee and promote the progress of humankind. Therefore, in the struggle against Fascism, the working class cannot have a permanent alliance with bourgeois parties and organizations—unless, of course, the working class gives up the struggle against capitalism as a system in decay . . ."

On the strength of their respective declarations of principle, it appears that Browder is a mere pink in comparison with the "true revolutionary," Jay Lovestone.

What I meant to prove by this piece, of course, was that our espousal of the "Democratic Front" proved that we were not impractical radicals, that we wanted to work with all people of good will to repulse the fascist threat and get on with the building of a better world. The party brass hats swiftly called me in and gave me hell for selling the party short in print. I was interrogated by the Disciplinary Commission of the District. They insisted that I should have written my piece in such a manner as to prove that promotion of the "Democratic Front" was the really radical thing to do in the present world situation, that the Communist party was the only truly revolutionary party, that all other so-called Leftist parties were strictly fakes and phonies. When I remarked that I had simply been poking fun at Lovestone, they abruptly reminded me that there was no place for humor in the serious discussion of revolutionary politics.

In the middle of this session with the Disciplinary Commission, the party leaders assigned to handle my intellectual guidance really got at the meat of our differences when they demanded to know why I had been reading a pamphlet by Lovestone, anyway? Was I not aware that he had been expelled from the party for treachery, that he was a dangerous renegade?

"Yes," I replied, "I know all those things, but I think I owe it to myself to read Lovestone or any other author of a political work to find out for myself just what these political struggles are all about."

Then the commissars blew their totalitarian tops. They informed me with an air of gravity that only "advanced revolutionary minds" were capable of comprehending the writings of such renegades as Lovestone and Trotsky. Henceforth, they told me firmly but gently, I would be expected to read only such political writings as were suggested for me by party leaders of long experience and profound political wisdom. In penance for my sins, I was instructed to write a treatise of ten thousand words denouncing Lovestone and proving that he was a stooge for the fascists.

It was then that I began vaguely to comprehend that there was no such thing as freedom of thought inside the official Communist movement. These men were telling me that I had no right to select my own reading matter. They were directing me to close my mind to the utterances of persons whom they described as "political adventurers and dangerous renegades." Their word was supposed to be powerful enough to establish the fact that the forbidden authors were wrong, and, therefore, there was no point in my reading such authors. In short, I was not to be trusted to judge for myself whether the authors had anything to say that might have validity for me. Mentally shocked into a daze by the impact of this blow against my belief that the party stood for decency and freedom, I could do nothing but nod in agreement to all that was said to me during the balance of the meeting.

Breaking faith with a political movement that one has believed in devoutly as the salvation of the human race is an experience full of emotional strain. When I realized that the Communist party insisted on chaining my intellect to the "line," as the price of staying in its fold, I knew that I could not and would not stay. But the physical act of making the break was something to be avoided as long as possible, like going to the dentist. For several days after my session with the Disciplinary Commission, I turned my problem over and over in my mind. To break with the Communists meant starting all over again from scratch in my efforts to make a place for myself in the ranks of the labor world.

In my local union, I was pegged as a Communist by the other shop leaders active in the local's affairs. I had never admitted or denied my affiliation with the party. Whenever anyone had asked me the direct question "Are you a Communist?" I had evaded giving a direct answer. But I led all the party's battles in the local and worked as a faithful cog in the party machine at larger labor conferences and conventions. My speeches were full of fire and fury, I battled for the rights of the underdog, and I did have a following. Even with the handicap of having opposition candidates whisper through the shop that I was a Communist, I was able to place high on the ballot during elections of delegates to important CIO conventions. This is typical of many Communists. I built my support and won my votes by working hard on grievances, collecting dues, signing up new members in the union, attending all meetings—in short, by doing a bang-up job for the union. By getting results, and by making plenty of militant speeches and writing fiery pieces for the shop paper and other papers, I perpetrated the great Communist deception that secures control of unions for the comrades. The workers who backed me with their votes were not impressed by the "Red-baiters" who described me as a Communist. They knew I was working hard for their interests and judged me accordingly. If a guy who worked as hard for the union as I did was a Communist—well, then, maybe Communists were good guys. And didn't Fountain say in his speeches that the bosses always called every guy a Red who wanted another dime an hour in his paycheck? And weren't the capitalist papers raving all the time about the communistic CIO? The CIO was the best thing that had happened to industrial workers in the history of America. If the bosses and the editors wanted to call it communistic, so what? Maybe it is communistic, and maybe communism is a good thing, some workers thought.

I describe this maneuver as a deception used by the Commies to win support and control, because I learned later that Communists are not really interested in doing things for the workers as such; they are interested in power harnessed to serve Russia. This was proven dramatically during the war when Commies betrayed trade union principles by such acts as selling piecework and scabbing on the striking Montgomery Ward workers. But at the time that I had to live with my problem of how to break with the party I did not know how much contempt the Communists have for principle.

When the deadline came for me to hand in the polemic against Lovestone which the party bosses had instructed me to write, I sent them instead a polite announcement that I was severing all my past political connections. From that day on I have—so far as the party is concerned—lived in that hobgoblin world inhabited by "Lovestoneites, Trotskyites, Lewisites, Coughlinites, and underminers of Big Three unity." These epithets, in CP jargon, connote darkness and evil, a world where all the party's enemies hatch plots to hamper the work of the faithful comrades.

It took me ten years to get around to the point of admitting without shame that I was once a part of the Soviet fifth column in this country. But I became grateful for experience gathered during my sojourn in the Communist party. My knowledge of the Communist pattern of political intrigue enables me to combat it more effectively at a time when I am certain that the drive of Soviet imperialism constitutes a direct threat to freedom and democracy.

On many occasions, when fuzzy-minded liberals or innocent laborites dispute my assertion that the Communists are in reality as reactionary as the capitalists and the Fascists, I can quote from my experience to prove my point. I can cite instances when I was instructed in party caucuses to thwart and corrupt the democratic process in the labor movement. I can relate how the party bosses tried to shackle my mind to the "line." I can spell out the reasons why Communists are totalitarian, and I can prove to political babes in the woods that it is impossible for Commies to be Left, liberal, or radical in the libertarian sense of these words.

9. New Beginnings

The first few weeks after my walk out of the Communist party into the role of a renegade were full of discomfort and loneliness. Most of my ex-comrades in Local 235 and in the entire CIO movement in Detroit, following party orders, turned against me and chopped away at my status in the union at every opportunity. The anti-Communists were too suspicious to take me into their ranks. By this time I was completely separated from my wife, having taken my two children to live with me in the home of a married sister. For a time I flirted with the notion of skipping the whole works and sliding back to my previous way of life—back to a routine of work, ball games, beer gardens, and hangovers.

January 1939, however, brought another crisis in the UAW-CIO. It caught me up in a whirlwind of factionalism that really blew Homer Martin out of power. Martin's downfall came about when he attempted to defy the UAW-CIO Executive Board majority that enjoyed the backing of John L. Lewis, Philip Murray, Sidney Hillman, and other top CIO officials. By then Martin's own backers on the board had dwindled to three members. With this slim and slipping grip on the loyalty of the top leadership of the UAW-CIO, Martin went on the air in a radio program and poured out a stream of strong accusations against his insurgent opposition. Under his orders, a squad of strong-arm men, most of them misguided union members who were loyal to him personally, seized the elaborate International Union headquarters in the Griswold Building in downtown Detroit. The board majority retaliated by sending its own flying squads to take over control of the union mailing lists at the Safran Printing Company plant on the East Side of Detroit.

The extent to which a disciplined political minority can gum up the workings of a labor organization was clearly demonstrated during this final blow-up between the Martinites and the anti-Martin faction. It was publicly revealed by the anti-Martin Executive Board majority of the UAW-CIO that Martin had been advised by a brain trust made up largely of agents of Jay Lovestone. Very few auto workers knew Jay Lovestone from the man in the moon. They did not know that he had been booted out of the Communist party for factional reasons, following his removal from a position of high leadership in the American section of the Soviet fifth column. When the inside story of the Homer Martin fight began to leak out, the auto workers learned plenty about Lovestone.

They learned that he had created a splinter Communist movement which was at first called The Communist Party Opposition. Later this outfit changed its name to The Independent Communist Labor League. Somehow the Lovestoneites got next to Martin and wormed their way into his confidence. Lester Washburn, a member of the UAW-CIO International Executive Board, who represented thousands of auto workers in Flint and Lansing, was a member of the Lovestoneite group. Martin hired Francis Henson and Eve Stone, two more followers of the Lovestone variety of communism, to work on the International Union's payroll. William Munger, who served the UAW-CIO at various times under Martin as Research Director and Editor, was another key person in the Lovestone group.

The Stalinist Communists hated the Lovestoneite Communists with a hatred more bitter than that directed toward any capitalist. They were infuriated at the spectacle of Lovestoneites manning strategic posts in the top structure of the UAW-CIO. This was one of the reasons why the Stalinists were so eager to see Homer Martin run out of the union. They wanted desperately to chop down the Lovestoneites at the same time. One day the anti-Martin faction turned up with a fistful of personal letters written between Jay

Lovestone and his agents in the UAW-CIO. These were intimate political documents, revealing how closely Martin had worked with the Lovestone clique. For a time the use of these letters was a great joke in the inner circles of the union. It was no secret that the Stalinists had obtained the letters by the simple device of sending their agents to break into the living quarters of Lovestone. A small thing like a burglary and the invasion of the privacy of a man's home were all in the day's work for the Stalinist agents.

Of course the Lovestone gang returned the hatred of the Stalinists with equal fury. Their factional hatred had, in turn, been largely responsible for the fury of Martin's anti-Communist crusade. So here was the UAW-CIO, composed mostly of honest union members trying to do a job for the workers, embroiled in a furious factional fight which was at least partly precipitated by the sectarian zeal of Marxist minorities entrenched on both sides of the factional fence. These minorities were not, of course, the exclusive cause of the factionalism. The real reason for it was the resistance of other union leaders to Martin's attempts to oust them. But the venomous interchanges between the CP and the Lovestoneites greatly intensified the struggle.

While Martin held the Union headquarters, and his opposition guarded the addressograph plates of the mailing list in the printing plant, a new headquarters was opened by the Board majority in the Fort Shelby Hotel. From this office a special convention was called to convene in Cleveland at the Hollenden Hotel on March 27, 1939. The election of delegates to this convention was accompanied by flurries of fist fighting and thuggery in many local unions. In my own local union we had a battle royal the last time Homer Martin tried to come to a membership meeting.

Martin announced on the Saturday before the meeting that he was going to appear at Local 235 the next day to tell "the truth to the Chevrolet Gear and Axle workers." To meet this threat, a group of us worked all night lining up our people to attend the meeting. We also invited flying squads from two other big locals to visit our meeting hall the next day—purely for the purpose of exchanging messages of "fraternal solicitude," of course. These preparations were made with the approval of the official leadership of the local union, a substantial majority of the local executive board having been converted to the anti-Martin camp.

When Martin arrived at the hall we were all set for him. On the platform we had Ed Hall, a leader of the anti-Martin faction in the International Union. Hall was a deep-voiced, paunchy, table-pounding battler. Adolph Germer, CIO Regional Director, was there, officially representing John L. Lewis and the national CIO office. We intended to give Martin the floor, then turn Hall and Germer loose on him.

The hall was packed when Martin came charging up to the door, escorted by a flying wedge of muscular henchman. Technically, he was still president of the International Union, and he asked to be admitted as such. All he could see of the door was two husky gearcutters from Plant One, standing shoulder to shoulder, wearing leather gloves.

"We'll send your message in and see what the meeting says," one of the gearcutters told Martin.

The sergeant-at-arms came in to the rostrum and told Joe Sawicki that Martin wanted in. Sawicki put the question to the meeting: "Shall we let Martin in?"

Someone made a motion that we let Martin in but instruct him to leave his goons outside. This motion passed almost unanimously, only a few Martinites dissenting.

Informed of this action, Martin's gang made one try at cracking the door, but the two gearcutters, backed up by the flying squads from other locals, laid the invaders out three deep on the sidewalk in front of the hall.

Martin then came into the meeting by himself, swinging a brief case full of papers to support his case. He was given the floor and began his address. Before he could get warmed up, the heckling began in earnest. Worker after worker jumped up and shouted insults at him. This was not part of our plan. We really wanted him to talk, so that Hall and Germer could chop him down in rebuttal. Several of us chased around the hall trying to quiet the boys down. But it was no go—we had done such a good job of undermining Martin in Local 235 that 95 per cent of the workers in that meeting did not want to hear what he had to say.

Frustrated and furious, Martin tried to play his trump card. "All good union men, follow me!" he shouted at the top of his voice and made for the side exit on the run.

It was then that my friend George Merrelli—a stanch Martinite up to that day—rose to a high point in his career. Merrelli was from my own Plant Two day shift; he ran a Fay lathe on the truck housing job, and we were locked in a battle for leadership of the shift. When Martin yelled his appeal, Merrelli leaped to the mike at the front of the hall and shouted: "Don't go out, fellows—stay here, stay with the CIO!"

Because of his standing in the Martin faction in our local, Merrelli's appeal carried weight. Only a handful of the most confirmed Martinites followed Homer out of the hall. Practically all of them came back later and remained loyal to the CIO after Martin marched his dwindling army into the AFL, where he stayed for a few months before fading out of the labor movement.

That was the end of Homer Martin in Local 235. We swung the local behind the Executive Board majority and sent our delegates to the Cleveland convention without any trouble. Out of eleven delegates to be elected, I placed fourth on the ballot with 485 votes, proving that I still had backing in the local.

The Cleveland convention opened with R. J. Thomas, a relatively recent convert from the Martin camp, presiding. Before being elected UAW-CIO vice-president at Milwaukee in 1937, Thomas had been a welder in the Chrysler East Jefferson plant in Detroit. A husky, tobacco-chewing auto worker, with a raspy high-pitched voice, he had led the organization of the workers in his plant, first as the leader of an independent union and later as president of UAW-CIO Local 7. Years later, while he was serving as international president, a newspaperman described him as "labor's undiplomatic diplomat." His strength in the union stemmed from his earthiness, his simplicity, and his bigness of heart—virtues that won him friends and followers who stuck with him to the bitter end of his seven years in the UAW-CIO president's office.

In his report to the convention Thomas revealed intimate details of back-door negotiations that had been held with the Ford Motor Company during the final months of Martin's regime. The objective of these secret talks, Thomas charged, was to take the UAW out of the CIO in exchange for the signature of an agreement by Ford. "The statement was made in my presence that if the United Automobile Workers of America would withdraw from the CIO Ford would then sign a contract," Thomas said.

There was no real contest in the election of a president to replace the discredited Martin, who had strayed so far from CIO industrial union principles. The filling of the presidency was wrangled out behind closed doors. Sidney Hillman and Philip Murray were at the convention, representing John L. Lewis; and it was their task to line up the convention behind their plan to put R. J. Thomas in the presidency and re-elect George F. Addes as secretary-treasurer.

Early in the convention the Commies tried to kindle a movement to run Addes for president. But a combination of political forces smothered this plot in a hurry. Hillman and Murray were obviously against it; they not only pressured local delegations to withdraw support from Addes, but worked on Addes himself to prevent him from accepting the nomination. Thomas and his backers sabotaged the Addes campaign in order to enhance the opportunity for R. J. himself. The Reuther caucus, not strong enough in itself to put up a candidate, but determined to stop the Commies from putting Addes in, strung along with Hillman, Murray, and Thomas.

Personally, although I stayed away from the Commies on nearly all other issues, I agreed with them on their plan to run Addes for president. Addes was a swarthy young Syrian who had come up out of the Auto-Lite plant in Toledo. His service in the union dated all the way back to the violent Toledo strikes in 1933. He was a loud, if not polished, speaker, and he had built his following in the union by giving the appearance of a determined and efficient leader destined to smash or circumvent all obstacles in his path to power. I backed his abortive boom for the UAW-CIO presidency in 1939 for several reasons. I believed that he had more experience and initiative than Thomas, who had been among the last to desert Homer Martin and was therefore too much of a Johnny-come-lately in the anti-Martin camp to suit my taste. There was also the fact that I still felt a wavering desire to work within the tactical boundaries of the party line.

But when Addes refused to run I trooped along with the overwhelming majority of the convention in support of Thomas for president and Addes for secretary-treasurer. All but one delegate from my local lined up the same way. There were two candidates against Thomas, but together they gathered fewer votes than some of the bigger local unions carried in the convention. R. J. was swept into the presidency, to remain until April 1946, when Walter P. Reuther defeated him in the first real contest ever held for the top office in the UAW-CIO.

The Cleveland convention set a record of endurance for democratic unionism. It lasted eleven tense days. There were many night sessions. The delegates sweated over intricate constitutional clauses designed to prevent the catastrophe of another Homer Martin. Section after section of articles of the constitution was voted back into committee because its wording was unsatisfactory to the finicky delegates.

While retaining all the safeguards of union democracy previously contained in the old constitution, the delegates wrote two new democratic features into basic UAW-CIO law. The first of these new provisions for protection of the rank and file against misuse of power by top officers was characterized as the idea of the "corporation council." My local union was among several representing General Motors workers which fought hard for the adoption of this plan.

As finally approved by the convention, the principle of the corporation council worked as follows: Workers from plants under contract with a single large corporation elected delegates to a geographic sub-council covering a certain group of plants. Each sub-council then elected delegates to the national corporation council. The delegates to this national corporation council elected a top committee which supervised and participated in all negotiations with management at the top corporation level.

First tested in General Motors, this arrangement served a double function. It provided a channel for a direct flow of ideas, suggestions, and grievances from the shop level on up to the highest strata of labor-management relations. In this manner, consciously or unconsciously, the machine-tenders in the auto industry took a pioneering step toward breaking through the barrier of impersonality that separates the individual worker in the shop from the policy councils of the big corporations.

The most important element in the corporation council, however, was its establishment of the organizational separation of the grievance procedure from the executive structure of the union. One of our bitterest gripes against the old-guard unionism of the AFL, for instance, was our disapproval of the consummation of agreements by top union leaders without the consent or participation of the rank and file. The UAW-CIO corporation council, as written into the constitution, virtually outlawed backdoor bargaining and sweetheart agreements.

The corporation council insured rank and file control over settlement of grievances and contract negotiations. Formulation of contract demands started in the local unions and boiled on up through the sub-councils into the national council and the top bargaining committee. Thus the final demands presented to the company and bargained over by the union officers and the corporation council committee actually reflected the desires of the people down below in the shops. Top officers could not bargain with the employers unless the top committee, made up exclusively of men from the shops, was present to check and observe the negotiations. When an agreement was reached between the negotiators of the union and the company, it had to be passed on down to the local unions for their discussion and approval before it could become effective. These safeguards against sellouts, designed by the auto workers to protect them from the evils of labor racketeering and union bossism, have become sacred organizational principles in the UAW-CIO. They stand strong and enduring, like a bill of rights, guarding the dues-paying members of the union from abuse by leaders unable to resist the corruption of power.

The other basic constitutional change fashioned by the determined delegates was the overhauling of machinery for the trial and expulsion of top union officers. Remembering the suspensions, trials, and expulsions which occurred under Homer Martin's manipulation of the International Executive Board, the delegates took the trials of international officers entirely out of the hands of the board. A constitutional provision was established that provided for a jury trial of suspended international officers, the jurors to be drawn from the credential list of rank-and-file delegates to the previous convention.

I engaged in very little of the customary political dealing and double-dealing that went on at the Cleveland convention. There were two reasons for this. In the first place, I was not an accepted member of any of the organized power caucuses. At the Milwaukee convention my Communist connections had opened the doors for me to all kinds of policy caucuses at high levels, but I was out in the cold at Cleveland so far as the CP was concerned. Politically, I was a maverick in that convention. The Commies wanted none of me, and the anti-Communists, gathered mostly in the Reuther caucus, still suspected me of being too close to the Communists. As for the Thomas crowd, I was leery of them because I felt that they were too newly divorced from Homer Martin to be trusted much. For this reason, I was pretty much a lone wolf for the eleven days of the convention.

The second factor which kept me out of politics was the fact that I was elected chairman of the convention Education Committee, and I worked hard getting out its report. It was mostly a non-political committee. There were a couple of Communists on it, but they didn't carry enough weight to control it. I was chosen chairman because of my fluency in discussing education at the opening session of the committee, and because the non-Communist members seemed to feel that I had no close connections with any power caucus.

After two meetings, the committee delegated to me the authority to draft an outline of a report. At the next meeting the draft I submitted was enlarged and amended in discussion and I went back to work to rewrite it. In its final form, as the following quotations will illustrate, the report indicated that the dose of Marxism I had absorbed was still fairly strong in my system. The report said, in part:

> We know that these [anti-labor] laws are being sponsored by the employers and their corrupt political agents. We can fight the laws now, but it is a bitter realization that, had the workers been properly educated, the enemies of labor would never have been elected to the legislative halls of government . . .
>
> Shall we wait until laws have been enacted making it a crime to belong to a labor union—and that is not so far-fetched as some people think—or shall we start now to teach our millions of American workers that in their hands they hold the greatest power in the world—economic and political power which can be used to obtain for them a maximum of food, shelter and clothing, of the good things of life, once they make up their minds to go out and get these necessities of existence . . .
>
> The days of rapid industrial expansion, the pouring of capital into new factories, new facilities of industrial production, are gone forever. It is no longer possible for the industrialists to profitably invest their surplus funds—profits that we workers have produced—in new plants and shops. It is no longer possible because, as most of us here so well know, the existing factories and plants are not being used anywhere near their potential productive capacity. Everywhere around us are idle factories, or factories operating part time, while the streets and relief offices are jammed with millions of unemployed workers [the recession of 1938 was lingering on into early 1939] . . .
>
> It becomes the responsibility of a trade union, in this hour of social distress, to sponsor and promote an educational program that will show the workers the correct path to progress. Such a program should prove to the workers that the only path to progress is in a powerful, united labor movement, a movement exemplified by the CIO, which can fight for, and obtain, through democratic processes, a more equitable distribution of the abundance of goods and services this country can produce. This knowledge that it is possible to produce plenty for all here in America should be the guiding motive in the educational program of any bona fide trade union. . . .

Most of the preamble to the report was as redundant with dialectics, and as laden with the language of the class struggle, as the foregoing few paragraphs. It was heavily economic. There was no specific reference in it to the virtues of liberty as a political institution. It reflected clearly the months during which the party commissars had hammered the materialist conception of history into my head.

In the final portion of the report, which outlined the specific recommendations of the committee for educational action in the field, our zeal for rank-and-file control went hog-wild. We proposed the election in the convention of a Regional Educational Director for each geographical region of the union. These Regional Educational Directors were to comprise an International Educational Committee, to have the power to meet at its own discretion or at the call of the International Educational Director.

We made it mandatory that all staff members of the Educational Department be required to pass a test based on merit, qualified ability, and experience. In another excess of zeal, we made it mandatory that local unions should include in their by-laws a provision requiring all elected local union leaders to attend at least one educational class per month. We forbade the International Union to spend any of the two-and-a-half-cents-per-month per-member fund for other than educational purposes—this being a common constitutional violation practiced when funds ran low in other departments of the union.

But for all our energetic efforts to concentrate the attention of the top union leadership on this program, few of the recommendations were ever carried out. I tried to run for the position of Regional Educational Director in the Michigan region, thinking my prestige as Committee Chairman would carry me through. But the power caucuses shouldered me aside in favor of another chap who had closer ties with the men that filled the full-time jobs. The job never amounted to much anyway, and in a couple of months the rest of the program was forgotten as the union focused its attention almost exclusively on the task of protecting its bargaining rights in an industry still hostile to the union.

When the elections were over the International Executive Board was divided almost evenly between pro-Communists and anti-Communists, with R. J. Thomas, the new president, sitting uneasily in the middle. Three of the board members were closely identified with the Communist party at the time. Several others were fellow travelers, including George Addes, who has never been a Communist party member. The pro-Communist faction could rely on eight members of the board, out of a total of eighteen. With Thomas in the middle, that left a balance of nine, made up of followers of Walter Reuther plus some independents and reformed Martinites.

However, largely because the star of Soviet foreign policy was still rather low in the skies, the new board didn't do too badly in the months that followed. It worked hard to get the union back on its feet, fighting Martin's secessionist union in strategic plants with large concentrations of membership. By the spring of 1940, when a vital National Labor Relations Board election was held in the plants of the General Motors Corporation, we were able to win the bargaining rights by better than 80 per cent.

It was in the closing hours of that hectic Cleveland convention that I made the acquaintance of Herb McCreedy, spokesman for a group known as New America, who was to convert me to another utopian political faith. But before I relate my experience with New America and its efforts to build an indigenous American radical party, I must touch on the critical General Motors strike of 1939, which really established the UAW-CIO and started Walter Reuther upward on his way to the top position he holds today.

10. Force and Violence

The armchair labor relations experts who counsel labor and capital to get together and live in harmony ought to study the General Motors strike of 1939 as an example of the impracticality of their theory. It was touch and go for the UAW-CIO that summer. General Motors refused to bargain with us except on a plant-by-plant basis, and, even in those plants where our committees were recognized by the company, the bargaining sessions were more or less of a farce. In eleven plants we were nearly helpless due to the presence of duplicate bargaining committees inspired and operated by Homer Martin's AFL outfit. We had voted Homer into oblivion in Cleveland, but, organizationally, he was still a thorn in our side. The corporation refused to bargain at all in the eleven plants where Homer's guys were operating, claiming that it didn't know which union represented the workers.

Two alternatives faced us. We could start the long and doubtful business of processing an unfair labor practices case under the National Labor Relations Board, or we could go on strike and use economic strength to compel General Motors to recognize the UAW-CIO as the bargaining agency for its workers. No one doubted that the future of the union was challenged by the refusal of GM to bargain nationally. Demands had been served on the company as far back as October 1938, but corporation officials had given us the old stall right along. GM was not convinced that it had to live with the CIO. The lesson of 1937 had apparently been forgotten by GM officials. Our membership was restive, and we had to produce some action—but fast.

Out of this crisis Walter Reuther came up with the idea that saved the day and set the union firmly on its feet. He proposed to strike the skilled operations in the GM plants and tie up tooling operations on the 1940 models, while the production workers went on working on the tail end of the 1939 production schedule. Under this strategy, the die-makers, tool-makers, maintenance workers, millwrights, designers, and engineers would cease all work on 1940 model jobs. The production workers would go on working for the few weeks left of 1939 production, and, when they got laid off, they would become eligible for unemployment compensation benefits. It sounded like a good trick—if we could work it.

To keep its hands clean for the record, the union made a last effort to get GM to bargain nationally. On June 8, Thomas, as president, and Reuther, as GM director, sent a letter to William Knudsen, GM president, asking again for the opening of negotiations on a national scale. In anticipation of the CIO strategy, Homer Martin chose that same day to try to pull off a rump strike in Flint and Saginaw, two key GM centers. Workers who were loyal to the UAW-CIO ignored the rump strike. It flopped with a heavy thud and was called off by Martin on June 14. By that time GM had replied to the UAW-CIO request for a reopening of negotiations with a letter repeating its offer of local bargaining operations, and reaffirming its assertion that it did not know which union represented the workers.

By this time the GM Council, as drafted by the delegates in Cleveland, had been set up and put into operation. A national GM negotiating committee had been elected. National demands had been formulated, including the thirty-hour week, the union shop, a steward system, and many minor improvements in the grievance procedure. When the strike votes were taken among the skilled workers, supplementary demands were drafted. These included a ten-cents-per-hour blanket wage increase, recognition of the union label, minimum hiring rates, time-and-a-half for Saturday work and double-time for Sundays, plus other fringe economic demands. The votes cast by the skilled workers were overwhelmingly for the strike.

The first plant to walk out was Fisher Twenty-one in Detroit, where the skilled workers set up their picket lines on July 6. We struck Chevrolet Gear and Axle the next day at the beginning of the day shift, and the battle of 1939 was on for myself and my buddies in Local 235.

We mobilized our pickets at five in the morning at the Local 235 hall. The turnout was gratifying to those of us who gloried in mass demonstrations of the economic power of the workers. Our skilled people were on hand almost 100 per cent. Their ranks were swelled by production workers from all shifts. I was working days at the time. I came to the local hall that morning at three to help get the strike under way. At seven I was to go in and work at my regular job, since I was a production worker and would not be on strike.

Picket signs were carried up out of the basement of the hall. They were tacked to two-inch-square sticks of hemlock sturdy enough to ward off the whacks of police night sticks. The sound car was going full blast, blaring out union tunes. Our local union sergeant-at-arms and guide buckled on their harnesses to carry the local's flag and the American flag into the picket lines. When the signal sounded we formed into ranks of four abreast and, several hundred strong, marched west on Holbrook Avenue to set up picket lines in front of the plant gates.

The Detroit police were on hand in force. Detroit's municipal government was then under the regime of Richard Reading, an open enemy of the CIO. Reading's police commissioner was named Heinrich Pickert, but we all called him "Heinie." Pickert took pride in personally directing the movements of his men in strike crises. That morning, however, although a number of police were on hand, everything went off smoothly. Our show of strength was sufficient to discourage any weak sisters among the skilled workers who might have considered cracking the picket lines. At seven o'clock we day-shift production workers went in to our jobs, and all was well—for the time being.

Production work went on in our plant for about two weeks

after the strike started. Then, as schedules were completed or as the lack of maintenance workers crippled operations, we were gradually laid off until very few jobs were working. We reported to the Unemployment Compensation Commission and filed for benefits. Then those of us who felt strongly about the strike gave our full time to assisting the skilled workers on the picket lines. I made a quick week-end junket to the Upper Peninsula with my sister and brother-in-law, taking my two kids up to stay with my grandfather for the duration of the strike. When I got back to Detroit I practically lived at the local union hall, going home only about every third night to shave and clean up. We had rented another hall upstairs over our strike kitchen and equipped it with cots for the faithful few who lived with the strike and were on hand for every crisis.

I was on the city-wide publicity committee, representing my local union. This work was under the direction of the late Eddie Levinson, who was at one time Labor Editor of the *New York Post*. Levinson had been hired by the UAW-CIO to work as its Publicity Director and Editor. Since he died in 1945 of a cerebral hemorrhage—probably brought on by working too hard and too fast for the labor movement that he loved—I have thought of him many times as he appeared to us that summer in 1939.

Our committee met every night at about nine o'clock at the old Local 157 hall located at 51 Sproat Street on the edge of downtown Detroit. The city-wide strike committee, headed by Ben Blackwood, a die-maker from Fisher Twenty-three, had its headquarters there. With Eddie Levinson's help and direction we wrote, edited, and published a legal-size mimeographed strike bulletin called the "GM Picket," which was distributed on the picket lines each morning.

In a hot, stuffy little room, Eddie sat at a desk in his shirt sleeves, a cigarette drooping from his mouth and the lights shining on his nearly bald head. He was thirty-seven years old at the time, with more than twenty years of labor experience under his belt. His energy was boundless, his spirit unflagging, his sense of news and timing and strategy keen as a knife. He worked like a whirlwind. Scribbling furiously with a swift pencil, he polished our crude manuscripts for retyping on the mimeograph stencils. When he was unsatisfied with our efforts, or when an idea hit him for a sudden piece of inspired writing, he whirled on his chair, hunched over his typewriter, and banged away with unbelievable speed, using only two fingers. When the writing job was completed for the night, he left us to crank out the thousands of "GM Pickets" on the mimeograph, while he hurried away to stay up most of the night planning strike strategy with the top committee. There have been all too few Eddie Levinsons in the labor movement, and the UAW-CIO lost one of its sturdiest champions when he slipped away to walk the last picket line with Joe Hill in August 1945.

We rarely finished our mimeographing before two or three in the morning. Then we snatched a few winks if our services were not needed on some picket line where danger impended. At six we were up and on the go, distributing our strike bulletins on the picket lines and gathering news for the next night's stint.

General Motors seemed determined to make the strike a test of economic power. High corporation officials agreed to open negotiations on July 14, but there was one flare-up of violence at Fisher Body in Pontiac on July 11, followed by a battle in Cleveland and two near riots in Detroit, before a settlement was finally reached.

On August 2 we received a phone call at Local 235 saying that the police were attacking the picket line at Fisher Plant Thirty-seven on Piquette Street near Hastings. We piled into all available cars and rushed over. When we arrived and plunged into the fracas, the street was thick with mounted police, surrounded by milling, struggling pickets. It was a hot, bright summer afternoon, and the air was filled with dust and the tumult of men fighting and cursing. Brickbats and rocks hurtled through the air, aimed at the mounted police. Inspectors and lieutenants, their gold braid gleaming in the sun, shouted orders like officers in a military battle. The battle broke up when tear gas shells began exploding in the streets. One worker was badly maimed by a tear gas shell that ricocheted from the pavement and tore into his chest.

My strongest memory of that skirmish is the sight of big Blaine Marrin, a leader of Local 157, who literally lost his shirt in the fight. As the battle subsided, he stood his ground on the picket line, his shirt hanging in tatters from his huge shoulders. Sweat poured from his shining skin, defiance glittered in his eyes.

"We showed them damn cops," he grunted, panting for breath, as he pulled out a handkerchief to mop his face.

At Local 235 we were in a more strategic situation, from which we waged a running battle with the police. Our union hall was located on Holbrook Avenue just a block east of the Hamtramck boundary. St. Aubin Street, running north and south along the east fence of the Chevrolet plant, marked the boundary, and within it we found political sanctuary. Hamtramck is a small municipality surrounded by Detroit and peopled largely by Polish workers. Its administration was friendly to labor and its police force gave us no trouble.

We therefore mobilized our troops inside this boundary. I remember standing on top of the sound car, clutching a microphone, and exhorting the pickets to stand firm against the enemy. Just beyond the picket line, across St. Aubin Street, I could see Commissioner Pickert leaning on his cane, standing at the side of his big black sedan. He was dressed in a Palm Beach suit and a Panama hat. Mounted police and patrolmen afoot stretched beyond him in lines along Holbrook Street, glaring at our pickets.

I pointed my finger at him. "There stands Heinie Pickert, ready to use his cops against us," I shouted into the mike. "This is how the system works. When you do not earn enough to live decently, and you go on strike to win higher wages for your family, they turn the police on you. They answer your demand for bread with clubs, guns, tear gas. Do you see now why we have to hold our picket lines firm, build our unions, and learn to march to the polls as we march on the picket lines—so that we may turn out the politicians who set the police against us?"

With words like these we nursed the morale of our forces. When we felt strong enough, we dashed across the Hamtramck boundary to exchange insults with the police. On August 3 we battled them openly for a few minutes after they started shoving us around. The skirmish was brief, and there was no tear gas this time. After bashing a few cops around with our picket signs, and being bashed some in return, just to show our strength, we retreated back into Hamtramck in good order.

Not all of the battles happened on the picket lines. There were many incidents in isolated spots away from the main lines of action. Arrogant anti-union truck drivers were frequently involved in these episodes. Once in a while such a truck driver would roar up to the plant and get himself escorted inside by a flying wedge of police, while the pickets heaped insults on him. Later he would come out and the cops would again form lines to escort him away. A half-dozen motorcycle cops would lead him down the street, guarding him for a distance of a half-mile or so from the plant. As soon as the cops left him, by some odd coincidence, three or four cars would slide out of the side streets and there would be a nasty traffic jam. The scabby truck driver was always in the wrong—and outnumbered. The outraged drivers of the other cars, aided by a few passengers who happened to be riding with them, would give the truck driver a working over. All this would happen in a few minutes. When the cops got back on the scene, there would be only a few curious pedestrians and motorists around giving mixed-up explanations. Truck drivers who met these accidents rarely came back to the plant.

Some of our guys met accidents, too. We never knew for sure who was responsible. It could have been goons inspired by employers, rival union zealots, or fanatic followers of the Black Legion, the Ku Klux Klan, or some such outfit. Russ Ferguson, one of the stalwarts of our Local 235 flying squad, was hospitalized after such an incident. He had driven downtown to the corner of Cass and Temple to pick up his wife, who worked in a beauty parlor. She was not quite ready and he went into a restaurant to get a cup of coffee. When he came out, three men jumped him and worked him over with blackjacks. As he slumped to the sidewalk, broken and bleeding, they leaped into a waiting car and sped away.

I am certain that I personally escaped such a massaging by close calls on a couple of occasions. Twice when a flying-squad car took me home late at night, we were followed by another car. I had my brother-in-law primed to meet me on the porch. He would hear the car coming, turn on the porch light, and step outside with his deer rifle in his hand. When the occupants of the pursuing car glimpsed him they stepped on it and raced down the street. But they did not give up easily.

One night, lacking a guard, I rode a bus to within two blocks of home and got off. Then I slipped in the back way, cutting through alleys and across vacant lots. I found the house open, dark, and reeking with a terrific stench. A front window was shattered; the rug in the front room was littered with broken glass. As I went out onto the front porch to get some air, a police car rolled into the driveway and my brother-in-law got out. Two cops came up the steps with him.

"What happened?" I blurted.

"Somebody threw a goddamn stink bomb through the window," he said. He had been away with the police trying to search for the bomb-tossers. Fortunately, I got through the strike with a whole skin—although all my clothes stank for several weeks.

On August 4 we had a mass meeting at strike headquarters on Sproat Street. It was called to denounce the company and the Mayor of Detroit for their efforts to smash the picket lines. George Addes was the main speaker. Walter Reuther and the top committee were somewhere trying to negotiate with GM officials. I was very tired that night. Sitting up front, trying to listen to the speech by Addes, I began to nod and doze off. I had been awake for about thirty-six hours. Ashamed, I slipped away and went downstairs to an alcove where there was a big old sofa upholstered with red leather. I stretched out on this welcome bed and relaxed. The voice of George Addes boomed away upstairs on the public address system.

The next thing I knew, it was morning, and newsboys were crying, "Extra!" on the streets. "GM Strike Settled!" they shouted. I rushed out and bought a paper. It was true. While I had been sleeping there, the negotiators had come to a sudden settlement.

Under the agreement, which was quickly ratified, the UAW-CIO was recognized as the exclusive bargaining agency in forty-two GM plants. It was a corporation-wide agreement, the first ever signed by the company. The Homer Martin rump union was banished from the eleven plants in which it had claimed bargaining rights. GM agreed to pay time-and-a-half for Saturday work in excess of forty hours a week, and double-time for Sundays. Economic adjustments were obtained which raised the minimum and maximum rates on many classifications. Differentials in wages were abolished between some plants and some areas.

The 1939 GM strike, like the sit-down strikes which preceded it and which fostered the development of the UAW, was a violent clash between two industrial giants competing for power. It established the UAW-CIO on a firm footing. Having bested GM in an economic struggle, we found it easy to solidify the union among workers employed by lesser corporations. Ford remained to be conquered, but that was a task for the future.

A turning point in the history of the UAW-CIO, the 1939 strike stands out as a justification of the strategic use of the strike weapon. By throttling a vital function of a large corporation with a stoppage of the work of a few hundred highly skilled workers, we won the confidence of the mass of workers employed in the auto, aircraft, and agricultural implement industries. They flocked to the union and strengthened its ranks. Utilizing our new strength, we moved forward, winning broad economic concessions in many plants. And this is as good a place as any to set forth my belief that the rough beginning of the UAW-CIO has paid off in benefits for the entire American community.

Pettifogging moralists are continually bemoaning the use of the strike weapon. They assail the economic strike as a forceful implementation of the theory that might makes right. They are even more critical of strikes in which workers fight scabs and police to win their demands. According to their reasoning, labor should keep on working, no matter how bad its working conditions may be, while waiting docilely for logic, law, and benevolence to bring relief. Had this reasoning prevailed in the larger affairs of men, America might still be a British colony—or the world might have been overrun by Hitler, Mussolini, and Hirohito.

Violence is relative. It exists in forms other than stoppages of work and brawls on picket lines. There are varying degrees of violence. Let us assume that an imaginary employer is paying his workers starvation wages and driving them like slaves in the plant. This is one degree of violence. But it does not stop there. The wives and children of the oppressed workers are also the victims of this violence. If they do not get the proper amount and quality of food, if they are ill-clothed and ill-housed, if they are denied sufficient medical care—all because of low wages—an enormous degree of violence has, in effect, been inflicted on them by the employers. Now suppose these workers go on strike, and maybe beat up a few scabs in the process, to win higher wages and improve their working conditions. The situation then resolves itself into alternatives of degrees of violence. Organized workers reason that the strike is the lesser of two evils—that there is less violence in a strike than in long years of waiting for a legendary blindfolded goddess to come to their rescue.

Arguing against the employment of force and violence in economic and industrial relations is no different from arguing against the use of violence under any circumstances, as the die-hard pacifists do. Pacifistic logic would not have approved of the American Revolution; it would have had us turn the other cheek to the Fascists and Nazis.

There will be violence in human affairs as long as governments —from the municipal to the global level—fail to act swiftly in relieving economic and spiritual injustice. Humanity is not yet civilized enough to wait in misery for the mills of morality to grind out their scanty measures of benevolence under the golden rule. Oppression will always incite revolt—until mankind orders its affairs so as to end oppression.

Labor does not revel in stoppages of work and slugfests on the picket line. We prefer happier and more orderly procedures for winning our demands. But democracy has not yet developed to the point where employers invariably treat workers as human beings; there are not enough employers who accept their social responsibility to use their property for the good of the community. Under these conditions, labor has no choice but to use its economic and physical strength in order to fight back when employers use their wealth to enforce unjust working conditions.

The strikes that accompany the building of a democratic labor movement are no more injurious than the labor pains that attend any birth. We had to strike to build the UAW-CIO. It is a sound democratic union today. It has secured economic gains for workers—and, for the great percentage of them, without striking. These gains have flowed through communities, benefiting labor and non-labor groups alike. The UAW is developing a philosophy of unionism that puts the welfare of the community above the welfare of labor as a group. It is fighting for housing, for medical care, for the abolition of racial and religious prejudice. These are aims whose worth outweighs by far the incidents of violence scattered behind us along the path of our march toward the lights beyond the prison.

11. Revolution by Thesis

It was inevitable that the passion for perfection which pushed me into, and out of, the Communist party would steer me into the fold of some other society of utopians. The radical idealist seems to be by nature a clubby creature. He has to have a star to steer his ship by, a faith to cling to, companions with whom to cry in his beer when dreams go sour. In the spring of 1939 I was drawn to, and became a member of, an organization known as New America, which carried on for only two years after I joined it. It was a happy juncture, in more ways than one. Not only did I find a new faith and enjoy a rich and gratifying association with an earnest assemblage of fellow idealists, but I also found a new wife in the ranks of New America.

The people in the organization were working visionaries of a high caliber. Dr. Harry Ward, its first chairman, had left the ranks before I joined. As I heard the tale from those who knew him, he was never able to adjust his thinking to the firm anti-Communist position developed by New America as one of its basic policies. While he disagreed with the Commies on some issues of strategy and tactics, he did not regard them as a threat to democratic values and was opposed to fighting them openly.

Ward was succeeded as chairman of the group by Richard Storrs Childs, who came from an East Coast family which had a long background of wealth and aristocracy. Despite his heritage of privilege and silver spoons, young Dick Childs was a genuine democrat with a keen, sensitive mind. His teammate in the top councils of New America during its heyday was Thomas Wright, who had been a Protestant minister and a professor of philosophy. Tom Wright was bouncing and benevolent. He was as full of energy and forceful intelligence as he was short, round, and bald. Propelled by a tireless passion for setting the world in order, Tom Wright, as National Director of New America, gave several of the best years of his life to what was at best a thankless task.

There were others: John T. Bobbit, a research historian; Day Krolik of Detroit, like Childs the son of a wealthy family; Emanuel Elston, director of a New York school of music; I. Krechevsky, teacher of psychology; Hugh Wing, English teacher; Paul Reid, church editor; and my friends Mary and Willard Martinson, who gave years of their youth to American progressivism—to mention only a few.

My first contact with New America came at the close of the 1939 UAW-CIO convention in Cleveland. I was approached there by Herb McCreedy, a scholarly, soft-spoken organizer for the group. There was little about "Mac" to suggest that he advocated a revolutionary drive for power and the construction of a new America. He had the appearance more of a shoe salesman than of a prophet of utopian social change. I learned later that my first impression had not been too far wrong. He had been a shoe salesman at one time in his career. But the depression had so diminished his earnings that he had turned his hand to the full-time pursuit of a more humane social order.

Despite his meek appearance, however, Mac was a persuasive talker and a top-notch organizer. He began to work on me, while we were having lunch together that day in Cleveland, by telling me that the people in New America had been watching me with interest for some time.

"You know, we like to see what happens to guys in the labor movement who get fed up with the Communist party," he said.

"You know about that?" I inquired diffidently.

"Oh, sure," he declared with quiet confidence. "We have our guys in the unions, too—and we know the score."

He then proceeded skillfully to sound out my political thinking. I explained to him my basic dissatisfaction with the Marxist strategy of radical operations as applied on the American political scene.

"The point the Communists miss," I told him, "is that political democracy has been a living, dynamic thing here in America for more than a century and a half. It's different here from the way it is in European nations, where lack of freedom has generated a higher degree of political militancy among the workers. There is no need in America to waste our time with Marxist mumbo-jumbo about dialectics and stuff; there is no need to idolize Lenin or obey Stalin. What we need in America is a homespun political organization that will harness the historic American sense of justice and fair play. We have our own democratic heroes—Paine, Jefferson, Jackson, Lincoln. If we have to have heroes and patron saints in politics, why not pay homage to our own Revolutionary founding fathers? What I mean is that American democracy has a dynamic of its own, bigger, stronger, and fuller of promises than anything the Marxists have been able to cook up."

"You're pretty much right about that," he said. "But, of course, you have to have basic economic understanding—that's the strong point of Marxism."

"What about this New America group?" I asked him. "Where does it stand with respect to Marxism?"

He told me that New America was essentially non-Marxist, but that its explanation of the decline of capitalism ran parallel to Marxist thinking at some points. In the two years that followed, I learned in countless skull sessions with my fellow New Americans that my new faith was in truth a native-born, if obscure, kind of American radicalism.

New America was born out of the ferment of ideas brewed in the depression. The organizers of the movement based its reason for being on three points: first, that the collapse of capitalism was inevitable; second, that fascism fed on the discontent generated by the decline of capitalism and threatened to become dominant in the world; third, that a democratic alternative to both fascism and communism, based on freedom and technological abundance, had to be organized and offered to the people, if democracy was to survive. New America was a kind of protest by democratic spirits who early recognized the totalitarian tendency of communism—an attempt to create a dynamic and democratic American radical movement. Yet, because many of its founders had gained their political experience in Socialist and Communist circles, it had to recover from a kind of Marxist hangover. By the time I became a member in 1939, the group had pretty much purged itself of Marxist thinking. But, by reading and talking, I discovered that it had possessed two distinct Marxist traits in its early days.

In the first place, its beginners thought it necessary to operate in an atmosphere of conspiracy. At one time members were listed in the organization's records with numbers instead of names. This indicated an obvious outgrowth of the old Marxist fear of getting kicked around by the capitalist state. Secondly, the group clung for years to the notion that a disciplined corps of revolutionary leaders was needed to direct rebellion in a period of economic and political crisis. This, again, was a throwback to the Leninist doctrine calling for a small, controlled, tightly disciplined party of professional revolutionists to act as the midwives of socialism. Even at the time I joined its ranks, New America still regarded itself as a training camp for intellectuals destined to guide the muddled masses out of the wilderness of a dying capitalism into democratic socialism.

A revealing example of the similarity between the expression of New America's early thinking and the jargon of orthodox Marxism is found in the report of Dr. Harry F. Ward to New America's first National Congress in Lorain, Ohio, July 3 to 5, 1936.

Our job, then [said Chairman Ward], is to continually explain to the American people who want these things [security and abundance] that they cannot get them under the profit system. . . . We must show them how to destroy and get rid of the profit system, and what to put in its place, and how to do it. . . . What about the forces that we have to work with that are going to do the job on the American scene? Our creative task is to develop these from their revolutionary potentialities into active revolutionary consciousness and will. . . . Remember what Lenin said, that when the masses start to move they always move faster than even the revolutionary organizations. . . .

Uninformed readers would gather from this fiery appeal that New America in 1936 was about to throw up barricades and lead a violent assault on Wall Street. To describe this kind of talk as the romantic ravings of crackpots, however, would be wrong —just as it would be equally wrong to mistake it for a menace to law and order in America. While New America's revolution never progressed beyond the point of finely edited theses on paper, the development of the organization itself indicated the extent to which the depression inspired people to search for a rational solution to America's troubles.

New America outgrew its Marxist hangover, but it never deviated from its basic belief that monopoly capitalism is a rotten system and that it is the duty of intelligent democrats to toil at the task of replacing it with something better. In a document known as the Basic Course, used to train New America recruits in the fundamentals of economic and political theory, this position was set forth in these words:

Through its own development the Profit System has so altered its environment by substituting potential plenty for actual scarcity, that conditions essential to its further growth no longer obtain. The wealth that society can create on the basis of new techniques and scientific knowledge, society alone has the capacity and the right to use. Social production demands social ownership of the machinery of production.

It was in its plans for replacing the declining profit system with a "New America" rooted in a socially controlled economy that the organization shook off Marxist doctrine and spoke its basic faith in the democratic way of life. This devotion to democracy and freedom as essentials of a society committed to human decency and dignity showed up in some of the later documents published by the organization. In a leaflet published in 1940, for instance, under a section headed "Political Democracy," New America stated that "the freedom and independence of the individual is the keystone of American democracy." An expansion of this point said:

We demand that all the guarantees of the Constitution and the Bill of Rights be maintained at all times and under all conditions. We are unalterably opposed to any social, political or economic discrimination or intolerance because of race, color or creed. We demand that the right of franchise be extended to all citizens of the United States regardless of race, color or creed and that all barriers to the franchise, such as poll taxes, be eliminated. We demand that the freedom of the press, the theatre and the radio be safeguarded from any dictatorial control by government or monopoly control by big business. We hold that the formal processes of government must be supplemented by free and independent associations of citizens representing their own interests as businessmen, farmers, professionals, workers and consumers.

This concern with the freedom of the citizen as an individual was not window dressing, as it is with leftist cliques that exploit democratic processes to gain power, and afterward hatchet democracy. In New America our faith in freedom was genuine and uninhibited. Nowhere was this faith more clearly shown than in the internal workings of the organization itself. Our loyalty was to freedom, not to the "line" of a know-it-all party claiming the divine right to identify the values of freedom either with Wall Street or with Moscow. Unlike the Marxists as a whole, and the Communists in particular, New America recognized no body of doctrine as sacred and unquestionable. Its members were free at all times to question or to challenge its policies and program; machinery was provided for the membership to shape its decisions.

Throughout its brief, energetic, and unsung history, New America grappled realistically with the root problem that has had humanity in an uproar since the turn of the century. Simply stated, the problem is this: When complex capitalist systems go haywire, causing needless want in the midst of potential plenty, must the citizenry of a nation give up its freedom to a police state in order to get security? Communists and Fascists see no problem whatsoever in this question. Their dogma enshrines collectivity, deifies political authority, and reduces the individual to a robot serving a super-state. But to the person who cherishes personal freedom and individual dignity, this question appears as the major intellectual challenge of our time. It runs like a theme song through all the organized social endeavors of people everywhere in this era of power politics on a global scale. As Walter Reuther puts it today in his speeches, "Can we fill our bellies without enslaving our souls?"

If the passion for writing theses and talking ourselves hoarse during policy discussions never achieved anything else in New America, it gave us a glimpse of an answer to this all-important question. By the time we reluctantly folded our political tent in the summer of 1941, we had worked out a set of democratic alternatives to economic statism. In the years that have passed since then, I have found no more intelligent and democratic plan for repairing our boom-and-bust breakdowns than that which New America formulated on its deathbed. In fact, I have noticed that more and more thinking people are independently coming up with ideas for action similar to New America's program as whispered faintly in its final thesis.

We rejected the totalitarian tactic of over-all state ownership of the means of production and distribution as a cure-all for capitalism's booms and busts. Absolute rule of the economy by the state, we argued, was bound to result in tyranny, no matter how noble the intentions of the clique or party taking power to lead the people to the "promised land." As an alternative, we drafted the following outline of a program, at the last national meeting of delegates representing our devoted little band of utopians, held in Chicago in the summer of 1940:

To uproot the causes of unemployment and depression, and get America off the boom-and-bust merry-go-round, we proposed a drastic reconstruction of the economic system. We put the finger on big business monopolies as the root of the trouble. To check monopoly we proposed public ownership of banking and credit, natural resources, and public utilities. Privately owned monopolistic industries—especially those which flouted the public will and refused to put their own houses in order—should also be transferred to public ownership, we declared. We urged the encouragement of genuine free private enterprise, the increased development of cooperatives, and competition, under federally policed rules, among private enterprise, public enterprise, and co-operatives. For agriculture, we advocated lower industrial prices, free access to credit, discouragement of corporate farming, and protection of the family-owned and -operated farm as the basic unit of agricultural production. We stressed the need for a re-vised system of taxation, based on ability to pay, and increased federal investment in public works, health, and medical care pro-grams. Finally, we called for protection of the basic right of Americans to organize for economic and political action—espe-cially the right of labor to organize and bargain collectively in all industries, private, public, and cooperative.

This, in a nutshell, was the outline of our program at the time of the unhappy end of New America. It was not a blueprint, not a sectarian doctrine; it did not stray from the path of American democratic procedure. It was the ultimate fruition of our years of writing theses and pondering over economic and political doc-trines; it was a set of ideas for democratic social change, designed to meet the threat of statism.

Conservatives will damn this rudimentary pattern for a mixed economy as a Red plot to communize America, and the Com-munists themselves will be equally swift to denounce it as a repair job on capitalism. It is neither. In essence, it is a suggestion that we apply the democratic technique in a practical effort to solve economic problems. Inherent in it are the bone and muscle of the democratic process built by the American people during the his-tory of our nation, and expressed in the Revolution, the Civil War, the periodic upsurge of agrarian rebellions, and, more recently, in the growth of powerful labor organizations. Cer-tainly a serious effort to carry out such a program would trample on the toes, and pinch the purses, of the rich and well-born, the highly placed. But when has a concern for the privileges of an aristocratic minority ever hampered the political style of Amer-icans when they took it into their heads to do a job for America? Since before the Boston Tea Party Americans have never been slow to use political freedom for getting things done in the inter-est of the community. It was this willingness to kick the top dog aside and give the underdog a chance—the belief voiced by Jefferson that "all men are created equal"—that carried America through its toughest times and made it a great democratic nation.

For all its faithful promises to help workers move toward the lights beyond the prison, New America never attracted many recruits from labor. However, we did not let this drawback slow down our activities among the workers. We had very positive ideas about what was good for labor—our best minds had drafted and polished fancy theses dealing with many phases of the labor movement.

I believe we were the first to challenge the deeply entrenched Marxist dogma which proclaimed the proletariat as the exclusive instrument of social revolution. On this score we battled Socialists, Communists, Trotskyites, and assorted deviationists, attacking the doctrines of each and all of them with equal vigor.

Our reasons for disputing the Marxist theory which designated the working class as the historic vehicle of social revolution were, I believe, based on very sound logic, the substance of which still holds true. We did not just scoff at and ridicule the fantasies by which Marxists seek to prove that it is the divine destiny of the working class to fulfill a historic revolutionary mission. We challenged their dialectical mysticism with logic and with factual reviews of social developments.

I summarized the meat of our arguments several years later in an article called "Labor in the Community," published in the 1945 Summer Issue of the *Antioch Review.* This summary bears repeating now, to make my point.

In Europe [I wrote] the labor movement developed a particular kind of political consciousness, best expressed by Marxism, which impelled the trade unions toward an admitted goal of social revolution. The lack of political democracy in most European countries forced working class organizations to focus their activities on a quest for political power. Out of this experience came the long-nourished notion, imported into the United States from Europe, that labor is inherently revolutionary in character, and that it is the historic mission of the trade unions to implement the overthrow of capitalism, peacefully if possible but by force if necessary, and to create a socialistic or communistic workers' state.

It is only recently—especially since the rise of fascism and the failure of European labor to stop its march to power—that there has developed in America the idea that perhaps the Marxist plan for social revolution does not fit the American scene. Discussion of this idea has been further promoted by the growing realization that total state ownership of all property does not necessarily bring freedom to the working class.

The fact is that American society is so divided into functional and economic groups that organized labor, as such, is a minority, and does not have the strength to attain political power of its own momentum. This is the first and most practical reason why a "Labor government" is impossible of attainment in this country. The next good reason why the trade union movement, as such, cannot be used exclusively as a base from which to launch an offensive aiming at basic social change is that trade unionism is too closely interwoven with the institutional pattern of capitalism to permit of its use as a revolutionary weapon. Trade unions attain popularity and strength by bending capitalism to the short-run interests of the workers, rather than by assaulting it frontally with destructive motives. Because of this fact, important sections of the labor movement acquire a vested interest in the institutions of capitalism.

We in New America used these arguments, not to defend capitalism, but to point out the dangers in excessive doses of agitation for a proletarian revolution. Lacking the power and the technical know-how to operate vital social functions after assuming or seizing power, it would be suicidal for labor, we argued, to pervert and dissipate its strength in a solitary attack on capitalist controls. Such a *putsch*, we reasoned, would only frighten the other sections of society into acceptance of fascism as an expedient defense against a proletarian bid for power. It was our firm belief that this was what had happened in Italy, Germany, and Spain.

Arguing this point, we called on all those portions of labor which would listen to us to shun the blandishments of the Marxist brethren. It was never our intention to belittle the importance of strong and democratic labor unions in the essential work of extending democracy from the purely political sphere into economic operations. Indeed, we understood that the task of building an economy of abundance and freedom could not be accomplished without the aid and leadership of labor. The first job, we insisted, was to keep the unions strong—and that meant a fight with the Communists, who are ever willing to sacrifice the workers' interests for the privilege of writing labor's resolutions on foreign policy. The second job was to cultivate a political understanding of our theory that capitalism could be replaced by a more humane and libertarian system only through the orderly rise to power of a progressive coalition government representing all functional groups in society.

So we wrote and talked about these theories wherever we could find workers to lend us an ear. With the discipline of faith and fervor, we used our positions of leadership in labor, what few we had of them, to advance this general outline of internal policy for building stronger unions:

That all decisions of policy remain in the hands of the rank and file;

That union leadership be granted powers only to the extent of carrying out the expressed will of the membership;

That a grievance structure, separate from the executive, be established for the settlement of disputes from below;

That elections be held frequently, and that executives be elected for short terms;

That salaries of leaders be consistent with the general income level of the working memberships;

That a numerical rather than a financial basis be adopted for representation at conventions.

In the summer of 1939 I went to a New America labor conference in Chicago to discuss this program. There, for two days, we sweated through wearing but lively sessions of discussion and review aimed at winning more recruits among the workers. During the conference I became increasingly conscious of the presence of a sharp-witted girl named Edith Maples from the Detroit District of New America. I had already met her a couple of times at the home of Herb McCreedy, where she roomed, but had not got around to really giving her the once-over.

My attention to Edith at that labor conference arose from a combination of romantic, practical, and biological interest. I had two children to bring up and I was sharing my sister's home—never a happy situation for kids. And there had been developing in the back of my mind for some time the notion that it would be a good thing to find a wife who would share my devotion to the quest for a better world. At any rate, I asked her to make the journey back to Detroit in a car with myself and two other New American fellows. It was a joyful journey, and the beginning of regular dates.

From then on Edith and I talked ourselves gradually into the notion of getting married, and finally, in May 1941, after the legal complications had been attended to, we were married in her home. It was a strange match in many respects, her family being rooted in the conservative environs of Dearborn, Michigan, close to the bastions of the Ford empire. In fact, she boasts that she was born on the site of the River Rouge Rolling Mill, where her father once had a farm.

Shortly after our marriage, in that same summer of 1941, the National Policy Council of New America, of which I was by then a member, met in Chicago to perform the melancholy task of self-dissolution. World War II was flaming across Europe, and American capitalism was perking up as the demands of Mars snapped it out of its hangover of depression. The American masses were in no mood for social revolution—by thesis or otherwise—since war production was fattening up the paychecks.

We had failed to attract any large following for our program, even after we quit thinking of ourselves as an elite leadership group and decided to build a mass organization. Competition was strong, what with labor organization flourishing and the New Deal attracting the allegiance of the rebellious masses. Under these conditions, New America just managed to hang on, and its finances were always as badly off as those of the impoverished prospects it showered with theses. Almost tearfully, we folded New America up and went our respective ways to keep the faith alive as individuals.

12. "Starve the War . . ."

The time I gave to New America, compounding theses and reaching for visions, did not diminish any of my activities in the union. I still worked eight hours a day banging Chevrolet brake shoes through a punch press or whipping them in and out of a reamer. And I still pulled my share of the load in the affairs of Local 235, serving as alternate committeeman on the grievance committee, and as a member of the by-laws committee and the education committee.

In the summer of 1939 the local began to publish a small nine-by-twelve-inch printed shop paper. I was assigned to serve on the editorial staff set up by the local union executive board to write and edit the paper. Since the other members of the staff were not as windy as myself, I fell naturally into the responsibility of writing all the long articles and editorials. In these pieces, banged out late at night or on Saturdays and Sundays on a rickety typewriter in my sister's basement, there is an amusing and revealing narration of my progress—along with most of America—from isolationism to interventionism.

I don't think that, prior to that time, I had felt any particularly strong emotions one way or the other about war. During the period of my membership in the Communist party I shared the excitement whipped up by the comrades in their crusade for aid to the Spanish Loyalists. Acting on party instructions, I was able to push a resolution through a Local 235 meeting demanding that America lift the embargo on shipment of munitions to the

Loyalist government. In the same manner, when the party decreed that all loyal members work to propagandize the boycott of Japanese silk, I peddled "Boycott the Aggressor" buttons in the plant and at union meetings.

But, by the time I neared the pinnacle of my political experience in New America, I had become a pacifist. The stuff I wrote during that period reflects my attitude. Here, for example, is a sample from the September 4, 1939, issue of the *Local 235 News*:

We American workers must be careful not to be stampeded into a war. American financial interests are committed to line up on the side of England. There will be another band-wagon crusade to "save democracy." But the war will not be a war to save democracy; it will be a war to "save profits."

The last war did not save democracy. Democracy was sacrificed in many nations. There is no real democracy in any of the so-called "democratic nations of Europe." Chamberlain and Daladier rule England and France in dictatorial manner. The workers are suppressed and regimented by governmental decrees. This is the "democracy" saved in the last war.

Our job of saving democracy must be done right here at home. And we don't need a war to do it. We have enough war on our hands trying to get a decent living out of General Motors. We have no business meddling in a European war—a war to decide which group of rich families shall get the most profits. . . .

In February 1940 I was still hammering away at the same line, echoing in my small way the rumblings of John L. Lewis, who was then still president of the CIO. Here is another sample from the *Local 235 News:*

Again, certain New Dealers seem to think that their first duty is to meddle in the European "merry-go-round of murder"—while millions of Americans are unemployed and in need of bread. Congress moves to cut WPA, to cut Farm Aid, to suppress labor's rights—while, at the same time, there is a definite plan hatching to loan American money to European countries.

We believe that the CIO speaks the desires of the American people when it says to Congress: Devote your energies to feeding, clothing and sheltering the American people—not by making America a base of supplies for the murder-mad cliques of European rulers—but by providing opportunities for American workers to produce the good things of life they need so badly today!

While I wrote and published these vehement views officially in the name of a UAW-CIO local with some seven thousand members, it is extremely doubtful that my sentiments reflected the genuine feeling of the people in the local. I was doing what so many people with strong opinions do—some willfully and some unwittingly: exploiting a position of trust and power to air my personal prejudices and cloak them in the sanctity of the organization footing the bill. This is a favorite trick of the Communists. They have effectively demonstrated how an articulate individual, strategically lodged in an organization and charged with the duty of expressing official policies, can distort such policies to reflect his personal opinions.

There were probably three influences which produced my passionate outbursts against American entanglement in World War II. For one thing, I was still suffering from the effects of the large doses of Marxist dialectics absorbed while I was a Communist. At one time I had practically memorized passages from Lenin, Strachey, and others, outlining the theory that war is an inevitable outgrowth of the decadence of capitalism. As a result of swallowing these doctrinal medicaments, I had fallen into the groove of Marxist maunderings indentifying war as a damnable affliction designed by brutal capitalists to perpetuate their domination of the human race. Thus incapacitated upstairs, and seeing only blacks and whites in a gray world, I was still a victim of propaganda artists clever enough to season their potions with just the proper amount of half-truths to make the whole dose stick in an unsophisticated mind.

There was also the fact that I was, at the time, an avid reader of the writings of Oscar Ameringer, publisher of *The American Guardian* and grand old man of American socialism. Then in his declining years, but still a powerful voice in the intellectual arenas of the labor movement, Oscar battled against the possibility of American intervention in what he called "Europe's bloodbaths" with every ounce of his vigor, until death stilled his loud and compelling voice. At the time of which I write, he was running the banner headline "Starve the War and Feed America!" across the top of the front page of every issue of *The American Guardian*. I thought the slogan a dynamic and persuasive one and used it extensively in my writing and talking against intervention.

Finally, I was influenced by the official position of New America, which at that particular time was strongly isolationist. In a document published in gaudy red and blue ink on white paper, dated July 4, 1939, and titled *A Peace Policy for the American People*, New America put itself on record as favoring:

> No American participation in any war except in case of direct attack upon our coasts and borders and the strategic points surrounding them . . . an embargo upon loans, credits and sale of armaments . . . public ownership of the armaments industry . . . defeat of all industrial mobilization bills. . . .

This policy, a strange and impractical mixture of pacifism and isolation, which resembled my own personal tendency to view World War II as a symbol of capitalist decadence, did not survive the year. It is to the credit of New America that its passion for freedom overcame its isolationism between July 4, 1939, and July 4, 1940. In the New America National Congress of 1940, *A Peace Policy for the American People* was pigeonholed abruptly and replaced by *A Program for National Defense*. It was no trick for New America to turn out a new thesis with a different slant on very short notice. Our new foreign policy stated:

> If Hitler wins in Europe he will be in control of a population of 400,000,000. He will be free to coordinate the productive power and resources of these 400,000,000 into a unified totalitarian system. These coordinated resources and capacities to produce will give him an economic weapon with which he will seek to destroy the economic unity of the Western Hemisphere. This totalitarian military might and coordinated economic power threatens the independent existence of our nation . . . we are now called upon to defend our democratic way of life with a new faith, courage and power. . . .

Having arrived at this patriotic frame of mind, we went whole hog and cut ourselves cleanly away from the isolationism and pacificism of radical orthodoxy. We resolved solemnly to support the creation of powerful military forces on land, on sea, and in the air; we recommended the registration of all males between eighteen and sixty-five and the inauguration of conscription; we urged the fortification of American outposts and bases around our boundaries. Armed with these bristling declarations of policy, we clamored for a "people's" program of national defense. We had new appeals to the public to plug for progressive social change. Our revised theme was that America could not defend itself efficiently against the menace of Fascist invasion under the status quo of monopoly capitalism. To expedite national defense, we argued, the industrialists, bankers, and landlords enjoying monopoly power had to be brought to heel and made to submit to democratic controls. Only more democracy could save democracy, we declared.

I managed this shift in policy all right, because it was made democratically. Our decision was not a decree handed down from the top. We threshed the matter out, pro and con, for several weeks before arriving at the final text of our program advocating national defense. This step promptly thrust us into violent combat with the Commies, who were screaming loudly against the "imperialist war." They were especially vicious in their attacks on President Roosevelt, whose bid for a third term was then shattering political tradition in this country.

Here, for example, is an excerpt from a line-following speech by James Lindahl—a leader of UAW-CIO Packard Local 190—taken from the proceedings of the Michigan State CIO convention held at Bay City in May 1940:

> We must go on record rebuking the Administration for the definite incitement to war. . . . I think those of you who have listened to President Roosevelt when he scared the country hysterical, pointing out how far from the United States Bermuda is, and such things, I think there is no question that the intent of the present Administration has moved toward involving us in the war. There is a point that I think we should make clear, because unless labor in conferences of this

kind rebukes the tendency and the course upon which the Administration has embarked, we shall be legislated into war without any resistance and without having anything to say.

Again, at the fifth UAW-CIO convention, held in St. Louis from July 29 to August 6, 1940, the party-liners lambasted Roosevelt all over the lot in the debate on a resolution endorsing him for a third term. A typical attack was voiced by Nat Ganley, who said: "I am not prepared to support a resolution which places this convention on record at the present moment as endorsing President Roosevelt for re-election. . . . An uncritical endorsement of Roosevelt puts us in the position of on the one hand endorsing the position of no involvement of America in war, and yet we say nothing on the Roosevelt changes in the neutrality laws of the United States. Even if you disagree with its final consequences, you will have to agree it shoved us closer towards American involvement in the war."

Though the resolution carried decisively, the agents of Moscow in our union were to fight a delaying action against American aid to the victims of Nazi aggression all the way up to the fateful flip-flop of June 22, 1941. And they were not alone that summer in sabotaging FDR's foreign policy or in setting political backfires intended to halt his third-term campaign. Their strategy coincided conveniently with the views of John L. Lewis himself. In her book, *The Roosevelt I Knew*,[1] Frances Perkins credits Dan Tobin of the AFL with reporting Roosevelt's revelation that Lewis had suggested himself in all seriousness as a candidate for Vice-President on the Democratic ticket that year —and had sulked away in a rage when the President dismissed the idea.

Word of the break between Lewis and FDR leaked along the grapevine from Washington to Detroit. It was hard to believe. Many Detroit workers, myself included, just didn't believe that the old man would go through with it. But on October 25, 1940, Lewis plunked his chips down with a clatter heard from coast to coast. Together with a group of New Americans, I listened to his radio speech, in the home of Herb McCreedy. We sat in

[1] New York: Viking, 1946.

hushed silence before the radio as he began to intone his ponderous sentences, his voice reaching into the homes of millions of attentive Americans:

> The present concentration of power in the office of the President of the United States has never before been equaled in the history of our country. How startling, therefore, is the spectacle of a President who is disinclined to surrender that power, in keeping with the traditions of the Republic. The suggestions of a third term under these conditions is less than wholesome or healthy. Personal craving for power, the overweening abnormal and selfish craving for increased power, is a thing to alarm and dismay. . . .
>
> Power for what? Personal and official power to what end? In all history, the unwarranted exercise of continuously vested authority has brought its train of political and social convulsions, for which humanity has paid an appalling price in loss of liberty, in disorder, tragedy and death. . . . Are we to yield to the appetite for power and the vaunting ambitions of a man who plays with the lives of human beings for a pastime?
>
> I say "No." . . .
>
> If not Roosevelt, whom do I recommend to do the job of making secure our nation and its people? Why, of course, I recommend the election of Wendell L. Willkie as the next President of the United States.
>
> It is obvious that President Roosevelt will not be reelected for the third term unless he has the overwhelming support of the men and women of labor. If he is, therefore, reelected, it will mean that the members of the Congress of Industrial Organizations have rejected my advice and recommendation. I will accept the result as being the equivalent of a vote of no confidence, and will retire as President of the Congress of Industrial Organizations at its convention in November. . . .
>
> Sustain me now, or repudiate me. . . .

As the last deep-toned cadence of his blast died away into silence, and the announcer began his chatter, those of us in the room just sat in astonishment, gawking at each other with our mouths open. Then somebody said, "Well, that's that." And we all began to talk at once.

Personally, I did not wait until November to begin the work of repudiation. The Executive Board of my local union was meeting the next morning, and I hurried home to get set for action. I stayed up late typing and polishing a resolution for presentation to the board. As the meeting got under way next day, I moved to suspend the regular order of business and take up the question of John L.'s endorsement of Willkie. Then I read my resolution, which appraised the value of the benefits won by labor under the New Deal, stressed the internal democracy of the CIO and its devotion to democratic procedure, and wound up with a thumping endorsement of FDR for the third term. There was little opposition to the motion to adopt the resolution. A couple of fellows quibbled a bit, but they were so heavily outnumbered and out-talked that they went along with a unanimous vote.

I immediately wrote the following two telegrams, which were adopted by the board and dispatched over the signature of Earnest Bennett, local president:

Mr. John L. Lewis
President
Congress of Industrial Organizations
Washington, D. C.

It is with regret that the Executive Board of Local 235, International Union, United Automobile Workers of America, affiliated with the Congress of Industrial Organizations, by unanimous vote, announces its inability to follow you in supporting Wendell Willkie for the presidency of the United States. We shall continue to support the official position taken by the St. Louis convention of our International Union in doing our utmost to reelect Franklin D. Roosevelt to the presidency of the United States.

President Franklin D. Roosevelt
The White House
Washington, D. C.

The Executive Board of Local 235, United Automobile Workers of America, affiliated with the Congress of Industrial Organizations, speaking for 8,700 organized automobile workers, has voted unanimously to reaffirm its loyalty to you, and pledge its wholehearted support of your campaign for reelection to the presidency of the United States.

The following reply was received from the White House:

Earnest H. Bennett
President, Local 235, UAW-CIO
2205 Holbrook, Detroit, Mich.
I am very grateful.

FRANKLIN D. ROOSEVELT.

I was pulled out of the shop by the union again that fall to rally voters for FDR. My strongest memory of the campaign is a vision of the closing of the polls on election day. I had been going full blast all day, supervising distribution of slates at the polls and coordinating crews of drivers hauling people to vote, in a neighborhood heavily populated with workers, in Detroit's Ward Twenty-two. As the balloting was about to end, I made a final quick check-up of the polls. It was a cold, drizzly night. At every polling place in my division there was still a long line of voters inching their way to the booths. Most of them had the grease and grime of the factory on their hands and faces. They smoked, talked, and joked, shivering in the rain as they shuffled along, keeping faith with the man who had given them the breaks.

John L. was repudiated with a bang. From then on his influence in the CIO declined steadily until he marched his miners out of it in 1942.

13. Super-Dupers and Flip-Flops

My political fortunes were at their lowest ebb in the UAW-CIO during 1940 and 1941. While World War II shifted into high gear and the gyrations of the American Communists kicked up rows that rocked our union to its roots, I was plugging away in the Chevrolet plant, working to rebuild my prestige and status, far behind the front lines of the political clashes that raised a clamor at the upper levels of union activity. I was unable to get elected as a delegate to either the 1940 convention in St. Louis or the 1941 convention in Buffalo.

The UAW-CIO was kept in a continuous state of tumult all through that period by an explosive combination of entangled and interrelated forces and factors almost too complicated to comprehend. To make sense out of the situation in which the union found itself at this time, it is necessary to break down the problems facing it into three rough groupings, all of nearly equal force and significance. These were: organizational and administrative problems; intra-union power politics and factionalism; and the over-all impact of the war on labor's rights and obligations.

Organizational and administrative problems were twofold. First there was the fact that the Ford plants, a major section of the industry under the jurisdiction of the union, were largely unorganized. Such a condition makes it tough for a union to bargain successfully with the employers it does have under contract. Management in the organized plants is quick to exploit such a weakness, by arguing that they have to keep labor costs down in order to meet the competition of the unorganized plants, which usually pay lower wages. In addition to the necessity of pushing organization in the Ford plants, the union faced opportunities for expansion all across the nation, due to the upsurge of industrial activity generated by the war. Old plants were being reopened, and new ones built, in many communities. The aircraft industry was mushrooming all over the nation. These demands on the resources of the union kept the leaders hustling day and night under heavy pressure to keep up with problems and situations springing up at all points of the compass. There were plants to be organized, contracts to be negotiated and serviced, new local unions to be chartered and set up, green union recruits to be trained for positions of leadership.

I can tell one story of an incident at the Ford Willow Run Bomber plant, illustrating the confusion typical of that period. It has to do with a new worker who came running up to the plant gate a few minutes late for his shift one day. As he tried to dash into the plant, a uniformed guard pulled him up short.

"Where's your badge?" the guard demanded.

"What badge?" the impatient worker replied, seemingly puzzled.

"Your plant badge—that round, shiny thing with your picture on it that we gave you when you hired in," the guard explained.

"Oh, that," the worker chuckled. "I sent that home to Maw in Tennessee—she always did want a picture of me."

Interwoven with these complications was the devious thread of Communist manipulation of workers for political purposes. It often reversed itself, switching adroitly from left to right and back again, but it never swayed from its purpose, to build a Soviet power network inside the American labor movement. With the membership of the union mounting at an amazing rate, and new leadership jobs opening up at an equal pace, the CP minority in the union had a field day. The swift growth of the union and its zooming influence in national affairs combined to intensify the political skirmishes for power at every level of leadership. At best the tenure of leadership at the top level was perched precariously on a shaky armed truce between the pro-

Communist Addes faction and the anti-Communist Reuther faction, while R. J. Thomas teetered uneasily on the fence. It is in this kind of tense and volatile atmosphere that the Communists are most adept at exploiting the power of their disciplined shock troops.

Finally, the war itself impinged on this snarl of threshing forces and tangled them into a more complex maze of erupting problems. Labor was asked, after Pearl Harbor, to pledge itself not to strike. Mediation boards were created to attempt to impose wage patterns from above under the sanction of governmental authority. Manpower difficulties cropped up in dozens of places. Allocations of materials, bottlenecks, and shortages bedeviled employment and production schedules.

Some labor leaders thrive on tough problems. Walter P. Reuther seems to be one of them. He demonstrated this late in 1940, when he popped up with his "Reuther Plan" for converting the auto plants to war production, while still giving his full attention to dozens of other complex labor problems. The Commies, of course, promptly denounced him with renewed vigor as a warmonger. Industrialists—who knew that he was right but did not care to admit that he was showing them up—pooh-poohed the idea with studied indifference. Reuther stood his ground, carried the idea up to the highest level of national defense strategy in Washington, and even got the ear of FDR himself. Months later, after Pearl Harbor, and long after the Reuther Plan had been sidetracked and lost in the jungle of Washington power politics, the essential features of his idea were carried out. Its importance in 1940, ignored by the press, was that it indicated the willingness of labor to give its technical know-how to the defense of democracy against Nazi aggression.

But the union was still too divided in its attitude toward the war, and too preoccupied with organizational problems, to give much attention to the gravity of the situation in Europe at that time. We could not know, of course, that two events were soon to explode, on June 22 and December 7, 1941, which made small potatoes of our previous problems.

Early in 1941 the Ford empire fell before a concentrated attack directed by the UAW-CIO. A ten-day strike marked the surrender of the last of the Big Three of the auto industry. It was a time of jubilance and rejoicing all up and down the ranks of the union. I was as happy as any union zealot can be—I had been tossed into the Dearborn jail three times for distributing leaflets at the Ford gates.

The toughness of the Ford management was legendary in the industry. One story about the plight of the Ford workers, used widely by union speakers in organizing talks, went as follows: A certain Ford executive with a reputation as a toughie was strutting through the plant when he noticed a worker seated on a nail keg, splicing some wires. Sitting down on the job was strictly against the plant rules in that building. Without warning, the executive kicked the keg from under the worker, spilling him on his rump. The worker bounced to his feet and smacked the executive into a tailspin.

"You're fired," the executive roared as he scrambled upright.

"The hell I am," the worker said. "I work for the telephone company."

Prior to the strike, called on April 2, organizers had been plugging away for weeks signing up Ford workers. Literature was distributed by the ton, radio broadcasts circled the clock; full-time organizers and volunteers wore out their legs tramping from house to house selling the union to Ford workers. As the campaign began to take effect, Harry Bennett, chief Ford strong-arm man, began to get jittery. His muscle boys, who had beaten up Walter Reuther, Dick Frankensteen, and a crew of organizers in the 1937 "Battle of the Overpass," seemed incapable of combating the union invasion. In a desperate rear-guard action, the company fired eight union leaders on April 2, 1941—and the plant struck.

The International Union promptly threw its full strength into making the strike effective. UAW-CIO members swarmed to the Rouge plant from all over Detroit. I went out the day after the strike started to put in my stint on the picket lines. A plan of battle worked out long in advance for just such an occasion was swiftly invoked. With the plant located as it is, at the hub of a network of roads crossing vast open fields closed in by Ford fences, it was simple to barricade these roads with parked cars and shut off the flow of traffic. Long before dawn the pickets were in complete charge. No one without a pass was permitted to cross the lines. Workers leaving were signed up in the union if they did not already belong.

Ford did not give up easily. Some groups of unorganized workers were goaded into attacking the pickets. There were some bloody clashes before the strike settled down to a war of nerves on April 3. Murray (Pat) Van Wagoner, then Governor of Michigan, assumed the role of top mediator, but CIO leaders had to keep the heat on him to prevent him from throwing state troops into the breach. When it became evident that the strike was highly effective, and the Ford powers began to budge, CIO President Philip Murray came in personally to take a hand in the negotiations.

The settlement agreed to on April 11 was a kind of truce pending a National Labor Relations Board election. Late in May the Ford workers voted overwhelmingly to choose the UAW-CIO as their bargaining agency. A myth was exploded. The voting was unquestionably evidence that the Ford workers, like other auto workers, wanted a union to protect their rights. Faced with this proof, the Ford Motor Company demonstrated again its yen for unorthodox industrial behavior by signing a union shop contract, the first major one in the industry. Wages were raised, seniority installed, and a grievance procedure designed.

History did not give us much time to gloat over our triumph at Ford's. On June 22, 1941, Hitler pounced on Russia, in violation of the Nazi-Soviet pact, and a swarm of synthetic pacifists in the labor movement turned their coats overnight. They began trumpeting loudly the necessity to "aid the people's war against Fascist aggression." I remember the day vividly because I was moving into a flat to set up housekeeping with my new wife when the papers came out announcing the invasion.

Hitler's global double cross caught the Commies in America completely off base. It was a time of tremendous turmoil in the breasts of the comrades, who were worn to a frazzle from beating the drums to keep America out of "the imperialist war." Party-liners were grinding out resolutions as a butcher grinds out hamburger and flooding the labor movement with attacks on FDR and his "plot to sneak us into a shooting war." Zealots, organized by the American Peace Mobilization, a Commie front outfit, were picketing the White House.

In the UAW-CIO, George F. Addes, International Secretary-Treasurer, told the Michigan State CIO convention in Jackson, Michigan, on May 22, 1941:

> I don't want any part of the European war. If we stop a moment to analyze what labor has won or what labor has gained since a year and a half ago, I believe then that every individual who believes in our democratic way of life wants no part of the war that is raging in Europe.

As they twisted their muscles in a titanic flip-flop, the Commies presented a most amusing spectacle. One of the funniest incidents happened in the Detroit and Wayne County CIO Council. UAW-CIO Plymouth Local 51, a strong CP outpost, had sent in a resolution denouncing the "imperialist war," to be acted on by the Council. Before the Council had time to act on the first resolution, Russia was invaded by the Germans, and the local sent in a second resolution appealing for aid to the victims of Nazi aggression.

The comrades had an even hotter one on their hands, however, in connection with a wildcat strike they pulled at the North American Aviation plant in California. Airing of the union linen dirtied in this strike demonstrated to 1941 convention delegates just how good the Commies were in manipulating a local union down the "line."

The strike was called on June 5, in direct violation of the orders of the International Union and in violation of a specific agreement made by the union with the National Defense Mediation Board not to strike the plant until the board had completed its findings. Dick Frankensteen, then UAW-CIO Vice-President in charge of the union's aircraft department, later discharged five International Representatives involved in the strike and revoked the charter of Local 683. When Frankensteen's action was appealed by the local to the Buffalo convention, the grievance committee brought the whole smelly affair out in the open for the delegates to judge and act upon. Though I was not a delegate to that convention, I remember how closely other active unionists and myself watched the Detroit newspapers to follow the proceedings of the convention.

Findings of the grievance committee, which split several ways before the issue was finally resolved, occupied the attention of the convention for days. The essence of the matter was contained in the report of the majority of the committee, a portion of which follows:

> The interference of the Communists into the strike gave basis to the charge of Frankensteen that the wildcat strike was engineered by Communists, inside and outside the union, who were interested in carrying out the policy they were then fostering inside trade unions. They were interested in demonstrating their effectiveness in obstructing national defense. Communist leaflets were distributed on picket lines.

Among the strike strategists blasted by Frankensteen was one Henry Kraus, a writer who had served as editor of the *Auto Worker*, official UAW-CIO paper, until he was fired by Homer Martin in the early days of the union. His part in the strike was attributable to Lew Michener, Director of UAW-CIO Region 6. It was Michener's influence that resulted in the loading of the Local 683 staff with people who were active in pulling the strike. Wyndham Mortimer, ex-Vice-President of the union, was also in on the strike as an International Union representative. His daughter was on the local union office staff. So was Dorothy Kraus, wife of the writer who wrote the leaflets.

In his speech to the convention defending his role in the strike, Mortimer tried to show that Frankensteen's antagonism toward Kraus was newly acquired and not worth much as evidence.

"Dorothy Kraus worked in my office, that is true," said Mortimer. "Is that a crime? And when Dick Frankensteen came to California about a year ago, he came into my office, and he saw Dorothy Kraus there, and he walked over to her and kissed her. I am not saying there was anything wrong with that kiss, purely a friendly kiss."

Delegates returned from the convention told me that when Frankensteen took his turn at the microphone to state his position, the convention en masse greeted him with puckered lips and loud smacking noises.

"If I am not blushing," he said, "I ought to be, because my wife is in the balcony." Then he went on to tell this story of the conduct of the strike:

I arrived on the West Coast three weeks prior to the time the strike was called. At that time I went into negotiations with the management of North American and the committee. I found that the committee had accomplished exactly nothing, that instead of arguing about the merits of their grievances and their cases and their contract, they were spending their time, if you please, arguing with the management that the management did not have the right to hire as they saw fit, but rather they had to hire regardless of race, creed, color or political affiliation. The management told them that there were government regulations, and yet they tried to force that language. Why? Because three members of your committee were registered members of the Communist party. Another was a member of the Young Communist League, and another, if you please, was art editor of a Communist magazine—every one of them—and that is what they were interested in and not in advancing the interests of these workers in the North American plant. . . .

On Sunday I went to the beanfield meeting. When I got out to this field I did not find hostility among those workers, I did not find bitterness among the rank and file, I did not find a lot of hostility in that crowd. It was only when I got close to the platform, where they had all of the outstanding leaders of the CP on the West Coast, if you want to know it, surrounding that, that I was heckled and booed and shoved around. That was the only time. And then they proceeded to put seven speakers on ahead of me, each of whom did a vicious job of tearing me down, each of whom raised one issue after another that did not bear on the North American case, what they were going to do to me, what my position was, what kind of a sellout I was, how I sold out for thirty pieces of silver, and all that sort of baloney. That is the stuff they were pulling.

Then finally I was given the opportunity to speak; at least, I thought I was going to be. I was introduced. I no sooner stood up than out of nowhere came a flock of slogans and platform banners all around the place. I want you to know that the striking Walt Disney American Federation of Labor Artists on the West Coast stayed up all night to draw these banners—and I want to pay tribute to the Walt Disney artists—they painted my face pretty well, and put it on the bodies of rats and skunks and snakes. I was heckled from the time I started to speak until the time I finished speaking. . . .

These revelations, complicated by an intricate parliamentary snarl, put that 1941 UAW-CIO gathering into the union's history as the "super-duper" convention. This term had special reference to the three-way splits that splintered two important convention committees, embroiling the delegates in a noisy wrangle and requiring many roll-call votes to settle the issues. The final result was a "super-duper" report by one lone committee member. Delegates rejected a four-member majority report, then knocked down a two-member minority report, before adopting the "super-duper" report by a roll-call vote giving it a scant majority of 98 votes out of a total of 3,029. The report adopted barred Michener from running for re-election as Regional Director. But CP influence continued strong on the West Coast. Three years later, at the 1944 convention in Grand Rapids, the delegates voted to put the region under an International administratorship following a scandal involving misuse of union funds to line up delegates in support of the Addes-CP faction.

Constitution committee members split in the same way on the issue of barring subversives from holding office in the union. Again the "super-duper" minority report was adopted, this time by a majority of 941 votes. The amendment to the Constitution thus adopted said: "No member of any Local Union shall be eligible to hold any elective or appointive position in this International Union or any Local Union of this International Union if he is a member of or subservient to any political organization, such as the Communist, Fascist, or Nazi organization, which owes its allegiance to any government other than the United States and Canada, directly or indirectly." Despite this amendment, dozens of known Communists continued to hold offices in the union.

The real test of power that year centered in a contest for the office of secretary-treasurer. Dick Leonard, then still a loyal member of the Reuther group, ran against George Addes and lost by 441 votes. As the delegates departed wearily for their homes, the top leadership was almost evenly divided, with tobacco-chewing President R. J. Thomas still straddling the fence. It was in this convention that the name of the union was changed to International Union, United Automobile, Aircraft and Agricultural Implement Workers of America, CIO.

Re-elected, Addes learned to look at the war in a different dialectical light. In May he had not wanted "any part of the European war." By November his heart was bursting with patriotism, and he told the National CIO convention: "The members of our union have accepted the idea and theory that it is all-important to defeat Hitler."

As the Nazi panzers raced across the holy soil of the Soviet Union, the necessity to defeat Hitler became a mania with the American Commies and their dupes. They were soon pushing proposals that sacrificed many of labor's most basic rights, and selling out the workers right and left, all in the name of defeating fascism.

14. "Forward with Fountain in '42"

On December 7, 1941, Local 235 held a regular membership meeting at Carpenter Hall in Hamtramck. During the disposition of the agenda, the Political Action Committee brought out a recommendation that the local send two members to Washington to lobby against the Smith-Connally Act. The National CIO had called for grass-roots action against the bill on the grounds that it proposed drastic limitations on the right to strike. The recommendation carried, and an election was held to choose the two members of the committee for the privilege of making the junket to the capital. Earnie Bennett and myself were named by the members to take the trip. Since it was necessary to get to Washington the next day in order to attend a briefing session scheduled by top CIO leaders for the hastily assembled lobbyists, we rushed over to the local office that Sunday to start working on our transportation. Before we could get reservations nailed down, the stunning news of Pearl Harbor came over the radio.

We canceled the lobbying journey when word came from Washington that the project was superseded by the urgency of getting the nation mobilized for war. In a few days the emergency hit the Chevrolet plant. Passenger car production was swiftly curtailed. I was working on the passenger brake drum assembly job at the time. As an alternate committeeman in the district in which the brake drum job was located, I had top seniority, so I was transferred to the truck brake drum line and kept on working. Truck production was stepped up. While the bulk of the workers were laid off, those of us left on the truck job got in lots of overtime and collected the fattest paychecks we ever earned in that plant.

Conversion of the Chevrolet plant to full war production dragged through the winter into the early spring of 1942, when the annual political campaign was kicked off in Local 235. It was certainly a mixed-up affair that year. There were four candidates bidding for the presidency of the local. I threw my hat in the ring and ran as an independent, in a determined bid to rebuild my political status in the union. With the usual modesty of a political aspirant, I prompted the formation of a "Plant 2 Rank and File Committee to Elect Clayton W. Fountain President of Local 235, UAW-CIO." This practice is as common in labor organizations as in any other political situation where pomp and propaganda are considered essential to the success of the campaign. No office-seeker wants to look like a self-starter—even if he is one. To make it appear to the electorate that he has organized backing, he persuades some of his friends to lend their names to his campaign literature.

My campaign pamphlet that year was weighted with the names of ten Plant Two rank-and-file members with varying degrees of influence in the shop. Across the top of the front page in bold type was the slogan "Forward with Fountain in '42." Under this timorous heading, the document carried the following glib recital of my alleged talents and capacities:

He has a wide knowledge of the labor movement, obtained by years of study and research and actual experience.

He is a capable public speaker with the ability to meet the management and express the needs and demands of the workers in direct, concise and convincing language.

He is a trained journalist, qualified to express the opinions of labor by effective use of the written word. [My only training was the experience garnered willy-nilly in three years of editing the local paper—discounting the couple of months in 1938 when I acted as an unpaid Detroit correspondent for the short-lived Communist *Midwest Daily Record*.]

He is a skilled parliamentarian, able to conduct orderly meetings....

He is a loyal American citizen, opposed to all un-American philosophies, as attested to in the following quotation from a letter he had printed in the *Detroit News* Letter Box on June 23, 1941: "We [the members of the CIO] will not allow the Communists or any other subversive group to use the CIO for subversive purposes. . . ."

The pamphlet then set forth a program for Local 235. I called for the winning of the war; for improved working conditions; for equalization of wealth; for liberty, security, and opportunity; for more rank-and-file participation in union affairs. I said that the union should become "a stronger force for doing away with graft, ignorance, corruption and crime in American public life. . . ." It was a large order, but strictly in the American political tradition.

At this point in the campaign, while my pals were plastering the plant with my propaganda, the political situation in the local was upset by a new development destined to have lasting effect on my future. Two weeks before the election, I got a phone call from George Merrelli, a member of our local serving on Walter P. Reuther's GM staff. He said he had something important to tell me. We agreed to meet the next night in a Hamtramck beer garden, with Earnie Bennett, ex-president of Local 235, who was then serving as executive secretary of the Wayne County Labor's Non-Partisan League.

I suspected a trick in the request for a meeting. George and Earnie were both UAW-CIO right-wingers,[1] high in the councils of the pro-Reuther group. They were backing Mike Lacey, another right-winger, for president of the local. I was still a lone wolf, attached to no power caucus. I thought they wanted to persuade me to withdraw from the race, to give Lacey a better chance to beat the left-wing pro-Communist candidate.

When I met them in the beer joint I found that, instead of tossing a monkey wrench directly into my campaign, they came bearing a gift. Over the beers they bought, they revealed that they were authorized by Reuther to offer me a full-time job that

[1] The term "right-winger" does not indicate political conservatism. It is applied in the labor movement to democratically minded anti-Communists. In the UAW-CIO we hold that our right-wingers are more militant than Communists can ever be—because Communists are opposed to freedom.

would take me out of the plant on a union leave of absence. This meant that I was to be taken into the pro-Reuther camp.

"Walter has been watching you for some time," Merrelli said, "and now he's a got a spot that he wants you to fill."

My pulse quickened by several beats, but I exploited the stoic qualities of my Indian ancestors and maintained a poker face. "What kind of a job is it?" I asked with a pretense of nonchalance.

"It's with the Blue Cross Hospitalization plan," Merrelli explained. He reviewed the steps by which the union and GM had acted jointly to install a new hospitalization and surgical care plan in the General Motors plants in Michigan. It was something new, offering the workers a method of prepaying the cost of hospitalization and surgery for themselves and their families.

"When we negotiated the plan," Merrelli explained, "the union asked the Michigan Hospital Service to hire two full-time union guys to take care of the grievances of the workers. Now they are ready to put the first guy on the payroll, and Reuther wants you to take the job."

"I'd prefer to wait until after the election to give you my answer," I finally told them. "Let's put it this way: If I make the grade as president of the local, I'll stick to the local; but, if I don't make it, I'll take your offer up."

They agreed, and we let it go at that.

When the votes were counted in the local primary election, I came within less than a hundred votes of placing for the runoff. That let me out—and it was my last fling at running for a labor union office. On March 11, 1942, my leave of absence started. I must admit that my feelings were a confused mixture of sadness and jubilance as I departed from the Chevrolet plant to start on my new job. I was happy to move up the ladder of the labor movement, but leaving the shop was much like moving out of a house full of memories where you have lived a long time. Thinking of how intimate I had been with many of the people in the plant, I vowed inwardly that my performance as a porkchopper would never betray the workers who were now hiring me to work for them.

The duties assigned to me as a union representative on the staff of the Michigan Hospital Service were neither very exacting nor very clearly defined. I shared offices in a downtown Detroit office building with three union brothers from the Chrysler plants, where the hospitalization plan had been set up a year earlier. Most of my work involved processing the complaints of workers fouled up in the red tape common to insurance systems. While the Blue Cross plan was non-profit in character, and not particularly inclined to bamboozle its claimants, it had its share of fine print and confusing procedures. The fact that it operated jointly with the Michigan Medical Service, another non-profit agency, which underwrote surgical service for GM workers, added to the kinks in getting the plans rolling.

Each of the plans had specified legal limitations on the scope of benefits. Grievances grew out of these restrictions. Some workers did not understand that they had to be bed-patients in a hospital to collect benefits. Others believed that they could go on collecting forever. Obstetrical benefits were payable only after a nine-month waiting period; this provision brought us many borderline cases that were tough headaches. If there was no hope of satisfying the aggrieved worker, we spelled out to him the provisions in small type in the contract, expressed our regret, and ended the case. But, if a gripe had merit, we fought the case all the way up to the top administration of the hospitalization services and used the power of the union to bargain for a favorable decision.

After I got the hang of handling the grievances, I found there were too few to keep me busy. I went out to visit GM locals all over the state, beating the bushes for beefs, but still did not have enough work to keep me out of mischief. So I dropped into bookstores and libraries, picked up several works on medical care plans, and stuffed my brain with dry data about hospital beds, weighted averages, and the high cost of an appendectomy. In a few weeks my shoptalk was well salted with medical lingo. To air my newfound knowledge, I wrote pieces for the labor press knocking the shortcomings of group medical care plans and boldly suggesting corrective measures. The point I hit hardest was the lack of consumer participation at the policy-forming level of the plans. This was waving a red flag at the medicos, who will not admit that a layman knows even enough to take a pill without their instructions.

One day John Mannix, then Executive Director of the Michigan Hospital Service, called me up to his office for a personal conference. After lauding my quickness in getting the pitch on the operation of non-profit hospital and medical care plans, he said he had a special job for me. His people wanted to get an enabling act passed by the Indiana legislature to make a Blue Cross plan possible in that state. He wanted me to go to Indianapolis, all expenses paid, to lobby for the act. I accepted quickly and did my best on the assignment, but, even with the help of the Indiana CIO boys, we couldn't get our bill through. The private insurance lobby, which opposed our bill, had the inside track with the legislators. We didn't get to first base.

I kept on finding extra work for myself. Together with my three colleagues from Chrysler, I helped draft a report on the union's medical care program. It was printed and distributed at the 1942 UAW-CIO convention in Chicago. Late in the year we promoted and helped to plan a Health for Victory Conference. It was held in Detroit with the participation of important figures in the medical world—most of whom uneasily praised our energetic concern with medical planning. And when the union revived its Medical Research Institute—a diagnostic clinic for workers suffering from occupational diseases or injuries incurred on the job—George Addes gave us expense money to tour the local unions and solicit support for the Institute. It was set up on a per capita tax basis, with participating locals helping to pay the freight. The clinic was opened at the union headquarters on West Grand Boulevard in Detroit; later it expanded into the old Edsel Ford home on East Jefferson Street.

In all of these activities we were exploring our way out of the cramped quarters of "unionism-as-usual." Instead of just paying lip service to the need of workers and their families for better medical care programs, we jumped into the game and started pitching. I believe the UAW-CIO is moving faster on this social frontier than any other union. As I write we have just hired a professional medical care administrator to coordinate and expand our Social Security

Department. This department handles group insurance, pensions, workmen's compensation, and unemployment compensation; and it operates the Medical Research Institute.

With a little persuasion we convinced the Blue Cross biggies that we could do the institution a lot of good at the 1942 convention of the UAW-CIO, which was to be held in the Sherman Hotel at Chicago. It ran from August 3 to August 9. Actually, there wasn't much for us to do there, but we promised to whoop it up for Blue Cross among delegates from other states. Our superiors thought that was worth trying and they let us go.

That 1942 convention was the dullest of the lot. With the exception of a few Trotskyites and other rugged individualists, everybody was for winning the war. The comrades were ready to back anything that would get another bullet on a boat headed for Russia. The dove of peace roosted on the rostrum throughout the conclave, so far as factional fighting was concerned. Until late in the convention, the delegates couldn't even find anything or anybody as a target for their usual barrage of boos.

Neither of the factions felt strong enough to try to knock the other side out. In fact, the leaders of both camps put their heads together and, by common consent, agreed to elect two international vice-presidents. The positions had been abolished in 1939 in an effort to prevent factional politics. One delegate from the Kelsey-Hayes unit of West Side Local 174 in Detroit rose to oppose the altering of the constitution on this issue. He unburdened himself as follows:

"We had five vice-presidents once. We had to call a special convention in Cleveland to clean them out. We did not go in there just with our sleeves rolled up; we walked in with baseball bats and brooms on our shoulders to clean them out.

"With two vice-presidents I am afraid it will be just as bad as five, maybe worse, because there will be two sides then and not five sides. Whenever the president goes away the vice-presidents will wonder who is boss. . . . We do not have to have any fellows in there with big titles who will get swell-headed with their titles and forget to go out on the road but sit in swivel chairs and not go out and do the job. . . ."

While this delegate may have spoken the feelings of a few other delegates who were suspicious of the newly found unity at the top level of the union, there was little open opposition to the change. The amendment carried by a voice vote, with only a few scattered "Nay" votes registered. The nominating speeches delivered for vice-presidential candidates were heavy with harmony. Walter Reuther was nominated by Dick Leonard, his fellow Executive Board member from Detroit's West Side. But the pay-off came, to the amusement of the delegates, when George Addes arose to second the nomination of the energetic redhead.

"I have watched Brother Reuther work," Addes orated, "and I have reached the conclusion that Brother Reuther is an able leader, an energetic leader, one whom I have become convinced in the last year is desirous of establishing, along with others of us, unity within this great organization. . . . I urge the delegates assembled here to cast a unanimous ballot for the nominee, Brother Walter Reuther."

Walter Reuther and Dick Frankensteen were elected vice-presidents by a voice vote. There were no roll calls that year. R. J. Thomas was unopposed for the presidency, and George Addes was also re-elected by acclamation to the office of secretary-treasurer.

The only exciting event in the convention came when the Constitution Committee recommended that the dues be raised from one dollar per month to a dollar and a half. All of the top officers were for the proposition, not only because they wanted to prove their faith in the newly established unity, but because there were sound administrative reasons for raising the dues. But the delegates would have none of it. They could stomach the re-establishment of two vice-presidencies, but the thought of raising the dues was too much for them. They had to assert their independence and their control over the officers at least once in the convention. So they shouted the dues increase down by a substantial majority.

The unity proclaimed by Addes could not, of course, endure; for it did not get at the root of factionalism. In a little more than a year, at the next convention, Dick Leonard, backed by Walter Reuther, tried to knock Addes out of his job and came near succeeding.

15. The Gruesome Twosome

Walter Reuther called me into his office on a wet, wintry afternoon in March 1943. The UAW-CIO top officers had by then moved into their present headquarters, at the corner of Cass and Milwaukee Streets, in the shadow of the General Motors Building. Thomas, the President, and Addes, the Secretary-Treasurer, occupied offices at the east and west ends, respectively, of the second floor. Reuther and Frankensteen, the two Vice-Presidents, had their quarters on the third floor.

When preliminary greetings were over, Reuther characteristically went directly to the point of our interview. He said he had been thinking for some time of putting a fellow on his personal staff to do writing, research, and so forth. Such a staff member, he explained, would work closely with him as a kind of administrative handyman. At that time, in addition to serving as Director of the General Motors Department, he had charge of one-half of the Washington office of the union, and was involved in several other vital union activities. The Washington portion of his work included manpower and contract procurement problems, plus responsibility for action on the consumer and cost-of-living front. It was about this time that he hired Donald Montgomery, former Consumer Counsel of the United States Department of Agriculture, to act as consumer counsel for the UAW-CIO. This was the first time in labor history that a major union had retained an expert to act in this capacity.

When he asked me if I would accept the job on his personal

staff, I nearly fell out of my chair. I accepted quickly, before he had a chance to change his mind, and from then on I fitted myself into the inner circle of Walter's close associates and began really to learn the score about union politics. I stayed in the job until May 1946, when Reuther promoted me to the post of Associate Editor of the official union paper.

In the months and years that followed my appointment to Reuther's staff, working closely with Montgomery, I helped to build the foundations for the UAW-CIO program of developing consumer cooperatives, now rolling in high gear. I taught classes, met with farm groups and participants in Rochdale cooperatives, built a system of communication and understanding between our union and these consumer-conscious forces. It was a long, slow, and tedious task, but the big consumer-owned cooperatives opening in industrial centers today are fruits of that early seeding by Reuther's staff members.

Shortly after I took up my new tasks, the Communist party kicked off its infamous drive to get labor on record in favor of the incentive pay system, better known in the shops as the piecework system. This was the same plan that had driven myself and other Briggs workers to pull our quickie sit-down strike in 1929.

A quaint sidelight on the concern of auto workers with speedups, incentive pay, and production schedules is revealed in the story of one slowdown in an important Detroit body plant. The membership of the local union in this plant had voted to press the company for a union shop contract in 1940. When the employer balked, a slowdown was called. Each day the union advised the management of how much it was going to cut production, almost down to the decimal point. Came the day when production was down 50 per cent. A shop steward, checking the schedule in his department, came across a sweeper pushing his broom down the aisle at a mighty fast clip.

"Hey," the steward yelled, yanking the sweeper down to a stop. "Don't you know production is down 50 per cent today? Slow down, brother."

"But I can't help it," the jittery sweeper protested. "You see,

I'm a nervous type; I have to work fast—I can't work any other way."

"Oh," the steward grunted, scratching his head in perplexity. Then an idea hit him. He called a machine repairman over and snatched a hacksaw out of his tool kit. With a few swift licks of the saw, he lopped 25 per cent off each end of the sweeper's broom.

"Here you are; that'll fix your schedule," the steward said, grinning as he handed the bob-tailed broom back to the startled sweeper.

Earl Browder, CP boss, who was still in the good graces of Moscow at the time, was reported in the *Daily Worker* of February 25, 1943, as having sounded the call for all good comrades to turn on the heat for piecework.

"It's patriotic to demand increased earnings based on increased production . . . war production could be doubled if this policy were applied," the *Daily Worker* quoted Browder as saying. By the middle of May, the party was carrying the fight into Detroit, home of the UAW-CIO and one of the national centers of war production. In a speech that was reprinted as a half-page advertisement in the *Detroit News* of May 14, 1943, Browder said:

> Walter Reuther has been conducting the same type of wrecking in the airplane and automotive industry. There, also, the basic problems of increased wage-income for the workers and increased production for the war go hand in hand and must be solved together. The obvious line of solution is to relate these two factors in such a way that increased wages help to expand production, and increased production furnishes the basis for the expansion of wages. That is the principle that has come to be known as the "incentive wage." But Walter Reuther, by the use of the most unprincipled demagogy and lying propaganda, has so far blocked the serious consideration of this solution in the UAW-CIO, he has forced the government to hesitate in bringing it forward, and under the slogan of fighting against the incentive wage, he has also created an ominous wave of strike sentiment. . . .
>
> Production is being increased every week and every month in most places. If the workers had not been blocked by Reuther from establishing the incentive rates, all of this increase in production would have meant increased wages for them. . . .

The willingness of the Communists to sacrifice labor's rights in the hopes of expanding production under the piecework system was in line with their general policy of the times. This policy was best set forth in Browder's book, *Victory—and After*,[1] in which he said:

> There is not, and cannot be, any literal equality of sacrifice as between workers and capitalists in this war. The workers must make the main sacrifice. . . . We must find a way to finance, organize and fight this war through to victory, a way which is acceptable to the owning class, industrialists, financiers, bond owners, with their important hired men. We must depend on the patriotism of the rich. . . .

Echoes of this line were quickly heard in the ranks of the UAW-CIO, where the Commies commanded several key locals and influenced the thinking of several members of the International Executive Board. George Addes advocated the piecework system; so did Dick Frankensteen. At the staff level, Addes had helped get key jobs for a number of henchmen who usually followed the Communist party line. Among these were James Wishart, Director of Research; Maurice Sugar, General Counsel; William Levitt, Director of Education; David Erdman, Editor of *Ammunition;* and Irving Richter, Legislative Representative. These were all appointive jobs; the directors in turn could appoint their own staff members—and so the staffs in these key departments were loaded with Commies. They were underfoot everywhere. Bill Levitt even hired Elizabeth Hawes, the fellow-traveling dress designer and author, who tried the UAW-CIO on for size and found it was too big for her. Later she wrote a book about the UAW-CIO that, according to reviewers, was sprinkled with inaccuracies and jibes at Reuther and his associates.

While these Commie agents, operating under the protection of Addes, ran loose among the rank and file of the union, Addes himself, aided by the unpredictable Frankensteen, tried to jam through an endorsement of piecework at the top policy level of the UAW-CIO. Addes personally raised the subject of piecework at a meeting of the International Executive Board held in Columbus, Ohio,

[1] New York: International Publishers Co., Inc., 1942.

starting March 5, 1943. Addes said he was bringing the topic up only to get a "clear" statement by the union on the matter. In the Board meeting he recited the arguments in favor of adoption of incentive pay. Then he told the press that he had not made up his mind on the subject.

Walter Reuther, Dick Leonard, and other Board members insisted firmly that the Board adopt a forthright statement of policy reaffirming the union's traditional opposition to piecework. After considerable debate this was done by a unanimous vote. Newspapermen had a hard time doping out why the vote was unanimous. The *Detroit Times* correspondent wrote on March 10:

> The unanimous vote on Reuther's motion was surprising inasmuch as several Board members stated last week that they were in favor of some kind of incentive pay. Their retreat on the issue was probably attributable to an avalanche of protests from rank and file members throughout the country at the time the matter was brought up for discussion by George F. Addes, Secretary-Treasurer.

The Board's statement said: "The International Executive Board reaffirms its traditional opposition to incentive payment plans." The statement also outlined minimum conditions on which the union would insist if incentive pay were to operate in plants where it already existed, or in plants where the workers exercised their democratic right to try it out if they wanted to. But on April 1, Addes sent out a mimeographed letter to local unions—supposedly to inform them of the Board's decision—in which he completely omitted the sentence setting forth the "traditional opposition" to piecework.

At the next Board meeting, held in Cleveland, Ohio, the week beginning April 20, Frankensteen introduced a resolution approving the introduction of piecework plans. He gave copies of the resolution to the press before he submitted it to the Board. Addes held a press conference at which he told the reporters he favored Frankensteen's resolution. The *Detroit News* of April 21 said: "Frankensteen was joined in his efforts to sell the Board on the incentive program by George F. Addes, International Secretary-Treasurer."

After airing their resolution in the press, Frankensteen and Addes condescended to bring it before the Board. The official minutes of the meeting, as edited by Addes, state: "Brother Frankensteen stated the proposal he wished to advance was not a radical change from the program adopted at the last meeting of the Board. It merely withdrew the statement that the union was historically opposed to incentive systems." Again, arguments raged. Reuther and his backers on the Board demanded a vote that would kill and bury the resolution. A motion was made to table it. The Reuther group held out firmly for a repudiation of the resolution. However, the motion to table carried by a small margin. But that was not the end of it. The Addes-Frankensteen group, with the Commies leading the parade, whooped it up for piecework right on into the 1943 convention, which opened in Buffalo on October 4.

Endorsement of piecework was not the only action by the Addes-Frankensteen-CP gang that summer. They openly backed government orders that struck hard at labor. When War Manpower Commissioner Paul McNutt tried to put through a labor freeze, Addes led a fight in the UAW-CIO to go along. He was defeated, but in Washington, Irving Richter, a CP-liner hired by Frankensteen to act as UAW-CIO legislative representative, continued to plug for a labor draft, in violation of union policy. When Executive Order 9328 was issued in an attempt to freeze wages, Addes presented the Board meeting held to act on it with a lengthy and lyrical document which actually praised the wage freeze order. Addes and his Board buddies battled for three days to try to get the union on record as favoring the wage freeze, but they were beaten down. Reluctant to give up, Addes used his office to send out a letter to all local unions which toned down the Board's blast at the wage freeze.

The democratic forces in the union, led by Walter Reuther and Dick Leonard, went into the convention determined to make a fight against the Addes-Frankensteen group and their policy of appeasing employers beyond the degree of cooperation necessary to promote the war effort. Our people in the plants were fed up with the efforts of the Commies to put across Browder's theory that the workers had to make the "main sacrifice." The fight took the form of an effort to oust Addes from the position of secretary-treasurer and replace him with Richard T. Leonard, who at that time was a faithful member of the Reuther group. I was active in writing, printing, and circulating our campaign literature, as well as in helping Eddie Levinson work with the press.

Up until the time of the vote, we worked all hours of the day and night to convince the delegates that the activities of Addes and Frankensteen in support of piecework, the labor freeze, and the wage freeze were good and sound reasons to toss them out of office. It was out of this battle that one of the quaintest and liveliest UAW-CIO political jingles was born. It was distributed on a mimeographed sheet by pro-Reuther delegates from Buffalo, New York, Linden and Trenton, New Jersey, and New York City; and it swept the convention like a popular song. Some of the words, sung to the tune of "Reuben and Rachel," were these:

Who are the boys who take their orders
Straight from the office of Joe Stalin [sung Sta-leen]?
No one else but the gruesome twosome,
George F. Addes and Frankensteen.

Who are the boys that fight for piecework,
To make the worker a machine?
No one else but the gruesome twosome,
George F. Addes and Frankensteen.

When it comes to double-talking,
Who is worse than Willie Green?
No one else but the gruesome twosome,
George F. Addes and Frankensteen.

The auto workers have their sideshow—
One is fat and one is lean.
Who are they but the gruesome twosome,
George F. Addes and Frankensteen.

There were several other verses, some of them unprintable. Early in the morning, late at night, or at almost any time during the convention, lines of delegates did snake dances through the corridors of hotels, singing this jingle at the top of their voices.

And, as Ollie Pecord, then editor of the *Toledo Union Journal*, put it, "Some of those leather-lunged lathe hands could really yell it out." Sometimes a delegate would stick his head out of a hotel window and bellow the first three lines of a favorite stanza down an airshaft. Promptly, somewhere across the airshaft, a husky voice would yell back: "George F. Addes and Frankensteen!"

The piecework issue came to the floor of the convention on the third day. A six-man majority of the Resolutions Committee, led by Victor G. Reuther, strongly restated the union's opposition to the introduction of piecework in plants where it did not exist. A three-man CP-line minority delivered a conflicting report which would have left the whole matter of choosing a wage payment system in the hands of the local unions.

R. J. Thomas, President of the union and chairman of the convention, promptly leaped astride the fence, although his position was not in jeopardy. Parts of his speech on the issue reflect his uneasy attempts to work both sides of the street. He said, for instance:

"I say calmly and considerately that there have to be ways and means worked out in some cases in the future—and I am not just speaking for the war, I mean for years ahead—whereby, if the workers after this war is over are able to get in and get wage increases, we are going to have to take into consideration more and more all the time if we can expect further wage increases of how to raise the efficiency if we are able to get more money."

This sentence, to those able to unravel it, would seem to indicate that Thomas favored the minority position. But his concluding paragraph made it clear that he wanted all the delegates and workers to see him as their champion, no matter what side of the issue they were on. He said:

"I am not wholeheartedly in accord with either resolution. The resolution which I think should come before this convention is that the officers of the union should not be permitted to go out and sell incentive pay plans, but yet the local union itself should have enough autonomous power to solve that problem within their own local without any help."

Addes and Frankensteen spoke for the minority report; Reuther and Leonard spoke for the majority. Then a motion was made and carried compelling all members of the Board to rise and be counted on the issue.

Finally, after the rank-and-file delegates had kicked both reports around for a while, the minority report was voted down and the majority report carried. Our next task was to attempt to translate the spirit of this repudiation of Addes and Frankensteen into votes against them in the election of officers.

When the votes were counted, Addes skinned back in by the very narrow margin of 70 votes out of 7,422 cast. On the first ballot for vice-president, Reuther defeated Frankensteen by 347 votes. Frankensteen came back on the second ballot and defeated Dick Leonard by 355 votes for the second vice-presidency.

The seventy-vote margin of victory for Addes was garnered by promising the Negro delegates a member on the International Executive Board. Prominent in the execution of this completely unscrupulous maneuver were the Communists, who always parade themselves as the most militant advocates of equal rights for all minorities. This is as good a place as any to debunk the myth that Communists really care about the rights of Negroes. All they want is the votes and backing for their program; they will promise Negroes anything to get that backing.

Our 1943 convention had more Negro delegates in attendance than had any other convention in the history of the union. This was due to the fact that we had waged a successful campaign to break down the employment pattern in the auto and aircraft plants, which gave Negroes only the most menial jobs of sweeping and mopping. It must be admitted that all major groups in the union fought side by side on this problem. But we Reutherites took our stand for the promotion or upgrading of Negroes to semi-skilled and skilled jobs they could perform because we really believed in equality. The Communists fought the same kind of battle because they wanted to win the support of Negroes for the CP line. This difference was brought clearly into the open in Buffalo in 1943.

The whole question of racial discrimination was brought to the floor of that convention in a divided report from the Constitution Committee. It centered around the first attempt of the UAW-CIO to establish what was called a "Minorities Department."

Majority Committee Chairman Melvin Schultz, of Local 12 in Toledo, Ohio, read the majority report to the convention, as follows:

"The International Union shall establish a department through which the problems of recognized minority groups within our International Union will be handled. The International President shall appoint a director for the Minorities Department subject to the approval of the International Executive Board."

The position of the Communists, backed by the bulk of the Addes-Frankensteen group, was that the director of this new department should be elected to the International Executive Board by the convention as a whole—*and that he should be a Negro as such.* The Commies had shrilled their backing for this kind of Jim Crowism in reverse long before the convention opened. In delegates' elections where large numbers of Negroes were involved, they had brazenly campaigned on the proposition of electing a Negro as a Negro to the International Executive Board.

Nat Ganley, then Business Agent of Local 155 and a member of the Central Committee of the Communist party of the United States, was the spokesman for the minority of the Constitution Committee on this issue. In the first draft of his minority report distributed to the delegates, Article 9, Section 2, of the Constitution was to include these words: ". . . the Director of the Minority Department of the International Union . . . shall be a Negro and a member of the International Executive Board nominated and elected by the convention as a whole."

Resentment against Ganley's proposition flared so high that he crawfished before the entire convention and deleted the words making it mandatory that a Negro be elected as a Board member and director of the new department. But he did not completely abandon the idea. In his speech to the convention he said:

"Although the minority report does not make it mandatory that a Negro be a director of the Minority Department, I feel confident that this great International Convention would want to demonstrate to the entire nation our policy of racial solidarity by electing a Negro member to this post."

Addes and Frankensteen spoke for the minority report, in keeping with their pre-election pledges to support the proposition. Walter Reuther and several of his followers denounced the minority report and urged adoption of the majority report. But perhaps the best speech on the controversy—which incited feeling to the point where two Negro delegates started slugging it out on the floor—was made by R. J. Thomas. In contrast to some of his sadder performances, this speech was one of the highest points in his career as a labor leader. Speaking in favor of the majority report, he said:

"If these individuals want a special place on our International Executive Board for a Negro, then I say to the delegates here the reason I think that is discrimination is because I am sure that those very same people would fight like hell if this convention went on record asking for such a thing as special seats in street cars for Negroes, or a special seat in a theater for a Negro, or a special room in a hotel for a Negro."

There are witnesses who swear that R. J. was so overcome with excitement when he delivered this speech that he swallowed his cud of tobacco.

When the vote came, both reports, surprisingly enough, were voted down. There can be only one explanation for this. Each of the big power caucuses certainly voted for its own proposal and against that of the opposition. There must have been a sizable minority opposed to both reports. Ineffective by itself, this minority was big enough to defeat both reports when aligned against each one in company with the competing caucus.

Much of the interest in the racial issue at that convention was directly attributable to the bloody race riot that broke out in Detroit in June 1943. Our union conducted itself with more dignity and honor in that most dishonorable situation than any other force in the community. While the rioting raged on the downtown streets, our members, Negro and white, worked peacefully side by side in the factories. The leaders of the union were quick to ask for decisive governmental action and for prosecution of the hoodlum elements responsible for the tragedy.

Just before the rioting died away, I remember, I drove Walter Reuther in my car, with a military escort, to Northeastern High School, where he made the main graduation address before a mixed audience of Negroes and whites. Everything went peacefully until the meeting was over. As the crowd began to drift out of the building, Walter and myself, accompanied by an Army corporal, went into the principal's office to make our farewells.

I stood near a window and looked out into a park across the street from the main entrance to the school. What happened was like a bad dream. Scattered through the park were young white boys and men, mostly in sweaters and slacks. Many had their sleeves rolled up; some had handkerchiefs tied over their hair to keep it out of their eyes. As if by a common signal, these fellows swarmed together into a mob on the sidewalk across the street from the school building. Most of the Negro students and parents turned eastward and walked parallel to the park. The mob of white males across the street began walking purposefully in the same direction. The policemen scattered along the edge of the park seemed to pay no heed to the maneuvers of the mob.

The corporal came to stand beside me, sensing my uneasiness. He shook his head in disgust.

"Look at those cops, standing there letting that mob form," he said sharply. "They could break that up right now before it gets started if they wanted to—but they aren't doing a damned thing, just standing there looking dumb."

The corporal was right. Walter and I stood there beside him and we could both see that a mob of whites was forming to attack the Negroes, many of them young students dressed in caps and gowns, clutching their diplomas. And the police, for the most part, looked the other way. A few cops made idle gestures toward directing the flow of humanity. Then the white hoodlums began to run across the street to get at the Negroes. A few policemen waved their night sticks helplessly, and shoved weakly at the hoodlums with their shoulders. Before our horrified eyes, the white hoodlums began to punch and maul the Negro students and their parents.

Just then, happily, two armored cars laden with military police rolled swiftly around the corner. The troops leaped out and swiftly scattered the white hoodlums, driving them back into the park with menacing bayonets.

I am still convinced that the riot of 1943 reached its deadly proportions for the same reason that the little riot described above was permitted to get under way: because the Detroit police sided with the white hoodlums and, in some instances, actually participated in the rioting. It is common knowledge that some of the Negroes slain during the rioting were the victims of trigger-happy police. The riot became an issue in the municipal election of that year, when the Negro community turned solidly against the administration of Edward J. Jeffries, then Mayor. Jeffries was re-elected, and in 1945, when Dick Frankensteen opposed him, the racial issue was again raised. White supremists inflamed the city with rumors that "niggers will move next door to you if Frankensteen gets in."

But, despite the white supremists, the trigger-happy cops, and the Communists—and all others who pour fuel on the flames of racial hatred—the UAW-CIO moved steadily forward with its program against discrimination. At the 1946 convention in Atlantic City, the constitution was amended to create a Fair Practices and Anti-Discrimination Department. Shelton Tappes, a CP-liner from Ford Local 600 in Detroit, tried, with another minority report, to renew the proposal for an elected director, but he failed. The delegates okayed a per capita tax allocation of one cent per month per dues-paying member to finance the work of the new department. And it was made mandatory that all local unions establish fair practices and anti-discrimination committees. Walter Reuther is now director of the department; he is assisted by Co-Director William H. Oliver, a young, personable, and highly intelligent Negro recruited from the ranks of the workers in the Ford Highland Park plant.

Between the 1943 convention in Buffalo and the 1946 convention in Atlantic City, we held one other convention, in Grand Rapids, Michigan, in September 1944. There again I helped Eddie Levinson work with the press, getting facts and information needed by the reporters, in between my political tasks of writing, editing, and distributing literature for the pro-Reuther caucus.

It was at this convention that Dick Leonard bolted from the Reuther caucus and ran against Walter Reuther for vice-president, and that the Communists confused the convention for days on the issue of the no-strike pledge. Opposition to Reuther reached its all-time peak that year. On the first ballot for vice-president, Frankensteen won 5,444 votes as against 4,528 for Walter Reuther and 385 for Dick Leonard. On the second ballot Reuther carrried 6,176 votes as against 3,477 for Dick Leonard and 364 for John McGill of Buick Local 599, an independent. This surprising outcome resulted from the policy of some large local unions, which was to keep the top leadership divided "for the good of the rank and file." Among the larger locals which voted for both Frankensteen and Reuther were Packard 190, Brewster Aircraft 365, and Delco Remy 662.

The issue of the no-strike pledge dragged on for months. The Commies were fanatically for the pledge, just as they were for incentive pay, because they wanted to produce more armaments to help Russia. They were so rabid against strikes that they even tried to break one. When CIO Retail Clerks struck Montgomery Ward—while the company was openly defying a War Labor Board order to bargain with their union—Harry Bridges' CP-controlled Longshoremen's and Warehousemen's Union crossed picket lines and scabbed on the Ward strikers in Minneapolis. Later Bridges came out for a no-strike pledge for "five years after the war." The bulk of the UAW-CIO membership was opposed to strikes during the war—but not to the point of giving up all of its rights. Leaders like Walter Reuther were for the pledge, but they wanted assurances from government and management that labor's rights would not be violated wholesale. Opposition to any kind of a no-strike pledge was fanned by a few Trotskyites, left-wing Socialists, and some sincere independent unionists who opposed it on principle. Our 1944 convention disposed of the issue, after a long, loud wrangle, by ordering a membership referendum to decide whether the pledge should be junked or kept. A heavy majority voted to abide by the pledge.

Another issue over which I tangled with the Commies in that period was political action. The CP was then loudly backing the Democratic administration. It screamed bloody murder when a group of independent progressives, former New Americans, Socialists, and Trotskyites launched the Michigan Commonwealth Federation in 1944. The MCF was intended to be a local third party, based on the support of labor, farmers, and assorted progressives. Its objectives were to promote a program of modified democratic socialism, to run candidates for state and local offices, and to join with other groups in agitating for the creation of a national non-Communist third party.

I was active in that endeavor, battling the die-hard Marxists who wanted to make it a "pure" labor party—for which I was roundly denounced by the Trotskyites as a "Red-baiter." Patterned after the Canadian Commonwealth Federation, the MCF ran a few candidates on the Michigan ballot that year, elected none. Its guiding spirits were my fellow former New Americans, Mary and Willard Martinson. Unable to compete with the powerful CIO-PAC for labor support, the MCF petered away and folded up after two years of fruitless organizing. It later joined with the New York Liberal party and other forces to form the National Educational Committee for a New Party—the voice of which was temporarily lost in the din when the Commies conjured up the Henry Wallace Progressive party in 1948.

16. A Look at the Books

When the General Motors workers poured out of the plants into their picket lines on November 21, 1945, to begin a strike that stayed on the front pages until March 13, 1946, they acted for the third time within a decade as the vanguard of the insurgent industrial union movement in America. In 1937 their sit-down strikes had cracked the stoutest rampart of the open shop, to set the pace for the unionization of mass-production industries. And, in 1939, when factional politics had sapped the power of the UAW-CIO, and GM refused to bargain on a company-wide basis, the GM workers pulled the strategic tool and die strike that set their union firmly on the forward path.

In the 1945-46 General Motors strike, the GM workers were out front once more, setting the pattern for the first substantial wage increase following World War II. But the strike did more than influence wage levels. It demonstrated dramatically that American labor can conduct collective bargaining on the basis of demands aimed at over-all community welfare, rather than on the narrow basis of "unionism as usual." The last GM strike, conducted under the leadership of Walter Reuther, opened the first act of a new and significant era in American unionism, an era in which labor might break away from the bonds of business unionism, to wage an economic struggle planned to advance the welfare of the community as a whole, and to lay the foundations for new economic mechanisms designed to win security without sacrificing liberty.

I was close to the scene of action when the story of the strike began on August 18, 1945. On that date, as director of the UAW-CIO General Motors Department, Walter Reuther sent a letter to Charles E. Wilson, GM President, setting forth the union's demand for a 30 per cent wage increase without price increases. In the letter to Mr. Wilson, Reuther said:

> On August 16, President Truman announced a change in national wage stabilization policy. His six-point labor policy for the reconversion period provides for the restoration of free collective bargaining, under which it is permissible to make general wage adjustments provided that such adjustments do not necessitate any increases in prices.
>
> With this policy we in the UAW-CIO are in hearty accord. We have maintained all along that the public interest demands effective, stringent price control; and we in the ranks of organized labor are proud of the role we have played in protecting the consumer interest against the pressure of war profiteers. . . .
>
> We oppose the special-interest, pressure-group approach of "Let's get ours—and the public be damned." . . . Our proposal for maintaining high labor income without any increase in prices is imperative if we are to achieve an economy of Full Production, Full Employment, and Full Distribution and Consumption. . . .

Reuther also suggested in his letter that General Motors team up with the UAW-CIO "to initiate the calling of an industry-wide conference for the purpose of establishing a uniform wage pattern for the entire industry." He said he believed that "an industry-wide conference at this time could come to grips with the basic problem of wages and the organization of production and distribution in the industry so as to achieve stabilized employment and the annual wage."

The novelty of Reuther's suggestions and demands seemed to stun GM into a brooding silence. Corporation officials did not get around to replying to his missive until October 3, six weeks later, when the union negotiators crossed the street to open discussions of the demands in the GM Building. Then GM press agents simultaneously released to the press and handed to the union representatives a lengthy letter rejecting the demands in their entirety as "unreasonable." The reply was signed by Mr. Wilson in person and indulged itself at some length in outlining corporate economic philosophy. Some of it follows:

> We shall resist the monopolistic power of your union to force this 30 per cent increase in basic wages. Such an increase in our plants would soon spread to the plants of all our suppliers and would affect all elements of cost. Automobiles would shortly cost 30 per cent more to produce. Prices to consumers would have to be raised 30 per cent. If wage raises in automobile plants forced such increase in car prices, the market for automobiles would be restricted. Fewer cars would be sold; fewer people would be able to afford and enjoy them; and fewer workers would be employed in making them.

Nor would Mr. Wilson have any of Reuther's suggestion for industry-wide wage negotiations. He said:

> We are not in a position to do this, and do not believe that it would be sound development for our country even if we were. . . . Industry-wide bargaining tends to disregard the peculiar or local interests of many groups of employees and of individual employers, to increase costs and prices and to affect adversely the interests of the people as a whole.

The October 3 meeting was as fruitless as early wage parleys usually are, and actual discussion of the union's demands did not begin until October 19. In the meantime, Reuther stepped up his cold war by proposing to the corporation that the negotiations be opened to the press and the public. I helped Frank Winn in the work of seeking public support for our demands. Reporters on the labor beat, assembled in Detroit from many points of the nation, leaped gleefully into the fray. They came early on October 19 and seated themselves comfortably in the conference room.

When the corporation executives arrived and found the reporters present, they promptly asked for a recess to take stock of this unusual situation. After chewing it over among themselves for more than an hour, they finally came back in with a formal statement, the gist of which was the following:

> General Motors has further stated that at any time the current collective bargaining has broken down or a strike occurs and it is

clear that there is no possibility of a solution by agreement between the parties, and a duly authorized public body empowered to investigate and report on the merits of the controversy assumes jurisdiction, we will not only be agreeable but will insist that the proceedings before such a body be open to the press and public.

In view of the fact that you [Reuther] have invited the press to the meeting with your union today without notice to and agreement with us, we can only conclude that you have decided that collective bargaining has failed in this case and you are taking the responsibility for breaking off negotiations.

Reuther replied that the union was unwilling to share GM's irresponsible and arbitrary attitude; he asked the reporters, with apologies for the shyness of the corporation, to leave the meeting in order that the negotiations might proceed. GM's refusal to open the talks to the press was but the prelude to its later display of an attitude that seemed to contradict all its professions of concern for the public welfare. While the corporation went on a spending spree to shout its love of the public from the roof-tops, its executives in charge of the negotiations exhibited a sullen secretiveness that prevented the public from appraising the economic merits of the dispute. And at every turn of the battle, the GM brass hats balked at any and all attempts by the union to bring the controversy under the jurisdiction of bona fide public agencies.

On October 19 Reuther and his aides began presenting to the GM negotiating committee a thoroughly documented recitation of economic arguments supporting the demand for a 30 per cent wage increase without price increases. As each section of the brief was delivered to GM and read into the record, we worked long hours at union headquarters mailing copies of it, clipped to interpretive press releases, to hundreds of newspapers, magazines, radio stations, heads of federal agencies, and congressional leaders of both major parties. This work was under the direction of my good and able friend, Frank Winn, later named UAW Publicity Director, who was assisted by Paul Sifton. Don Montgomery, the union's Consumer Counsel, did a capable job of marshaling our economic facts. At the conclusion of the presentation of the brief to GM, the entire document was published under the title of *Purchasing Power for Prosperity*. It has become a standard reference work in the economics departments of many schools and colleges.

Our economic arguments, in brief, were as follows:

First, that the post-war return to the forty-hour week, the loss of night-shift premiums, and downgrading to lower-paid jobs had slashed the weekly wages of GM workers 23⅓ per cent. If wartime levels of take-home pay were to be maintained, a 30 per cent increase in wages was necessary to compensate for this cut. Quotations from President Truman, the National War Labor Board, and Director Vinson of the Office of War Mobilization and Reconversion were cited at length to substantiate the desirability of maintaining wartime levels of take-home pay.

Second, that the UAW-CIO insistence on a wage increase tied to a pledge by the corporation not to increase prices flowed from a genuine desire to achieve lasting prosperity. To promote employment and expanded production in the post-war period, we argued, it was necessary to divert a stream of national income away from profits and dividends and into consumer purchasing power. Our brief stressed this point as follows:

"Our economy could not tolerate in 1929 the high business profits and large savings of the wealthy of that year even though the economy was then operating at close to full employment and the national income as a whole was rising. How can it tolerate the even higher profit margins of 1946 at a time of mass unemployment and sharp drop in the national income?"

Third—and this was the stinger that outraged GM—that General Motors could easily grant the 30 per cent wage increase without boosting prices and still enjoy profits juicier than any harvested before the war. To back this point we delved deeply and accurately into the economic history of GM. We pointed out the startling fact that a thousand dollars invested in GM stock in 1917 had multiplied itself twenty-six times in twenty-eight years—adding up to a total of $26,044.65—at an average yearly rate of 93 per cent of the original investment. We cited past performances, when wages and profits had risen out of all proportion to price increases. From 1936 to 1941, to be specific, we pointed out, GM prices had gone up only 16.6 per cent, but wages had gone up 37.3 per cent and profits had soared by 61 per cent. This had happened, we pointed out, because total output went up 21 per cent and output per man-hour 12 per cent in the same period. Don Montgomery projected GM's profit potential by multiple correlation analysis to show that future profits could easily absorb the 30 per cent wage increase without increasing prices.

These demands and arguments, presented in a scholarly fashion, rocked the GM Building, shook Wall Street, and aroused an unprecedented amount of interest and comment in the press. Here was no exhibition of table-pounding, no shouted threats of "come across, or else." Instead of trying to browbeat the boss into line, or to cut a sly deal with him at the expense of the consumer, the union was firing broadsides of cold, hard facts to prove its point. It was breaking with the past by insisting that its wage demands be settled within a framework of economic policy keyed to the welfare of the nation and the interests of the consuming public.

We put our departure from "unionism as usual" in the following words:

> UAW-CIO does not base its demands on short-run selfish considerations, but is basing them on enlightened long-run considerations which identify the true interest of the union with the general interests of the public.
>
> The UAW-CIO demands not only do not conflict with the public interest, but actively promote the public interest. The easy way to get wage increases is to conspire with industry to get price increases from OPA, getting wage demands met out of prices at the expense of the general public. This is the philosophy of "The public be damned!" . . . We do not want our wage demands met out of price increases. . . .

The repartee inside the conference room, dealing with the relationship between wages, prices, and profits, was both enlightening and entertaining. Here is a sample from the official transcript of the negotiations:

> Mr. Coen (of GM): Is the UAW fighting the fight for the whole world?
>
> Mr. Reuther: We have been fighting to hold prices and increase

purchasing power. We are making our little contribution in that respect.

Mr. Coen: Why don't you get down to your size and get down to the type of job you are supposed to be doing as a trade union leader, and talk about the money you would like to have for your people and let the labor statesmanship go to hell for awhile?

Mr. Reuther: Let's talk down where we can understand each other. Let's get down on our level. Say we modified our demand and we want X per cent wage increase, and don't talk about prices and profits, talk about X cents we think we want, would that help the situation?

Mr. Coen: It would change a hell of a lot.

Mr. Corbin (of the UAW): Do you mean if we came in here with a 30 per cent wage demand and offered to join with you in going before OPA for a 30 per cent increase in the price of your cars, you would talk business?

Mr. Coen: We don't ask you to join with us on the price of the cars. It is none of your damn business what the OPA does about prices.

Mr. Reuther: The question I am trying to put is this: I am trying to say, how much of an increase are you offering us, and how much of a price increase are you going to ask to cover that up?

Mr. Anderson (of GM): On the first part of your question, up to this moment we don't know what it amounts to.

Mr. Reuther: But it will be the difference between——

Mr. Anderson: It will be the difference between them. What we do about prices, we figure that is our business what we do with it.

Mr. Reuther: You don't think that is something we ought to talk about here?

Mr. Anderson: That gets back to the old question again, whether or not we are going to let the union run our business by determining our prices.

Negotiations continued in this spirit, enlivened by frequent exchanges of salty shop profanity, from October 19 to November 19. GM unbent to the point of admitting Department of Labor conciliators to the conference room as observers—without voice. Reuther pressed his cold war another step by filing a complaint with the National Labor Relations Board on November 8, charging GM with unfair labor practices on the grounds that it was refusing to bargain in good faith with a certified union legally representing its workers. By November 15 the corporation had begun a slow retreat; it offered a flat 10 per cent increase in wage rates, but the offer was tied to a formula for using the increase to get higher auto prices out of the OPA.

Reuther and the union's top committee for GM called a national conference of delegates from General Motors plants to meet in Detroit on November 19, to review the negotiations and consider GM's 10 per cent offer. The conference promptly rejected the 10 per cent offer as unsatisfactory. But the delegates made one more attempt to avoid open warfare on the picket lines. A proposal was drafted and dispatched to GM offering to submit the dispute to arbitration. Under the arbitration machinery suggested by the union, each side was to choose one arbitrator, and the two thus chosen were to select a third. The union stipulated that both parties agree to submit all books and records called for by the arbitrators and that any wage increase awarded not be used as an excuse for raising car prices. A deadline of November 20 was set for GM to reply.

The corporation replied that it would answer the arbitration proposal on or before November 23—obviously defying the deadline and inviting a test of economic power. On the morning of November 21, from coast to coast, GM workers laid down their tools and took their places in the picket lines. All plants had, of course, taken strike votes under the Smith-Connally Act and had followed the UAW-CIO constitutional requirements for secret ballot strike votes and authorization of the strike by the International Union.

While the workers maintained their vigil on the picket lines, Reuther sent invitations to a broad list of prominent Americans asking them to judge the merits of the dispute. They were asked to come to Detroit and study the transcript of the negotiations to date, and to form a free opinion as to whether the union was justified in asking for a wage increase without a price increase. Fourteen people accepted the invitation, including Leon Henderson, Bishop William Scarlett, Professor John Hanna, and Professor Harry A. Overstreet. Dr. Henry Hitt Crane, pastor of the

Central Methodist Church in Detroit, served as chairman of the committee formed by these people. I worked at the job of publicizing the committee. Later, as the strike lengthened, I worked with a city-wide publicity committee—just as Eddie Levinson had done in 1939—getting out a daily mimeographed Detroit strike bulletin. Another bulletin that I edited went out weekly, and sometimes oftener, to all GM locals.

Members of the citizens' committee spent December 4 and 5 studying the transcript and questioning representatives of the union. GM representatives refused to appear. On December 6, the committee issued a report which said, in part:

> . . . we recommend that any fact-finding commission appointed by the President be authorized and directed to determine what increase in wages can be given on the basis of the corporation's ability to pay without increase in prices. The corporation's ability to meet a wage increase is a sound factor in the determination of wages, both in good times and bad.
>
> From the record it is clear that the union in its refusal to accept a wage increase that involves price increase has lifted the whole matter of collective bargaining to a new high level by insisting that the advancement of labor's interest shall not be made at the expense of the public. The union has shown a sense of social responsibility that indictates its growing maturity and is certainly to be commended.

General Motors was not impressed. It struck back on December 10, while thousands of pickets paraded around the GM Building in Detroit, by canceling its national agreement with the UAW-CIO. Until then, wages were the only matter in dispute, but GM's reprisal threw the whole issue of collective bargaining in its plants open to renegotiation. Reuther told the press that the corporation's counterattack was not too significant; it simply meant that GM was maneuvering in an attempt to strengthen its bargaining position.

Shortly after the cancellation of the agreement by GM, President Truman appointed a fact-finding board to investigate the dispute and make a recommendation in the public interest. It was made up of Lloyd K. Garrison, of the University of Wisconsin; Milton Eisenhower, of Kansas State College; and North Carolina

Supreme Court Justice Walter P. Stacy. The board opened its hearings on December 20. Once again the union presented its documented case for a wage increase without a price increase. GM quibbled as usual. Corporation representatives appearing before the board inquired whether ability to pay was to be a factor in its determinations. They were unwilling to recognize the jurisdiction of the board until this question was answered.

President Truman answered the question on December 28, when he sent a memo to Mr. Garrison, chairman of the board, containing instructions to consider ability to pay as a factor in the case. GM, speaking through Walter Gordon Merritt, a special attorney hired for the occasion, denounced the consideration of ability to pay and withdrew from the hearings in a fine corporate huff. This was the same Walter Gordon Merritt who won his legal spurs in 1909 representing the D. E. Loewe Company when it successfully prosecuted the Danbury Hatters under the Sherman Act.

In publicizing our claim that GM had the ability to pay, we used a union slogan demanding "a look at the books." The terms "ability to pay" and "a look at the books" were employed to dramatize the union's detailed statistical analysis of GM's financial structure with which it supported its demand for wage increases without price increases. When, later in the spring of 1946, some newsmen attending the UAW-CIO convention reported Reuther as saying that the issues of ability to pay and looking at the books were just public relations gags, not taken seriously by the union, they misquoted him. What he said was that the union did not actually want to examine the corporation's records, but that we did want GM to bring in economic facts to prove that it did not have the ability to pay the demanded wage increase without increasing prices. At every press conference before, during, and after the strike, Reuther made this point clear: Whenever GM should bring in the economic evidence to show that it could not meet the wage demand—and hold its profits up to pre-war levels—without increasing prices, the union would scale down its demands. Ability to pay has always, of course, been a major argument presented by employers who wanted to cut wages. But they act as if they never heard of it when the heat is on for a wage increase.

On January 10, 1946, the presidential fact-finding board issued a report recommending a nineteen-and-a-half-cent wage increase, which, it declared, could and should be paid without increasing prices. It also recommended reinstatement of the previous national agreement between GM and the UAW-CIO. And it suggested that the nineteen and a half cents could be paid on the basis of 1941 production and profit levels. This substantiated the union's argument that even higher wage increases without price increases were possible under the high production levels projected by GM for 1946. A conference of UAW-CIO delegates from GM plants promptly voted to accept the recommendations of the board, with the stipulation that, if GM did not likewise accept within a specific time limit, the union would reinstate its demand for 30 per cent. GM climaxed its performance by rejecting the recommendation.

By this time the workers were feeling the pinch of the strike, although we were doing our best to help them. Other sections of labor responded nobly to our appeal for help. Hundreds of thousands of dollars poured in to assist the strikers. Money came from many non-labor people who expressed support for our fight against price increases. Reuther and all his staff members had voluntarily agreed to contribute their salaries to the strike fund shortly after the strike was called. It was the least we could do. To all those loud-mouthed critics of the strike who screamed that Reuther was drawing his pay while the strikers went hungry, the answer is that the record will show the opposite. Reuther and the rest of us on his staff gave our paychecks to the strikers. More money was raised by setting up a National Committee to Aid the Families of GM Strikers. Many liberal citizens worked with this committee to aid the strikers; the most notable performances were turned in by Eleanor Roosevelt, Helen Gahagan Douglas, Senator Wayne Morse, and Elizabeth Janeway.

While the strike was in full swing, we had some trouble stopping rumors. One evening when Frank Winn and I came out of the Book-Cadillac Hotel, where the International Executive Board was meeting, we saw the first edition of the *Detroit Free*

Press, running a banner headline saying settlement of the strike was near. It was news to us. We hurried over to the *Free Press* Building, two blocks away, to check on where labor reporter Art O'Shea had picked up his dope.

O'Shea insisted he had his information from a confidential source high in the union. He was backed up by Walter Ruch, of the *New York Times*, who had filed a similar story. Both refused to divulge the source of their tip. It was our belief that a staff member close to R. J. Thomas had planted the rumor, thinking it would kindle political fires under Reuther. The strike went on for some time after that.

The Commies had until then given critical support to the strikers. They sniped at Reuther for "jumping the gun" and argued that he should have held back until steel and all big industries could go out together in a general strike. The steel workers did go out in January. Within the UAW-CIO, while factional politics simmered below the surface, we kept a fairly strong united front behind the GM strike. Thomas, Addes, Frankensteen, and Leonard repeatedly put themselves on record in support of the union's strategy. When they reversed themselves in the convention that followed shortly and blasted the strategy of the strike in an effort to discredit Reuther, their criticisms had little weight.

Then the Commies pulled what they thought was an effective trick out of the bag. Several plants in the GM empire were under contract with the CIO United Radio, Electrical and Machine Workers of America, a union tightly controlled by CP-liners James Matles and Julius Emspak with the help of fellow traveler Albert Fitzgerald. The UE struck these plants weeks after the UAW-CIO members in GM had manned their picket lines. But, once they had struck, here was an opportunity to demonstrate the solidarity of the working class, the spiritual kinship of labor to which the Commies are always quick to pay lip service. All the GM workers were out on strike. The steel workers were out, too. Comrades from coast to coast had been yelping shrilly about the power of a general strike. But, suddenly and without warning, the strategy of the general strike seemed to turn sour on the tongues of the commissars commanding the forces of the UE-CIO. While the UAW-CIO was pressuring President Truman to put the heat on GM in support of the nineteen and a half cents recommended by his fact-finding board, UE-CIO quietly and secretly met with General Motors and settled for eighteen and a half cents.

It was one of those things. R. J. Thomas felt constrained to join Reuther in blasting the UE-CIO for its betrayal. Word must have gone out from party headquarters that Reuther was getting too much build-up out of the GM strike. In such a situation, the comrades are never above cutting a deal with an employer to chop down opponents of their policies. This time the Commies used the UE-CIO to set a wage pattern that cut Reuther's bargaining power out from under him.

The Communists and General Motors were not far apart in their strategy. Both were out to get Reuther. The secret eighteen-and-a-half-cent settlement was a natural for them. It generated faint rumblings of dissatisfaction in the ranks of the GM strikers and intensified the necessity for Reuther to win a quick settlement of some kind. Then GM and the Commies both sat back and gloated.

Some newsmen covering the strike were certain that GM was purposely prolonging the strike to weaken Reuther's position in the union. The UAW-CIO Top GM Negotiating Committee felt the same way and expressed its feelings on March 6 in a press release which said:

> General Motors is trying to play union politics. They consider the several million dollars it will cost them to continue the strike a cheap enough price if they can put an end to the union's advocacy of higher wages without price increases or turn out of office the union leadership which advocates that kind of economic thinking. . . .

Early in February the government gave way to industry pressure for price increases. Banker John Snyder, assigned by President Truman to handle the price problem, retreated before the heat applied by the steel trust. He okayed a steel price increase of $6.25 per ton. General Motors was assured on March 10 that the new price policy would apply to the auto industry. Relieved, GM officials began to negotiate in a fashion indicating eagerness to get the strike settled. A settlement was reached in a round-the-clock negotiating session on March 13. Gains in the settlement included the eighteen-and-a-half-cent increase plus other concessions which the union calculated to be equal to the additional penny recommended by the fact-finding board. Union security was obtained in the form of an irrevocable check-off of union dues, and there was some improvement in a vital contract clause recognizing seniority as a factor in promotions and transfers.

Thereafter the torrent of inflation widened the break Snyder had blasted in the dam. Auto manufacturers had received three rounds of price increases from OPA by August 1946. Price control was washed away by the flood that followed. The Department of Agriculture acted to weaken controls on food prices. Congress balked and would not extend controls beyond June of that year. President Truman kicked the debris of price control under the rug with his executive order abolishing it in November. The song of "wage increases without price increases" was ended, but the melody was destined to ring sharply through the months and years that followed.

The lesson of the 1945–46 GM strike was that collective bargaining and working-class economic action on a national scale can be conducted in the interest of the entire community. It was a good fight; it won the UAW-CIO many friends, even though our wage-price position was weakened by the government's retreat before industry's grab for profits. Despite the opposition of General Motors, of the Communists, and of the business-unionism politicians inside the UAW-CIO—all of whom were critical of the strategy used in the strike—Reuther went on to win the presidency of the union. After his election, he restated his policy in these words:

> We condemn the discredited policy of old-line labor leadership which pretends to promote the interests of the workers by conspiring with management, as in the coal industry, to exact higher prices from consumers. In the division of the spoils of that policy the workers have always come out second best while employers have found it easy

to shift the blame for higher prices away from their own profiteering and on to the minor wage gains which go to the workers. Labor will not make progress toward the high standards of living which it is able to produce so long as it seeks to advance its interests without regard to the interests of all other workers and of the community of which it is a part. We shall realize and hold on to our gains only by making progress with the community, not at the expense of the community.

In late 1945, Commies and business unionists alike sneered at "Reuther's cockeyed economic theory." In 1947 it had become the gospel of the national CIO. The GM workers had gained another beachhead in the battle for a better tomorrow.

17. Boardwalk Ballet: Act I

The 1946 UAW-CIO convention, which opened March 23 in Convention Hall at Atlantic City, was probably the most rugged and rambunctious gathering in the history of the union. It convened just ten days after the settlement of the hard-fought General Motors strike. Newspapermen came from far and wide, their pencils poised to report the impending bid of Walter P. Reuther for the presidency of the union. Few observers in the know doubted that the tireless redhead would run for the top spot.

Reuther's decision to make the race was not nailed down officially until a mass caucus was held on the evening of the opening day of the convention. But some of his closest supporters had been trying to smooth the way for the contest for some time. For one thing, they tried hard to neutralize the opposition of George Addes, who was top man in the enemy caucus. First they worked on some of the more competent non-Communist members of Addes's staff. The argument used on these people was that, if Addes would keep hands off while Reuther challenged Thomas for the top spot, there was nothing to stop Addes from being second top man for a long time to come. That would be the sensible way to solidify the union and eliminate factionalism, with a minimum of political hatchet-work, our people argued. Some of the Addes guys agreed with this thinking and said they would try to get their man to accept the proposition.

Addes appeared to give this offer his serious consideration. Some Reuther people, including myself, were impressed with the way

Addes responded. His conduct during the GM strike had been almost above reproach. Little incidents cropped up to fan our hopes that he was ready to make a deal. One such episode happened at a meeting of the Top GM Negotiating Committee in Reuther's office during the strike. On that occasion, when Charles Beckman, a CP-line committee member from Fisher Local 45 in Cleveland, tried to apologize for the conduct of the UE-CIO during the GM strike, Addes responded quickly and explosively.

"To hell with the UE," Addes said and proceeded to dress Beckman down with a tongue-lashing. Events like these encouraged us to think that he might be contemplating a shift away from his Communist allies.

When the chips were down, however, Addes came out openly in support of Thomas for president. His apparent strategy had been to play along with our offer of a deal based on a Reuther-Addes team in order to insure that we would not groom a candidate to contest his position as secretary-treasurer. But finally it became evident that all bets were off, and we junked the notion of ever cutting a deal with Addes.

The boom to make Reuther president of the union was kicked off in Detroit on March 10, while the GM strike was still in progress, by a committee of presidents of seventeen large local unions. In its statement to the press, the committee put itself on record as follows:

> A large majority of the union's membership feels strongly the need for a change in the administration. . . . The membership feels the need for a change to carry out a vigorous, intelligent and progressive program in order to eliminate the factionalism which has divided our forces for several years. . . . We know and respect Reuther's refusal to devote time to any activity other than fighting and winning the GM strike. It will not, however, be necessary for him to divert his attention from the strike to a political campaign. His acceptance of the candidacy will make his election certain, without further effort on his part.

After declaring that "The incumbent president [Thomas] has perpetuated himself in office only by fostering rivalry between Reuther and Addes," the committee declared itself as favoring the re-election of Addes as secretary-treasurer. This was done to woo the support and votes of certain non-Communists in the Addes faction, even though by this time Addes had already publicly pledged his support to Thomas. There was still a powerful block of independent rank-and-file members in the union who were fed up with Thomas and would vote for a Reuther-Addes team, no matter what Addes himself said or did.

Campaigning to elect Walter Reuther president of the union was an exciting experience for most of our people. There had never before been a real contest for the office. Francis Dillon, first UAW president, had been appointed by William Green under the AFL charter in 1935. In 1936, at the South Bend convention, Homer Martin had been elected by acclamation under an agreement worked out by the leaders before the election was held. Martin had had no opposition in 1937 at Milwaukee. R. J. Thomas got in through a compromise in 1939 and was returned to office by acclamation, or with only token opposition, at each succeeding convention. The only really sharp political fight for power, after the upheaval that blew Martin into oblivion, had erupted in Buffalo in 1943, when Dick Leonard came within seventy votes of trouncing Addes for the job of secretary-treasurer. Now, for the first time in eleven years, the union that bragged so loudly of its militant democracy was about to engage in a serious contest for its presidency.

There was little time that winter to carry out an extensive campaign in the delegate elections conducted by the local unions. I went out to my local union to vote for a pro-Reuther slate but did no campaigning. In a few key areas, where the membership was heavily concentrated, we did get out some literature and hold meetings to rally votes for our candidates. The bulk of the locals were touched only lightly, if at all, by the vote-gathering activities directed by the higher councils of the power caucuses. Reuther followers were too deeply involved in the GM strike to give anything but secondary attention to politics. It was no secret, of course, that we believed the winning of the strike would help Reuther's candidacy more than anything we could do.

Before the convention opened, it was clear that the Addes-Thomas-Leonard caucus, brain-trusted by the Communist party, was going to pick on the General Motors strike as the key issue. The *Daily Worker* harped away at the charge that Reuther had "jumped the gun" in calling the strike, that he had kept the workers out too long, and that he had settled for too little. Commie puppets in the local unions picked up this line and echoed it across the land. R. J. Thomas himself, while never expressing open criticism of the strike on the floor of the convention, supported the Commie attacks when he told newspapermen in Atlantic City that the strike was called too early and settled too late. We countered that one by publishing direct quotes from press releases issued in Thomas's name all during the strike, in which he stated his complete agreement with the strike strategy and its conduct. When the campaign got really hot, I spent hours in an Atlantic City print shop getting out leaflets supporting Reuther.

Oddly enough, an open discussion of the merits of the strike never came up on the convention floor. This hurt Reuther's candidacy. We would have welcomed a free-for-all debate expressing the views of the top officers and the delegates with respect to the strategy and conduct of the strike. The Addes-Thomas-Leonard strategists and the Communists were afraid to risk the outcome of such a democratic discussion. With Thomas in the chair, the anti-Reuther forces controlled the agenda. Secure in their control of the convention machinery, they kept controversial committee reports off the floor before the elections. Reuther's powerful oratorical ability was his ace in the hole—and they knew it. So they steered clear of a showdown. Reuther was thus prevented from speaking on any important issue, let alone defending himself against the charges of lousing up the strike.

In an effort to shame the opposition into an open discussion of these charges, we published a stinging pamphlet challenging Thomas to debate Reuther. Thomas ducked the challenge, refused to match himself against Reuther on the platform. Attacking on another front, one of our delegates made a motion to hold a night session for the purpose of staging a debate between Thomas and Reuther. Addes was in the chair at the time. He ruled that the motion would involve changing the rules and would thus require a two-thirds majority to carry. After a flurry of hectic debate among a few delegates, the vote was taken. It was evident to those of us on the platform that the delegates standing up in favor of the motion had a clear majority, possibly a two-thirds majority. But Addes, ignoring scattered demands for a roll call, ruled that the motion had lost for lack of a two-thirds majority. Despite the fact that a majority of the delegates felt Thomas should meet Reuther in an open debate on the charges made against the conduct of the strike, the opposition was afraid to meet this test. This refusal of Thomas to face his opponent on the platform may have alienated enough democratically minded delegates to lose him the election.

Unable to dispute the popularity of Reuther's program for dynamic unionism extending beyond the bargaining table into the community, and afraid to face his forces in a free discussion of union issues on the floor, the Commies and their stooges worked overtime their favorite weapon of character assassination. They spread the lie that Reuther was plotting with David Dubinsky, head of the International Ladies' Garment Workers, and John L. Lewis to take the UAW into the AFL. To attempt to prove this absurd charge, they cited the fact that Dubinsky had contributed several thousand dollars to the GM strikers.

R. J. Thomas toyed with this fairy tale in his report to the convention, but did not express the accusation openly before the delegates.

"There is a man in the American Federation of Labor who, during our General Motors strike, gave money to the workers of General Motors," Thomas bellowed. "And I say to you quite frankly I have worried about that situation. That same man, during the fight in our union when this union ousted Homer Martin from the presidency, that same man gave twenty-five thousand dollars to whip the UAW-CIO. And that man is none other than Dave Dubinsky. . . . I say to you I don't believe that the Automobile Workers can be whipped from within any more than they can be whipped from without."

Thomas was trumpeting the CP line in a last desperate effort to bolster his faltering fortunes as a labor leader. On March 27 the *Daily Worker* ran an editorial which said: "The enthusiastic response of the UAW convention to the speech of President Murray [who had just addressed the convention] reflected the concern of the overwhelming majority of the delegates over the threat to the unity of the CIO and its largest affiliate. This threat comes from those within the CIO who are allied to the Lewis, Dubinsky, Woll clique in the AFL."

The editor of the *Daily Worker*, in typical Communist fashion, had hung his editorial on the peg of a single paragraph in Murray's speech, which said: "Oh, I had a committee come over to see me in Washington last week and they said some people in New York were interested in splitting up this organization. I said, 'I don't give a damn who those people are in New York, they can't do it, they are not going to do it; whether they are alleged leaders of the American Federation of Labor makes no difference—they are not going to do it!'" Out of these two sentences the *Daily Worker* wove a fabric to disguise Reuther as a devil designing to take the UAW into the AFL. Of course the editor also heaped his blessings on Thomas and Addes.

It was difficult, as it always is in such strained political situations, to judge the impact of Murray's speech. There is no doubt that the word of the president of the CIO carries considerable weight with the average convention delegate. That the workers do not, however, regard the presidency of the CIO as a shrine of infallibility was demonstrated in 1940 when the Lewis endorsement of Willkie fell on deaf ears so far as the rank and file was concerned. Nevertheless, the UAW-CIO delegates in 1946 greeted Murray with an ovation, received his remarks with rapt attention, and applauded him with another ovation.

His every word was weighed for political implications. Would he endorse Thomas? Would he frown on Reuther's candidacy for the top job? What would he have to say about the GM strike and its relation to the over-all strategy of the CIO in the recent wage increase battle?

In his soft Scotch burr, gesturing dramatically and building involved sentences up to climactic conclusions, Murray led the delegates through a long oratorical hallway to the issue of the GM strike. Then, in angry, thunderous tones, he blasted at the rumor that he had had a hand in the decision of the President's fact-finding board to recommend only nineteen and a half cents for the GM strikers. He said:

Another very erroneous rumor got afloat, due to a statement attributed to a high officer of the General Motors Corporation, that I, Philip Murray, had done the detestable thing of going to the members of the GM Fact-Finding Board for the purpose of having that Board allegedly reduce the so-called recommended wage increase from 24 per cent to nineteen and a half cents, the contention being that Murray went to the Board for that purpose because he, Murray, did not believe, according to these rumors, that he could get a 24 per cent wage increase in the steel industry.

That, of course, was a diabolical, detestable lie, manufactured out of whole cloth by a high officer of the General Motors Corporation, and circulated throughout the union for the purpose of creating division among CIO workers. I detested that ugly rumor because it attacked the integrity of the President of the CIO and it also questioned the integrity of the members of the GM Fact-Finding Board—positively untrue, wholly preposterous and circulated by a defamer of defamers for the purpose of injuring the Congress of Industrial Organizations.

From this climax, he coasted down into an outline of the CIO program and purposes. Then he built his way upward again toward a carefully worded appraisal of the UAW-CIO political situation. Treading a tightrope between the different hopes and expectations of the factions that hung on his words, he admonished the delegates to guard the unity of their union. Nearing the end of his speech, he teetered ever so slightly and brought joy to the Thomas backers with these words:

Before I close, I wish to express also my appreciation to the officers of your International Union for the splendid spirit of support they have manifested towards me personally in the conduct of my work as President of the Congress of Industrial Organizations. That goes to Secretary Addes, Vice-President Reuther, Vice-President Frankensteen, and to this great big guy for whom I have a distinct fondness, the President of your Union, R. J. Thomas . . .

Thomas backers, reaching for straws to prop up their man, clutched happily at this "distinct fondness" for the "great big guy" and almost beat fence-riding delegates to death with it for the balance of the convention. The fact that Murray was distinctly fond of Thomas, they argued in a frenzy, was unquestionable proof that the CIO chief wanted R. J. voted back into the top UAW-CIO spot. In our camp, we felt that a few wavering delegates might slide over to Thomas as a result of Murray's quaint bestowal of a weak blessing on the incumbent president, but it did not worry us. We had estimated the support for Reuther and believed ourselves in possession of a slender but safe majority. Our job was to hold that majority and to work faithfully to add to it.

The Reuther forces were greatly outnumbered in the convention by the political workers for Thomas. Almost the entire International staff was present to campaign in accordance with the preference of various department heads. Reuther had the certain support of his own staff and that of seven regional directors; they could beat the bushes for stray votes. Two regional directors were on the fence, after a fashion, and their staffs were divided in loyalty between Reuther and Thomas.

Members of some minor organizations were working on Reuther's behalf, too. A few Socialists, most of them key leaders in local unions, were intensely active in the pro-Reuther caucus. Another group with considerable influence—but not nearly the weight attributed to it by the Communist press—was the Association of Catholic Trade Unionists. The ACTU is concentrated in Detroit, but has a few outposts scattered around the country. Trained and directed by the Catholic Church to build democratic unionism and to fight Communism within labor, the ACTU people have earned the violent hatred of the CP. Nor is the party the only group that looks with suspicion at the ACTU; most orthodox leftists, remembering historical incidents when the Catholic Church has fought on the side of reaction, do not trust the Catholic trade unionists. My own opinion is that this mistrust is out of place. From personal experience with ACTU unionists, I have come to believe that their loyalty to the union is unquestionable. Speaking for myself only, I would say that the ACTU has made an important contribution to the ousting of Communists and fellow travelers from the UAW-CIO leadership.

On Thomas's side, there were the staffs of the president, the secretary-treasurer, one vice-president, and nine regional directors. In addition, the Communists were there in force, from New York, Detroit, and all points of the compass. They threw in every stunt, gag, and trick they could think up to influence the voting. Not the least in their bag of tricks was the importation of glamorous female comrades who worked the swing shift in hotel rooms at night to convert delegates to the Thomas cause. Some of these babes got taken in by smarter and lustier delegates on our side, who pretended they wanted to be converted—both for the joy of it and for the practical purpose of wasting the time of the CP Mata Haris.

Intimidation was another tactic used widely by the Commies. There was one particular case that I personally know of in which the CP pressure boys browbeat a zealous Reuther follower into switching his vote. The delegate was from the deep South. I had made his acquaintance a couple of years earlier at a regional summer school in the mountains of Tennessee. He was a bright young Negro, unschooled, but filled with instinctive intelligence, eager to work for the cause of labor. I talked to him early in the convention and he swore that Reuther was his man forever. About a day before the voting took place I happened to notice that a Negro member of the opposition staff had that delegate in a corner and was really laying down the law to him. I hung around until the confab broke up, then got the delegate off to one side. Believe it or not, he just wouldn't talk to me about Reuther. His eyes were sad and full of misery. Nothing I could say would induce him to confide his troubles to me or to indicate what had been said to him. Later, during the roll calls, he voted straight down the line for the Thomas slate. Thomas Starling, Director of Region Eight, told me later that he had found out that the delegate had switched because of threats of physical violence.

At another point in the convention a fist fight broke out on the floor while Local 669 was voting on a vice-presidency. R. J.

Thomas, acting under power granted to him by the rules adopted earlier in the convention, appointed a committee to investigate intimidation of delegates. In the months that followed, this committee became a kind of traveling sideshow. Thomas and Addes sent it into pro-Reuther locals to harass and bluff the local officers. It spent many thousands of dollars of union funds for expenses and was still going strong when the pro-Reuther majority at the 1947 convention stopped its activities. Once, while reporting to the International Executive Board, the committee admitted coyly that it had discovered one delegate who had been intimidated. Pressed for details, a committee spokesman said that a delegate from Local 669 had said that he was pro-Reuther but had been pressured into voting for Thomas!

The roll-call election for the office of president of the UAW-CIO on March 27, 1946, was probably as tense and dramatic as any political crisis that will ever occur in a labor union. A delegate from Local 1, carrying one vote (for the workers of the Buchanan Steel Products Corporation in Buchanan, Michigan), cast his vote for Reuther. Thereafter, the voting went down the roll call from local to local for several hours. Whenever a large local voted in a block for either candidate, partisans burst into long, loud cheers. As the cheering subsided, the voice of the chief teller droned the number of the next local on the list. Hundreds of people sat hunched over their roll-call tally sheets, figuring furiously to compute the accumulating totals to three digits past the decimal point.

Suddenly a group of Reuther supporters surrounding their candidate on the platform picked him up, hoisted him to their shoulders, and began shouting hoarsely with joy. He had a mathematical majority—even if the rest of the locals voted against him, he was in! The largest union in the world had finally elected a leader in a close and hard-fought contest waged on the basis of programs and philosophies. Flash bulbs illuminated the platform as press photographers worked their shutters madly. A few Thomas backers muttered that it was all a trick to influence the locals which were still to vote. But when the adding machines stopped clicking Reuther had won by the scanty margin of 124 votes out of 8,765 votes cast—each vote representing a hundred dues-paying members.

George Addes, as acting chairman, introduced the new president to the convention. The delegates erupted into a wild uproar of applause. I stood at the end of the press table, weary and with all my nerves tightened by emotion, as Reuther began to speak. Tears ran down my face and trickled onto my shirt, and mine were not the only wet eyes in the hall.

"There is much work to be done in the world," Reuther said, in tones vibrant with feeling. "We won the war. The task now is to win the peace. We have the job of mobilizing America, the labor and progressive forces, so that we can be certain that there will be just as determined a fight on the home front to make the peace secure as was demonstrated by our boys on the battlefront to make victory possible.

"I stand here humble—humble at the great task that you have given me. Let us go home when this convention is over motivated by the same spirit that motivated us back in 1936 and 1937 when the only thing you could get for belonging to the union was a cracked head. Let's be motivated by the simple loyalty we have in our hearts. Let's be guided by the sincere desire to place the union's welfare above any personal consideration or any personal differences."

The end of the fighting, however, was not yet in sight. George Addes was re-elected by a unanimous vote. Then, out of the bigness of their hearts, the unpredictable delegates blessed R. J. Thomas with a vice-presidency. On the next ballot, since Dick Frankensteen had two months earlier announced that he did not choose to run, Richard T. Leonard defeated John W. Livingston, the Reuther candidate, for the second vice-presidency. In the regional elections for International Executive Board members, all incumbents but one were returned. Melvin Bishop was replaced in Region One (Detroit) by Emil Mazey, a leader of Briggs Local 212, who at the time was an Army sergeant in the far Pacific and did not even know that he was a candidate. The Briggs delegates, who held the balance of power in Region One, ignored all persuasions and used their power to get the Reuther caucus to approve Mazey's candidacy.

Some people said that in the election of Reuther as president we had won a battle but lost the war. He was surrounded by three hostile top officers and could count on only seven of the International Executive Board members, out of a total of eighteen, to support his policies. It looked like tough going until the next convention. The Communists would not give up. There was to be no rest for those of us who wanted to build the UAW-CIO into a force pledged to fight for security and liberty, against both the commissars and the capitalists.

18. Comrades in Retreat

It could be said that the period from March 31, 1946, to November 9, 1947, was a prolonged recess in the UAW-CIO convention. For, despite the solemn pledges of unity voiced so loudly on all sides when the 1946 convention adjourned, the eighteen months leading up to the next convention were but one long skirmish of union politics. The UAW-CIO was a house divided against itself. The dynamics of democracy decreed that it had to resolve its internal conflict or disintegrate.

Reuther's opponents lost no time in taking the initiative. At the first regular International Executive Board meeting held after the 1946 convention, George Addes displayed his power. He introduced and steam-rollered through the board meeting a statement of policy that deliberately repudiated most of the main points of Reuther's economic and political philosophy. Protests voiced by Reuther and his seven supporting board members were invariably smothered by the weight of a vote of fourteen to eight. We dubbed the Addes power clique on the board the "mechanical majority," because it voted with the precision of a well-oiled machine.

On the appointment of key department heads, however, Reuther played his opponents off against each other to considerable advantage. By a scant majority, Victor G. Reuther was confirmed for the all-important post of Director of Education. By the same scant margin, Frank Winn was okayed as Publicity Director. Walter worked this out by trading the directorship of the Competitive Shops Department to R. J. Thomas. Eager to make a comeback in 1947, Thomas undoubtedly felt that the large staff assigned to this department (whose task was to organize unorganized plants all across the country) would be of strategic value in rebuilding his shattered political forces. To get his hands on this staff, Thomas persuaded a few board members to vote—against the wishes of the die-hard Addes followers—for the appointments of Victor Reuther and Frank Winn. Reuther's strategy paid off later. In his report to the next convention Reuther cited figures to show that Thomas had not succeeded in organizing the strategic unorganized plants.

Most of the CP-liners lodged at the top level of the UAW-CIO were retained by the "mechanical majority" despite all of Walter Reuther's efforts to remove them. These included Maurice Sugar, General Counsel; Jim Wishart, Research Director; Allen Sayler, Radio Consultant; and Irving Richter, Legislative Representative in the Washington office of the union.

Before that first 1946 board meeting adjourned, Reuther submitted his own draft of a program for the union, after the Addes-Thomas-Leonard majority had railroaded through its statement of policy. The Reuther draft reaffirmed the philosophy of democratic unionism in a positive way and stressed the necessity for labor to work for the welfare of the community as a whole. It was rejected, practically without discussion, by a vote of fourteen to eight.

In May 1946 I was appointed by Walter Reuther to serve as Associate Editor of the *United Automobile Worker*, official publication of our union. This placed me in the Public Relations Department, under the direction of Frank Winn. The short interval of ten years, packed with excitement, had passed since the spring of 1936, when I first started boning up on grammar and pecking out atrocious verses on my installment-plan typewriter. I was pleased with my progress. With no formal training in writing, and with no orthodox experience in reporting and editing, I had inched my way upward to the post of labor journalist assigned to edit and make up the official publication of one of the largest labor unions in the world.

Oscar Ameringer once wrote that "running a labor paper is like feeding melting butter on the end of a hot awl to an infuriated wildcat." This statement referred particularly to Oscar's bouts with labor leaders in the general melee that accompanied efforts by John L. Lewis to purge Alexander Howat and Frank Farrington from the United Mine Workers in 1910–11. So far as we were concerned, it was an understatement. Like Ameringer, UAW editor Frank Winn and, to a lesser extent, myself were buffeted about by labor politics. We were caught between our desire to publicize democratic unionism and the demands of the belligerent Addes caucus for space in our paper. The hostile "mechanical majority" had created an editorial committee of three, composed of Reuther, Addes, and Leonard. Reuther was hopelessly outnumbered on this body. But by a constant process of give and take, we managed to keep both sides pretty well satisfied for a while. In addition to our political problems, we struggled with the headache inflicted on every labor editor: that of trying to publish a lively and objective paper containing enough news to offset the routine accounts of coups pulled off by the top leaders to "protect the workers from the greedy bosses."

Despite the pressure of these problems, I squeezed out time enough to learn the rudiments of photography. The Publicity Department had a press camera when Frank Winn and myself moved into our new offices, and I took on the job of learning how to operate it. By the fall of 1946, again without benefit of formal training, I had set up a darkroom at UAW headquarters and was turning out creditable prints of photographs of union activities.

Much of my time that summer was taken up in serving on the staffs of several of our summer schools. I taught classes in labor journalism, in the development of cooperatives, and in the techniques of bargaining for group-insurance social security plans. Between classes I took pictures for the Education Department magazine, *Ammunition*, as well as for the *Auto Worker*. In the evenings I played my guitar, sang folk songs, and led group singing. For one month I acted as temporary editor of *Ammunition*, after Vic Reuther had discharged Dave Erdman, a Commie-liner who had been hired by Bill Levitt. The following month, I helped the new *Ammunition* editor, Lewis Carliner, whom we hired away from the Department of Agriculture, to break in on his job with the Education Department.

It is impossible to account for the political strength built up by the Reuther forces in the eighteen months between the 1946 and 1947 conventions without giving credit to the Education Department of the union. After sweeping out the debris bequeathed to him by the CP-liners previously in charge of the department, Victor Reuther began the job of building a staff devoted to the principles of democratic unionism. With the help of such loyal aides as Joe Kowalski, Brendan Sexton, Mildred Jeffrey, Ed Lee, Clay Lowndes, and Lewis Carliner, he speeded up the long-overdue establishment of the department as a source of information, assistance, and ideas for action needed by the local unions.

There was nothing "political" about this overhauling of one of the most vital departments of the union. The staff simply slaved to produce pamphlets, radio scripts, movies, and other visual-aid materials, organized smooth-running and fruitful classes, conferences, and summer schools—in short, performed so excellently that the membership was impressed with the quality of the leadership of the department. Under the impact of this approach, scores of rank-and-file members decided for themselves that they wanted more of the Reuther program for democratic unionism.

They learned for themselves, by using their own judgment, that the pro-Reuther bloc in the union was rooted in the democratic faith. And with this conviction, they saw through the falsehoods spread by the Communists, who pictured President Reuther as a "tool of the employers and imperialists." When the time came to elect delegates to the 1947 convention, the sweat, energy, and intelligence expended by the Education Department paid off in the strong locals hitherto held by the opposition.

While all this was going on, the political fight simmered below the surface. There were no serious outbreaks, however, until the national CIO convention opened in November at Atlantic City. Two events at that conclave highlighted the growing tension between pro-Commie and anti-Commie forces. First, Philip Murray forced the adoption of a resolution, written by three pros and three antis whom he had appointed to a special committee, which put the pro-Commies in the dubious position of "resenting and rejecting" themselves. The resolution said: "We . . . resent and reject efforts of the Communist Party or other political parties and their adherents to interfere in the affairs of the CIO."

The CP was sorely stung by this spanking. Accustomed to having Lee Pressman, the party-lining CIO General Counsel, draft and present all CIO convention resolutions in phrases that praised the CP with faint damns, the Commies were outraged at this strong statement labeling them as a force inimical to the interests of labor. Weak as the resolution was, it cracked one of the most vital and valuable armor plates constructed laboriously by the comrades over a period of many years. In calling the Communist party by its right name, and criticizing it openly in a CIO convention, the delegates knocked the party off its pins for a moment. Torn away by a few blunt words, and shattered before the spotlight of public opinion, was the shield of dishonesty the Commies had forged to make them immune from criticism. The entire CIO convention had uttered the unspeakable words, had blasted the Communists as Communists, had said they were bad for the labor movement. A myth that had endured since the founding of the CIO collapsed and left the CP exposed to the kind of criticism most deadly to its plots, that of democratically minded trade unionists.

Later in the convention, the CPers staged a comeback that saved their faces a little and salved their wounds. CIO protocol demands that the president of each major CIO national and international union be honored with a CIO vice-presidency. In accordance with tradition, Walter Reuther, as UAW-CIO president, was placed on the approved slate of candidates for vice-president of the National CIO—but so was R. J. Thomas. There was a vacancy—created when Murray forced the withdrawal of CP-lining Reid Robinson, chief of the Mine, Mill and Smelter Workers—and Murray insisted that unity would be served by awarding the spot to Thomas.

We spent the early part of the winter of 1947 preparing economic data to support a demand for a new round of wage increases. The UAW-CIO set its demand at twenty-three and a half cents. Don Montgomery, UAW-CIO economist, turned his talented mind to the preparation of a brief entitled "Wages, Prices, Profits," designed to justify the demand. He was assisted by Nat Weinberg, a new Reuther appointee to the UAW-CIO Research Department, who had worked for the government.

But before Reuther could get the brief circulated to help build public opinion behind our demand for the twenty-three-and-a-half-cent increase, R. J. Thomas raised questions that forced a delay in its release to the public. He said he was not satisfied with the economic reasoning in it, although he had raised no serious questions when Reuther presented the outline of it to the Executive Board.

While the release of the brief was being held up by Thomas's protest, and while Reuther was negotiating with General Motors for the increase, the United Electrical, Radio and Machine Workers again settled with General Motors, for an increase of eleven and a half cents per hour plus six paid holidays. The raise was computed to be the equivalent of fifteen cents straight across the board. Public opinion was swiftly rallied by the employers and the daily press, and the fifteen-cent increase became a pattern. The GM workers in the UAW-CIO were plenty sore, but there was nothing they could do about it. They were again the victims of a CP political maneuver. The Commies had used the UE-CIO to prevent Reuther from getting the credit for winning a raise that would set the pattern for 1947. This was more important to them than the extra few cents per hour—badly needed by the workers—that might have been won had the UAW-CIO succeeded in leading the way.

In the early summer of 1947, Reuther appeared to be gaining strength steadily. He had suffered no serious losses in the local union elections held during the winter and early spring, and had made several important gains. With the November convention coming on fast, the Addes-Thomas-Leonard-CP caucus became desperate. Everyone knew that the outcome of the battle between the pro-CP and anti-CP forces in the CIO hinged largely on what happened in the UAW. As the auto workers went, it was said in informed circles, so would go the CIO. With relations between Russia and the democracies going sourer every day, the Commies hungered for a coup that would fortify their position inside the CIO. So they put all their chips on an attempt to pull a fast one, and this effort stands out in labor history for its contempt of democratic procedure and for its sheer audacity.

There had been a running fight for years inside the CIO over the jurisdiction of the plants manufacturing farm implements. Two CIO unions were operating in the field, the UAW-CIO and the Farm Equipment Workers-CIO. Both held collective bargaining contracts with a number of important farm implement manufacturing companies.

In secret meetings, members of the Addes-Thomas-Leonard "mechanical majority" agreed with the top leaders of the FE-CIO to merge the two unions and bring the full voting strength of the FE-CIO into the November UAW-CIO convention. Reuther was never advised of these meetings nor invited to attend them, although they were held in the hotel where he was registered in Chicago, where the UAW-CIO Executive Board was meeting. On June 11, 1947, just as Reuther was about to leave the board meeting to catch a plane for an important speaking engagement in the East, the Addes group launched the merger proposal.

All efforts of Reuther and his seven supporting board members to delay action on the merger were overridden by the "mechanical majority." Only one vote shifted the fourteen-to-eight line-up. On a motion by Dick Gosser, of Toledo, to set up a committee of five to work out a sound constitutional merger, one board member switched sides and voted with Reuther, but in the final show-down roll call he was back on the other side. The motion to adopt the merger, which carried by the usual majority, stipulated that a referendum vote of the local unions was to be completed by July 15. Locals were to vote on the proposal in membership meetings—by secret ballot or by show of hands, as they chose—and their votes were to be counted on the basis of their voting strength at the preceding convention.

The chips were down and the battle was on. In the following six weeks, officers and staff members on both sides rushed around the country, debating the issue before local membership meetings. All of the odds were on the side of the Addes group and its Commie bird dogs, who were beating the bushes to flush votes for the merger proposal. In terms of staff members available, we were outnumbered. The Commies had shrewdly picked a time of the year when membership meetings were poorly attended, many workers being away on vacations. To make our arguments against the merger stick, we had to beat down the charge that we were opposing admission to the UAW of thousands of workers whom we had always claimed as potential members.

Our only hope was to stick to the facts, expose the completely undemocratic character of the merger proposal, and put out trust in the good sense of the UAW-CIO membership. Shooting from the hip, as it were, we plunked away at the merger on the following points:

1. It would undermine the industrial (as opposed to craft) union principle in the UAW constitution by setting up an autonomous FE Division inside the UAW-CIO.

2. It would also violate our constitution by giving the FE Division power to elect an International Executive Board member on a craft basis.

3. It specifically proposed to guarantee the jobs of all the officers and staff members of the FE-CIO.

4. It would have committed the UAW-CIO to assuming all the financial obligations of the FE-CIO (which neither Addes nor FE President Grant Oakes could document with a CPA audit until the fight was practically over).

5. It was designed to give the FE-CIO local unions full voting power at the coming convention of the UAW-CIO, as if they had always been members of our union. This was in flagrant violation of a clause in our constitution which limits the votes of new locals by a ceiling computed on the basis of the amount of per capita tax they pay prior to the closing of the books when the convention is called. And, with customary Commie thoroughness, it would have given the FE-CIO locals a chance to vote

twice on the issue—once as FE-CIO locals voting to merge themselves with the UAW-CIO, and again as UAW-CIO locals voting to seat themselves in the UAW-CIO 1947 convention. We estimated that the adoption of the merger on these terms would give Addes an additional block of 450 solid anti-Reuther votes at the November convention of the UAW-CIO.

6. There was no provision whatsoever in the UAW-CIO constitution for the kind of referendum vote dreamed up by the "mechanical majority" to cloak its coup with a spurious membership sanction.

We tore the merger to pieces by citing the above points. We showed that a number of mergers had been consummated by the UAW-CIO with minor independent unions in the past within the procedural framework of our constitution, but that the membership had never before been asked to approve such a merger by a referendum vote. This proved, we argued, that the sponsors of the merger wanted to get off the hook and hang the responsibility for the merger on the membership. Finally, we affirmed our belief in unity and our desire for a sound, constitutional merger. We clinched this latter point by offering to support a merger that would follow the pattern used by Philip Murray's Steel Workers to absorb the Aluminum Workers of America. I carried the ball in my own local, which rejected the merger by a two-to-one vote.

When the votes of the local unions were tallied late in July, the merger proposal had been knocked down by the UAW-CIO membership by a majority of almost three to one. It was an omen of perilous days ahead for the Addes-Thomas-Leonard caucus.

19. Boardwalk Ballet: Act II

Some philanthropist with a little good sense and a lot of money ought to erect a monument at Atlantic City, New Jersey, to commemorate the bouts in labor politics that have taken place there in recent years. It was there that John L. Lewis biffed Bill Hutcheson in the eye on the eve of the founding of the CIO. It was there, too, that Phil Murray ascended to the CIO presidency when Lewis abdicated after his endorsement of Wilikie boomeranged. And it was to Atlantic City that Walter Reuther returned late in 1947 to avenge himself for the fate that had encircled him with hostile Executive Board members early in 1946.

With our confidence bolstered by the membership's rejection of the FE merger trick, we took off our gloves and girded up our program for the election of delegates to the 1947 convention, scheduled to open November 9 at Atlantic City. We were convinced that more than one political head would roll on the boardwalk this time.

From late July until early October, the Commies threw everything but their hammer and sickle at Walter Reuther. Acting through the Addes-Thomas-Leonard caucus, they unleashed a campaign which ranks among the bitterest in American labor history. Here are some examples:

With the hired brains of a three-hundred-dollar-a-week press agent, they published a twenty-four-page magazine entitled *The Bosses' Boy*. This document endeavored to prove that Reuther was the darling of American big business. We laughed that one off.

Seizing upon the unauthorized use of Reuther's name on a statement put out by the National Planning Association favoring increased productivity, Fisher Local 45 in Cleveland, a CP stronghold, flooded the union with charges that Reuther was a speed-up artist. We answered that one with photostats showing that Addes and Thomas had both signed NPA statements in their time. If the NPA was a "Wall Street outfit," as Local 45 and the Commies charged, Addes and Thomas were as tainted as Reuther with the stench of mammon.

Perhaps the most fantastic absurdity of the campaign came out of Chicago on the Associated Press wire. It told how an unidentified "citizens' committee" was being formed to promote a 1948 Republican ticket consisting of Senator Robert A. Taft for President and Walter P. Reuther for Vice-President. Drew Pearson got sucked in by that one; he broadcast it on one of his Sunday night radio programs. When our friends in Chicago tracked this whopper down, the master mind behind it was found to be an attorney who had for years represented John L. Lewis's District 50 of the United Mine Workers in the Chicago area. This was not the only indication that the old ham actor from the coal pits was pulling strings and greasing palms to encourage the attacks on Reuther. It was the old story of strange bedfellows all over again, with Lewis and the Commies temporarily skipping their hatred for each other to scratch backs for a mutual political advantage. When queried by the press, Reuther charged openly that Lewis, in the hope of taking over a portion of the UAW, was pouring money into the Addes-Thomas-Leonard caucus.

Our replies to these accusations, however, were only a minor part of our campaign material. We concentrated our energies on the presentation of a program designed to strengthen the democratic structure of the union and to clean up sloppy financial practices responsible for the squandering of union funds. Facts and figures were presented in our literature to show that the Addes group had padded the payrolls of board members who changed to their side. Bill Stevenson, anti-Reuther board member from Detroit, during a meeting of the board invited other members to change sides and get their staffs enlarged. Juggling of funds and unauthorized loans were exposed, to show that International Union money had been poured into locals where cash was needed to finance political machines.

We urged the creation of an International Union Board of Trustees as a corrective for these loose financial practices. To give the local unions a more effective method of checking on the actions of the top leadership, we proposed the keeping of verbatim minutes of International Executive Board meetings for the perusal of dues payers wanting to know what was going on upstairs. The "mechanical majority" had always rejected motions made by pro-Reuther board members to initiate the keeping of verbatim minutes. Before the convention was opened, we made it so hot for the Addes caucus on this issue that they backed down and approved the keeping of verbatim minutes.

Beyond this, we spelled out in great detail the new kind of unionism we were trying to build beyond the experimental stage. With a top leadership united behind a common program, we told the membership, it would be possible to make greater strides in such directions as getting wage increases without price increases, building co-ops, winning health plans, promoting racial equality, and strengthening the role of the union in every kind of social endeavor. For the first time—excluding previous isolated cases—our candidates for places in convention delegations conducted their campaigns openly as backers of what we called "the Reuther program for democratic unionism." Reuther's picture was printed on sample ballots and on leaflets which spelled out his program in shop language. Behind this strategy was a strong belief that the great majority of the auto workers understood Reuther's program, and approved it, but had never had a real chance to register their approval.

In September we threw our campaign into high gear through a bold stroke that caught the opposition completely off guard. Reuther wrote and published in the September *United Automobile Worker* a hard-hitting report to the membership. This action was required of him by the constitution, and Addes had no legal grounds for trying to prevent the publication of the report. But we knew that, if Addes found out that we intended to print the report, he would try to hold it up. So we went ahead without telling Addes—although he could have found out about it if he had been smart enough to post a lookout at the printing plant in Indianapolis.

The final editing of the report took place while the International Executive Board was meeting in Buffalo, New York. I handled the Indianapolis end of the job, editing copy, writing heads, checking proofs, and sending them air mail special to Buffalo. In Buffalo, during the evenings and far into the night, Reuther, Frank Winn, Jack Conway, and Don Montgomery read the proofs, made final corrections, and sent the proofs back to me. Phil Cornelius, the head of the printing firm, sensed that something was cooking, I think, but he played it down the middle and did not look at the report or tell Addes that anything was in the wind.

I must confess that I was somewhat jittery. At any moment one of Addes's staff members might have breezed into the plant and upset our plans. But, happily, no one from the opposition ever showed up, and the dynamite-laden twelve-page issue of the *Auto Worker* was put to bed without a hitch. When the stereotypers were rolling the mats for the rotary press plates, foresight prompted me to have them make an extra set of mats of the inside four pages containing Reuther's report. With these carefully wrapped and stowed away in my car, I took off for Detroit.

The board meeting had been adjourned by the time the paper began arriving in various UAW centers. As usual, a bundle shipment was broken open and laid out on a table in the lobby of the International Union office in Detroit. In a short time people were popping up from all over the place to get copies and read the report.

Reuther had pulled no punches in drafting the document. He had analyzed the sources of factionalism in the union and put the finger squarely on the "mechanical majority" without mentioning names. He blasted political patronage, squandering of funds, organizational and administrative incompetence, and interference by the Communists in the affairs of the union. Then he wound up with a punchy but brief summary of his program for democratic unionism, followed by a call to arms aimed at the rank and file.

The shoe Reuther had fashioned fitted so perfectly that all hell broke loose in the reaction to his report. A board meeting was called, and the Addes group blasted Reuther all over the lot, but the invectives showered on him did not break either his bones or his will. To cap the expressions of outrage, R. J. Thomas introduced a resolution which contained, among other wordy fantasies, the proposal that the name of the Taft-Hartley Act should be changed to the "Taft-Hartley-Reuther Act." To soothe their smarting dignities, the members of the "mechanical majority" solemnly adopted the resolution by the usual vote of fourteen to eight. Then they authorized Addes, Thomas, and Leonard to print and mail to every member an answer to Reuther's report. Reuther then asked the permission of the Board to mail to the local unions his reply to the charges that he was in favor of speed-ups. The board said, by a fourteen-to-eight vote, that he could, but that his communication was subject to the approval of Addes.

In the midst of this uproar, Reuther processed a purchase requisition for the reprinting of fifty thousand copies of his report. Addes blew up. He refused to okay the expenditure of the funds necessary to pay for the reprints. But his triumph was short-lived. In a matter of hours, I had my extra set of page mats in a print shop in Detroit, the plates were cast, and the reprint was on its way to UAW centers all over the country.

As the returns began to roll in from the shops where delegate elections were completed, our confidence mounted. We not only held our own in the plants we had counted on, but we were making heavy inroads into locals that had always been in the Addes camp. In desperation, the Commies tried all kinds of tricks to halt the tide, but it continued to wash them backward. At the Motor Building of the Ford Rouge plant, for instance, they rigged the election for a short, two-hour period on a Sunday, instead of running it all day as was customary. Our boys protested, but did not get far. So they shook the bushes to get their people out to the meeting. The pro-Reuther candidates won nine out of ten delegate positions. Then the Commies, who controlled the administration of that particular unit of Local 600, turned around and ordered a new election for the same reasons that our people had protested in the first place. Our guys went to work again. On the second ballot they took all ten delegates.

Before the UAW-CIO convention opened in Atlantic City, the CIO national convention was held in Boston, in late October. There was no appeasement of the Commies at this session. Secretary of State Marshall was invited to speak, and he accepted. When his speech was finished, a resolution endorsing the principle of the Marshall Plan was introduced. The Commies quibbled over it but did not stage a real fight against it. Then R. J. Thomas was detached from his CIO vice-presidency. No one had to guess any longer about where Philip Murray stood.

Late in October, the Reuther forces held a national caucus in Detroit at which it was revealed that we had enough delegates—if we could hold them—to do a long overdue job of house cleaning. The caucus chose to run Reuther for president, Emil Mazey for secretary-treasurer, and John W. Livingston of St. Louis and Richard Gosser of Toledo for the two vice-presidential posts.

There was never any doubt about the outcome of Act II of the UAW-CIO "Boardwalk Ballet" after the 1947 convention got under way. Although the "mechanical majority" had a majority on every convention committee, the Reuther forces lost not a single issue on the floor. The first test was on setting the date for the election of officers. A majority of the reporting committee, favoring the Addes-Thomas-Leonard view, recommended the holding of the election of top officers on the fifth day of the convention. A pro-Reuther minority recommended that the elections be held on the third day. The minority report carried by a heavy majority.

The next test was on a resolution to comply with the Taft-Hartley Act provision calling for the signing of non-Communist affidavits. Again the reporting committee was split, the majority being against signing, and the minority in favor of signing. Debate was long and furious. But the minority report, instructing UAW leaders to sign the non-Communist affidavits, carried.

When Philip Murray came to address the delegates, his words were again weighed for political implications, and there was no mistaking his meaning this time. He said: "I have no words that can flow from me that would provide adequate appreciation for the splendid support that little redhead has given Phil Murray since his incumbency." Questioned later at a press conference, he said that he endorsed Reuther for re-election. Pressed by newsmen to say whether he was endorsing any of the other officers for re-election, he said bluntly that his endorsement of Reuther was the only comment he cared to make on the elections.

By this time the opposition had conceded the futility of trying to defeat Reuther for the presidency. They refused to run a major candidate against him. But Local 45, the Commie-controlled Fisher Body local in Cleveland, Ohio, which had master-minded the charges that Reuther was a speed-up artist, refused to back down. It nominated John DeVito as a protest candidate. Another candidate, Edward Murphy of Local 205 in Detroit, was also nominated. Between them, DeVito and Murphy polled 339 votes. The bulk of the Addes-Thomas-Leonard followers registered their disapproval of Reuther by withholding their votes. Delegates representing 1,219 votes abstained from voting. Reuther polled 5,593 votes. The campaign to "repeal Reuther" had fizzled.

Everyone agreed that the real test of strength would come in the voting for the job of secretary-treasurer. Addes, the incumbent, was the recognized leader of the anti-Reuther forces and was certain to poll the maximum strength of the opposition to Reuther.

Emil Mazey, our choice to oppose Addes, had a long record of militant union work, despite the fact that he was only thirty-four years old. He was known in Detroit as the firebrand from Briggs Local 212. He had been involved in many strikes and clashes with the police. As a reporter put it in a newspaper story after the election, "Mazey has taken on the employers, the police, the Congress and even the high command of the U. S. Army at various times in his stormy career." The latter reference was to Mazey's organization of a drive to bring the GI's home from the Pacific, and to his exposure of wastage of Army supplies, when he was a sergeant stationed in the Philippines.

Our delegates held the line even more strongly than many of us expected. Mazey polled only 760 votes less than Reuther. He defeated Addes by a majority of 2,234 votes. In the balloting for the vice-presidencies, Thomas and Leonard were swept out in turn by Gosser and Livingston. Later in the convention, when the regions voted for their board members, our people defeated all but four of the old "mechanical majority." Since the convention even these four have indicated a new willingness to mend their ways and work with the Reuther administration. In Region One, Michael F. Lacey, a leader from my own Chevrolet Gear and Axle Local 235, was elected to fill the vacancy created by Mazey's promotion.

At a party thrown to celebrate our victory, Walter, who normally does not smoke or drink, fulfilled one of his campaign promises: he puffed on a cigar and tossed off a shot of whisky—to the delight of the happy delegates.

The next day, after the new Executive Board was sworn in, he said to the delegates: "We are the vanguard in America, in that great crusade to build a better world. We are the architects of the future, and we are going to fashion the weapons with which we will work and fight and build."

20. Brotherhood versus Buckshot

Editorial comment on the outcome of the 1947 UAW-CIO convention, with few exceptions, conveyed the impression that the triumph of the Reuther forces foretold a turn toward conservatism in the auto union particularly, and in the CIO generally. This misapprehension grew, as usual, out of the inability of many publishers and editors to understand that communism and conservatism are blood brothers under the skin. Victimized for years by the myth that communism is a manifestation of progressivism, they could only interpret the blitzing of the Commies at Atlantic City as an indication of more conservative UAW-CIO policies.

Reuther did his best to dispel this illusion in the closing hours of the convention. In reply to specific questions thrown at him in press conferences, he spelled out the reasons that a democratic union cannot be truly progressive when it is hampered by Communist control. He pointed out the similarity between Communist contempt for human liberty and the disregard of the corporations for human dignity. The UAW-CIO would be committed in the future, he assured the reporters, to a program of practical militance that would be anything but conservative. If proof were wanting, the performance of the union in the months since November 1947 have given ample weight to his prophetic commitment.

When I returned late in November from a week's vacation of deer hunting in Northern Michigan, the UAW-CIO was busily donning its own version of the new look. In a few weeks the groundwork was laid for a thoroughgoing reorganization of its financial, administrative, and organizational machinery. The emphasis was on efficiency, plugging of financial leaks, and stimulation of the staff personnel assigned to organization.

I was immediately drawn into the preparations for a hard-hitting organizational drive. The campaign was designed to take up the slack in partially organized and poorly organized plants, where factionalism had in the past resulted in sloppy organizational work. Over-all supervision of the drive was assigned to Vice-President John W. Livingston, who, as Director of Region Five, had done an admirable job of building the membership throughout the Southwest.

General Motors was chosen as the target for the first phase of the drive. The GM agreement was due to expire in the early spring of 1948, and the strategy of the union was to consolidate the membership in preparation for the 1948 negotiations. It just happened that General Motors was itself concluding a morale-building act called the "My Job Contest." It had solicited letters from the workers telling what they liked about their jobs. Prizes, including cars and other GM products, were awarded to the winners. The best crack describing the GM call for letters telling "what I like about my job" came from the *Wage Earner*, publication of the Association of Catholic Trade Unionists in Detroit. This paper said editorially: "There ain't no negative in that sentence, chum."

In a spirit of competition for the loyalty of the workers, the union launched a "Build the Union" contest in General Motors. GM was formally asked to sell GM products to the union at a discount—so that the UAW-CIO might also offer GM-made prizes—but for reasons of its own the corporation rejected the request. Unabashed, we secured a Ford and a Packard for the top prizes in the GM organizational drive. In front of our Detroit headquarters, directly across the street from the towering General Motors Building, we put these two prizes on display.

A huge banner under the Ford said: "There's a Ford in the future of a GM worker." Under the Packard another banner said: "Ask the GM worker who wins one."

The drive turned out to be well worth the effort put into it. More than twenty-five thousand new members were signed up in the GM plants. This greatly strengthened the hand of the union in getting ready for the 1948 wage negotiations. The drive was then extended to other plants within the union's jurisdiction.

Late in February 1948 I was sent to the West Coast to do publicity work on an aircraft organizing job. Out of this assignment came a new appointment for me. Because of the increase in aircraft employment resulting from the growing strain in American-Soviet relations, the Aircraft Department staff was increased, and I was transferred to that department to do publicity in connection with the rebuilding of the union in booming aircraft plants.

On the evening of April 20, shortly after starting on the new assignment, I went to a meeting sponsored by the Detroit Chapter of Americans for Democratic Action. A guest speaker had been invited by the ADA to tell of his visit to Czechoslovakia just before the death of Jan Masaryk. His grim account of the terroristic Soviet rule behind the iron curtain heightened my appreciation of the political freedom we enjoy in America. I was certain that nothing like that could happen in our country.

After the meeting, I went straight home with my wife. I had scarcely fallen asleep when the phone rang. As I answered it, I wondered sleepily who was calling at that late hour. It was a friend in Flint, Michigan, who is editor of a weekly labor paper.

"Can you wire me the details of the shooting of Walter Reuther first thing in the morning?" he asked sharply.

"What!" I exclaimed, awakening with shock.

"Don't you know about it?"

"No, when did it happen?" I asked in a kind of a daze. I had talked to Walter just that afternoon at an International Executive Board meeting in the Book-Cadillac Hotel.

"About an hour and a half ago," my friend replied. "I heard it on the radio. He's in the New Grace Hospital. Someone fired a shotgun at him through his kitchen window—the radio says his right arm is shot off."

I said good night to him, blundered back into the bedroom, and sat down on the edge of the bed. My wife shared my shock when I told her what had happened. I could not get to sleep for hours. Political terrorism had come to America, I felt.

Next morning I rushed down to the office. It was in an uproar, with phones ringing constantly, telegrams arriving, people coming and going and cursing under their breath. Frank Winn, who had been up all night at the hospital, held a bottle of coffee in one hand and a telephone in the other. Another long-distance call was waiting for him. He interrupted his conversation long enough to tell me to get out to the hospital and coordinate the press relations.

I went to the hospital and stayed there almost constantly for four days and four nights—until things began to quiet down. There was a crew of reporters, still photographers, and newsreel men hanging around all the time, except in the smallest hours of the morning. Telegrams poured in by the bushel. Hundreds of flowers arrived. And a guard of two police detectives and two unionists patrolled the hallway leading to Walter's room. Medical specialists walked softly in and out of the room, whispered to each other in soft voices.

About noon of April 21, which happened to be my birthday, I slipped into Walter's room when a nurse left the door open. He lay on his back, with his right arm, tightly bandaged and swollen out of shape, suspended in a traction apparatus made of metal and ropes. He was conscious and smiled wanly at me without turning his head.

"They're trying to beat us down, Clayton," he said with a little crack in his voice. He was still pretty well loaded up with drugs and did not have very effective control of his nerves.

With a lump rising in my throat, I walked over to the side of his bed.

"You know they can't do that to us, Walter," I said softly. I picked up his left hand and squeezed it for a minute. "We've got the same thing in us that Joe Hill had—and they haven't made guns that can kill our spirit of brotherhood."

His smile was a little brighter for a moment. "You're damn right; they can't stop us, not even with buckshot," he said with a faint trace of spirit in his voice.

Despite the fact that the buckshot had smashed the bone of his upper arm into several fragments and mutilated the flesh severely, medical science—combined with his good health and fighting spirit—swiftly put him on the road to recovery. And I think the entire union staff worked hard to try to make up for Walter's temporary inability to lead us, and to speed his recovery with reports of progress on the union projects under way when he was struck down. [1]

I was suddenly called away from the hospital in the middle of the night to catch a plane heading for Peoria, Illinois, where we were bidding for the bargaining rights in the huge Caterpillar Tractor plant. Lewis Carliner, Editor of the UAW-CIO Education Department magazine, joined me on the plane, and we plunged into what turned out to be the toughest and fastest organization job ever staged by our union.

The Peoria assignment grew out of the refusal of the leaders of the CIO Farm Equipment and Metal Workers Union to sign the non-Communist affidavits required by the Taft-Hartley Act. The Caterpillar management withdrew its recognition of the FE-CIO. The FE-CIO struck the plant on April 8 in a frantic attempt to force the company to renew its recognition of the union.

The FE-CIO leadership was especially desperate because the UAW-AFL, a fifty-thousand-member remnant of the Homer Martin bolt out of the CIO in 1939, had petitioned the National Labor Relations Board for a representation election in the Caterpillar plant. Knowing that FE-CIO could not get on the ballot, because of its defiance of the Taft-Hartley procedure, Ray Berndt, Director of UAW-CIO Region Three, intervened in the NLRB hearing. He demanded a place on the ballot for the UAW-CIO, after it should have met the necessary legal requirements. The International Association of Machinists, an independent union, also intervened, asking for a separate craft election in the toolroom. The NLRB denied the IAM craft petition but placed it on the ballot for the entire plant bargaining unit. The first election

[1] The indictment in October 1948 of Carl Bolton, a former minor official of Ford Local 400, aroused new interest in the Reuther shooting. But no one in the union was yet certain of who had done it, or why.

was ordered for May 12. About sixteen thousand workers were eligible to vote. They could choose between the UAW-AFL, the IAM, the UAW-CIO, and "None." The campaign that followed was one of the weirdest in labor history.

The FE-CIO had built a machine based on a strong Communist unit in the Caterpillar plant which used many questionable tactics to put across the party line in Peoria. When the first two UAW-CIO organizers checked in at the Père Marquette Hotel early in April, a gang of armed muscle men quickly showed up to give them the pitch. Pistols were stuck in the organizers' ribs, they were taken downstairs and checked out of the hotel, then driven thirty miles out of town and told to get rolling and keep rolling. When the UAW-CIO returned, late in April, we brought a crew of our own big enough to prevent a repetition of this stunt.

At the hottest stage of the campaign we had close to one hundred full-time organizers in Peoria. Vice-President Livingston came in to lend his experience and help to Regional Directors Ray Berndt and Pat Greathouse. The city was broken down into districts. Crews of organizers went from house to house all day long and well into the night, searching out the Caterpillar workers, talking to them, giving them leaflets. Carliner and myself bought up all the radio time we could get, spent hours knocking out scripts, and scurried to and from newspaper offices with copy for full-page ads. We arranged to have two airplanes, one with a banner and another with a public address system, in the air on election day. I called Central States Cooperatives in Chicago, and they rushed down a refrigerator, a radio-record-player, and five pressure cookers to give away as door prizes at a mass meeting scheduled for the night before the election.

Word came to us that a plot to break up our mass meeting was afoot. Livingston, Berndt, and Greathouse got on the telephones and put in swift calls to South Bend, Rock Island, Moline, St. Louis, and Chicago. Two hours before the mass meeting was set to open, on the evening of May 11, buses began to pull up in front of the hall. A hundred auto workers from other cities piled out of them; they were assigned to the front of the hall to protect the meeting. The FE crowd watched from across the street, but stayed away. About six hundred Caterpillar workers turned out for the meeting. They heard speeches by Livingston and Victor G. Reuther, and adopted a resolution expressing their intention to return to work on Thursday if the UAW-CIO won the election.

It was rough going on the day of the election. FE campaigners were out in force, with plenty of Communist shock troops from Chicago to help them. They pleaded with the workers to vote for "None." This was the peculiar angle of the election. While FE sought to persuade the workers to vote for no union, the Caterpillar management wrote letters, bought ads, and put on radio programs urging the workers to vote for any union, but to vote for a union of some kind. FE guys argued that a majority vote for no union would be a vote of confidence for them. The company wanted to get rid of the FE, and was willing to bargain with any of the other unions that could get a majority.

The election was held in the Peoria Armory. Workers going in to vote had to walk past long lines of campaigners for all sides, who littered the streets with literature.

"Vote 'no' for FE-CIO," the FE stalwarts chanted.

"A vote for 'no' is a vote for Joe," our guys sang back at them.

The FE people wore their voices out insulting us. They called us scabs, finks, raiders, and union-busters. We kept our tempers, but we threw our choicest adjectives back at them. At one point a crew of Commie gals danced in a circle, singing: "We'll dance around Reuther's grave—we'll dance around Reuther's grave."

It was a critical day all the way around. The papers came out with a story reporting that the Chrysler workers had walked out in a nation-wide strike to back up their demands for a 1948 wage increase. By eight o'clock, when balloting ended, our people were worn to a frazzle. FE had us outnumbered about three to one. We had a job of it getting our boys away in cars in gangs big enough to prevent FE from jumping them. After the last car pulled away, in a shower of FE insults, I went inside with five other UAW-CIO observers to watch the counting of the ballots. When the count was concluded, the UAW-AFL was out in front with some 4,700 votes. We were second with about 2,500; FE was third with a "no union" vote of 2,000; IAM trailed with a little over 1,000. The vote was inconclusive; there would have to be a runoff between UAW-AFL and UAW-CIO.

But we still had a big headache on our hands. The company had announced that the plant would be open in the morning for those Caterpillar workers who wanted to go in to their jobs. State troopers were in town to patrol the gates. Our meeting had passed a resolution saying we favored going back to work if we won the election. We had not won the election—but a lot of workers would be going back anyway. If the FE pickets chose to make a fight of it—and we had every reason to believe they would—we would have a nasty decision to make. Should we help our people who wanted to go back to work fight their way through the FE pickets? We postponed the decision, holding all our organizers together in the Jefferson Hotel, waiting for an FE radio broadcast scheduled for midnight. Silence hung heavy in the room as we waited for the announcer to introduce the FE speaker. Then we breathed a sigh of relief as he announced that the strike was called off. There would be no fighting at the plant gates.

I could not stay for the runoff, having been ordered to Baltimore on another organizational assignment. Our people who did stay worked harder than ever. When the runoff ballots were counted on May 20, we had trounced the AFL by a majority of more than two thousand votes. The plant was ours, after a two-week campaign starting from scratch.

On May 25, still in Baltimore, I read the story of the settlement of the 1948 UAW-CIO wage demands on the General Motors Corporation. It was big news. After a five-month cold war, started at the turn of the year by the refusal of Big Steel to grant a wage increase of any kind, the big business "no-raise" front had collapsed. GM had broken the ranks of the Wall Street alliance. UAW-CIO had done it again.

The terms of the GM settlement were unique, and they were destined to have far-reaching repercussions in American labor relations. A wage increase of eleven cents per hour was granted. Eight cents of the increase was earmarked as an adjustment to compensate for the increased cost of living. Three cents was designated as an "improvement in the standard of living." A formula was set up providing for wages to rise and fall with the ups and downs of living costs. If prices continued to go up, wages would rise one cent per hour for each 1.14 per cent increase in the Bureau of Labor Statistics cost-of-living index. But, if prices went down, wages could be cut no more than five cents of the eight cents cost-of-living adjustment. If prices continued to go down thereafter, the wage level would hold, and the buying power of the workers would go up sharply. And, no matter what happened to prices, GM committed itself to continue adding at least three cents per hour per year for "improvement in the standard of living." While many newspapers, most of big business, and a few rival unions jeered at the settlement, its meaning for American labor was not obscured by the babble of comment. A powerful American corporation had openly conceded the validity of Walter P. Reuther's argument that workers were entitled to get higher living standards as a result of advances in industrial technology. No invective could dissolve the three-cents-per-hour-per-year improvement factor. It was not a bag of gold—but it was a concrete admission by a vital segment of industry that the machine-tenders have at least as much right as the stockholders to get a cut of the technological pie. Labor was seated at a table previously reserved for plutocracy. Future negotiations might enlarge the size of the serving. Perhaps GM's concession was a sign of a new era of industrial peace.

With the front broken by GM, Chrysler gave in and settled the 1948 strike on May 28 with a thirteen-cents-per-hour increase, more vacation pay, and a raise for salaried workers. Norman Matthews, UAW-CIO Chrysler Department Director, pointed out to the press that teamwork in the leadership, and solidarity in the ranks of the union, under its new united leadership, had made possible the 1948 wage gains. He said: "The Chrysler strike and the militant spirit of the Chrysler workers contributed to the substantial gains won by the General Motors workers and their victory in turn made possible the settlement won in Chrysler. . . ."

After leaving the hospital in May, Walter P. Reuther wrote in his column in the May *Auto Worker:*

In this struggle, we in the UAW have made enemies. And those enemies have struck back in the wild, misguided belief that a shotgun in the hands of a hired killer can murder the ideas and idealism of our movement. . . .

The momentum and power of our new kind of labor movement cannot be stopped and thrown back by slugs from a shotgun. The social and economic democracy for which we struggle is a practical vision that cannot be clouded or killed by assaults on one man. . . .

I have left my hospital bed more determined than I have ever been to work unceasingly for the practical realization of the aspirations and hopes we all share. Let us go forward with banners high, confident that we can build a world where men can live in dignity, freedom, security and peace.

21. "Give Me Liberty . . ."

I sat sweltering in a hotel room in Washington, D. C., on July 14, 1948, the third day of the National Democratic Convention, listening to a broadcast of the proceedings. The announcer's voice was excited as he gave a blow-by-blow account of the fight led by Americans for Democratic Action to include a forthright civil rights plank in the Democratic party platform. It was a knock-down, fight-to-the-finish battle between the white supremists of the South and labor and liberal elements from the rest of the nation. My wife Edith was there with the Detroit delegation, helping to carry out the strategy of the ADA group. Prominent in the floor fight for civil rights were young progressives such as Hubert Humphrey of Minnesota and Helen Gahagan Douglas of California. When the announcer told of the success of the libertarian bloc, I felt like joining in the cheers that came over the air from the turbulent Convention Hall in Philadelphia.

Listening to that broadcast describing a new victory for human rights I remembered milestones on the long road I myself had traveled. In twelve years I had been transformed from a backwoods bumpkin, lured into the factories by promises of fat paychecks, to a zealous full-time labor representative. I had learned a lot, accomplished a little, grown to appreciate the inner satisfaction resulting from hours, days, weeks, years spent on the battlefront of freedom. I had gone hungry, walked picket lines, been roughed up by the police, been thrown into jail, worked around the clock—all for the cause of labor and democracy.

And still the fight went on. The battle at Philadelphia was a part of it, linked by bonds of human suffering to the struggle out of which I had come. The right of a worker to demand a voice in the shaping of his destiny is no different from the right of a Negro or a Jew to be treated as a human being. The pangs of hunger and the shame of segregation are equally hurtful. If there is one thing of which I am proud, it is that I have learned in these twelve years to fight as hard as I know how against every manifestation of man's inhumanity to man.

Perhaps the most lasting lesson rooted in my mind during this period is the one which taught me to understand the relationship between bread and liberty. I started in the labor movement by revolting against unemployment, depression, low wages, and corporate dictatorship. The experience of combating these evils drove me into a search for a more permanent answer than the day-to-day tactics of pure and simple trade unionism. Collective bargaining, I learned early and fast, was okay as far as it went, but it didn't go far enough. It was at this point that the Communists snared me with their bait of a utopia that turned out to be a police state.

After I learned that the heaven on earth promised by the Communists was to be one in which commissars would stick guns in the backs of people to force them to eat strawberries and like it—if there were any strawberries—I was never again in doubt about the value of freedom. I learned to recognize the superiority of liberty over security, to realize that a man in jail may have absolute security. Knowing this, I worked my way to a meeting of minds with the independent, democratically minded Americans who have the guts to make a fight for both liberty and security.

I am convinced that the CIO has developed out of the heritage of a free people. The patron saints of our democracy—Tom Paine, Tom Jefferson, Abe Lincoln and such—stand guard over the spirit of independence that gives American workers the backbone to organize into unions and stand up for their rights. It is the same spirit which prompts a mechanic at a ball game to tell the banker in front of him to sit down. When cops push us around on the picket lines, this spirit of independence gives us the courage to stand firm for our belief that justice is on our side.

What I mean by this is that it seems a little silly to have spent a hundred and seventy-two years telling Americans that they are their own political bosses, running a government "conceived in liberty and dedicated to the proposition that all men are created equal," and then spring a Taft-Hartley Act on them. We of labor know better. Liberty has been in our blood too long for us to submit to either capitalist politicians or Communists who are bent on giving all power to an elite group selected to run the show from the top. The Taft-Hartley Act forbids me as a unionist to spend union funds on behalf of a candidate running in a federal election—even though the membership of my union democratically authorizes me to do so. In 1937 General Motors fired me off my job for daring to try to organize a union. And in 1938 the Communists would have thrown me out of the party—if I hadn't beat them to it by quitting—because I wanted to enjoy freedom of expression. I defy anyone to show me any difference in principle among these three acts of suppression of my rights.

It seems to me that my experience of learning the economic and political facts of life is an example in miniature of what is happening in the world. Evidence is all around us that capitalism has lost the power to sustain itself—that it is a senile system stumbling blindly from boom to bust to war to inflation and back again. No capitalist nation, not excepting America, has enjoyed a stable period of lasting prosperity, security, and peace in the last forty years of world history. And as the people, including workers like myself and my fellows in the auto industry, learn that the old system cannot fill public needs, we are compelled to look for new ways of making society operate democratically.

Labor is not out of character in leading the quest for saner ways of producing and distributing goods and services, extending civil rights, battling for political freedom. American workers have a long and proud record of working for representative government, for free public schools, for universal suffrage, against child labor, against slavery, against discrimination. Our gains on these fronts date back to the Revolution. I believe sincerely that the powerful unions organized in basic American industries during the past decade are going to carry on in this tradition of democratic action.

And in which direction shall we travel? If capitalism has lost its dynamic, there is no hope down that lonesome back road. World War II seemed to prove the futility of trying to prop up capitalism with dictatorship and militarism—even though Hitler and Mussolini did their best. Communism stands exposed before the world as a police state that denies its victims all of the human rights won so painfully by mankind through ages of struggle. Which way shall humanity turn at this juncture?

We of the UAW-CIO think that we have an answer suited to help America build its democracy into a force powerful enough to back up the world-wide fight for freedom.

In March 1948 the UAW-CIO International Executive Board, complying with a mandate of the convention held in November 1947, adopted a resolution which stated that our "official political objective" was to be the formation of a genuine progressive political party. Its principles were to be as follows:

1. It shall welcome into its ranks industrial and white collar workers, working farmers, small business men, professionals and every individual and every group honestly committed to winning economic security and abundance without surrendering fundamental freedoms.

2. It shall not serve as the mouthpiece or errand boy for any other political party or movement and it shall oppose all forms of totalitarianism, both the Communist variety on the left and the Fascist variety on the right.

3. It shall be dedicated to fair play and equality of treatment for all groups and individuals, and shall fight against all forms of discrimination and for full civil rights for all people everywhere.

4. It shall place human rights above property rights and shall advocate a program of full production and full employment based on democratic controls in every area of our economic life where the public interest is directly and vitally at stake.

5. It shall be a popular movement built from the grass-roots upward, encouraging the maximum degrees of activity at the ward and precinct levels, with final authority resting in the rank-and-file membership.

Commenting on this decision in the August 1948 edition of the *Auto Worker*, UAW-CIO President Walter P. Reuther said:

It is not enough to be against corporate monopoly that grows and tightens its hold upon our lives each year. We and the government we elect must be for something. For example, for an economy that is both free and enterprising, for government expansion and even operation of necessary productive capacity when private enterprise refuses to expand, for producer and consumer cooperatives, and for government authorities patterned along TVA lines to save and restore our remaining natural resources.

Such a government, so elected, will not fail us. It will not depend upon a "good man" in the White House and "good men" in the Congress. As our government, loyal to our principles and our program, it will serve us in the necessary planning and action for prosperity and peace and against depression and war.

To know Walter Reuther is to know that the "us" and the "we" used above do not mean the UAW-CIO, or even labor as a class—they mean the American community. He expresses himself that way as a matter of habit, because he never deviates from the principle of building a union that makes community welfare the keystone of all its policies and programs.

I am confident that my union will hold fast to this principle of basing all its actions on what is good for the community as we move into action to build that "genuine progressive political party." Our goal is a simple one. We want the American people to have a chance to make an intelligent choice of political objectives. To make such a choice possible, someone has to take the initiative in herding the monopolists, the price-fixers, the grafters, the white supremists, the inciters of religious hatred, and the labor-haters all into one political party that stands for such things. Conversely, someone has to lead off in building another political party, made up of the groups listed in the UAW-CIO political resolution, standing for full production, full employment, economic abundance, full civil rights, and racial and religious equality. It seems to us in the UAW-CIO that there is no other way to create political alternatives that make sense.

We believe that this task of forcing a political re-alignment dividing the democrats from the totalitarians is most urgent. The hopes of people around the world who cherish liberty above all things are at stake in the decision facing the American people. Our brothers and sisters in England, with whom we are in close contact, have elected a government which is doing a job most of us in the UAW-CIO admire and respect. We believe British socialism is proving one thing: that a society can plan to curb privilege in the interest of community welfare without sacrificing basic freedoms. In our own way, we of the UAW-CIO are promoting projects that we think run parallel to the pattern of progress in England. We are committed to public operation of basic and monopolistic industries—as in the TVA—with checks on bureaucratic power reserved to the people. Likewise, we are building Rochdale cooperatives in the industrial centers where our union is strong, to prove that democracy can be made to work in the market place. These are indications, we think, that Americans can make a decision to move forward democratically.

We in the UAW-CIO do not think that decision can be made in the interest of democracy by retreating—by smashing labor unions, by kowtowing to the rich and privileged, by persecuting racial and religious minorities, by turning our backs on global problems, by delivering our destinies into the hands of political or economic masters. We do not want America to go backwards, to give political power to our plutocrats, our racial supremists, our religious bigots, and so insure the triumph of rightist and leftist police states in other parts of the world. If that were to happen, we believe the Fascists and the Communists would then battle it out, over the dead bodies of democrats, for control of the earth. There would be nothing but concentration camps and firing squads for labor in such a disaster.

But I have no blueprint, no cure-all to prescribe for the troubles of humanity. This much I can and will say: The auto workers from whose ranks I speak have shown in a modest way what can be done by putting democracy to work. We have put extra dollars in the pockets of our people by organizing—but that has not been our major gain. The accomplishments of which we are most proud are in the field of human engineering: persuading employers to respect our individuality, learning to work together for a common objective, breaking down the barriers of racial and religious hatred—living, working, playing, learning together as people. None of these accomplishments is one hundred per cent complete, because labor as a group cannot do these jobs alone in a democracy.

That is why we are moving out, joining with other democratic groups, into the fields of political and social action, to try to convince our fellow Americans that they should help us to make democracy work in America, so that America can do her share in making democracy work in the world. The outcome of the 1948 national election already seems to justify that program. With the issues taken to them nationally by President Truman—and locally by a labor movement finally sold on the importance of political action—the people responded with a democratic vigor that startled the world. Civil rights, labor's rights, social security, democratic planning for abundance—these are the goals for which the people voted. The vote was a rejection of both communism and monopoly capitalism, a repudiation of reaction and white supremacy; it was an affirmation of faith in working democracy.

I think America has shown that with hard work, vigilance, and plenty of exercise of our democratic freedoms we can use popular control of our free government to keep marching toward the lights beyond the prison.

Index

Index

Adams, Elmer C., 45
Addes, George F., 68, 74, 85, 86, 100, 101, 106, 114, 141, 144, 147, 148, 154, 156, 157, 160-63, 164, 165, 166, 183, 187-88, 189, 190, 191, 192, 193, 196, 197, 199, 200, 201, 204, 205, 207, 208, 209, 210-11, 212, 213, 214, 215
Agriculture, Department of, 185
Allan, Billy, 90
Aluminum Workers of America, CIO, 207
American Federation of Labor, 48, 69, 84, 99, 102, 107, 147, 189, 191, 192
American Guardian, The, 132, 133
American Peace Mobilization, 144
Americans for Democratic Action, 218, 226
Ameringer, Oscar, 132-33, 201
Ammunition, 160, 201, 202
Anderson (of General Motors), 178
Anderson, Sherwood, 44
Andy (friend of the author), 25-26, 30, 44, 45
Antioch Review, 126
Associated Press, 209
Association of Catholic Trade Unionists, 194, 217
Auto-Lite plant (Toledo), 100

"Battle of the Overpass" (1937), 142
"Battle of the Running Bulls," 72
Beckman, Charles, 188
Bennett, Earnest, 137, 138, 149, 151
Bennett, Harry, 35, 142
Berndt, Ray, 220, 221
Bishop, Melvin, 197
Bishop, Merlin, 70
Black Legion, 113
Blackwood, Ben, 110
Blue Cross Hospitalization plan, 152, 153, 154, 155
Bobbit, John T., 119
Bohn Aluminum & Brass Company, 70
Bolton, Carl, 220 *n.*
Bosses' Boy, The, 208
Bridges, Harry, 170
Briggs plants, 37, 158, 197; Mack Avenue plant (Detroit), 26, 27, 28-29, 158
Browder, Earl, 46-47, 48, 90-91, 159, 160, 162
Buchanan Steel Products Corporation, 196
Buckley, Jerry, 35
Budenz, Louis F., 80
"Burying Ground by the Ties," 7

Callahan (Chevrolet plant superintendent), 53
Canadian Commonwealth Federation, 171
Carliner, Lewis, 202, 220, 221
Carpenter Hall (Hamtramck), 149
Caterpillar Tractor Company, 220-23
Central States Cooperatives (Chicago), 221
Chamberlain, Neville, 131

Chevrolet Employees' Association, 43
Chevrolet Motor Division, General Motors Corporation, 22, 39, 42, 43, 50, 51, 52, 57, 60, 61, 65, 66, 112, 130, 139, 149, 150, 152; Drop Forge, 68; Gear and Axle (Detroit), 38, 48, 50, 52, 60, 61, 64, 76, 97, 109; Plant One, 98; Plant Two, 42, 52, 53, 54, 60, 99, 150; Plant Three, 57, 60; Transmission plant (Toledo), 68
Childs, Richard Storrs, 118-19
Chrysler Corporation, 19, 37, 153, 154, 222, 224; Jefferson plant (Detroit), 68, 99
Civil Rights Federation, 75
Cobb, Clint, 32
Coen (of General Motors), 177, 178
Communist Front, *see* Civil Rights Federation; National Negro Congress
Communist International, 85
Communist party of the United States, 28, 35, 46, 47, 51, 54, 63, 64, 66, 67, 68, 69, 70, 71, 75, 76, 77, 78, 79, 80, 81-82, 83, 84-85, 87-88, 90-94, 95, 96, 100, 103, 104, 105-106, 118, 119, 120, 121, 123, 125, 126, 128, 130, 132, 134, 139, 140, 141, 143-44, 145, 146, 147, 148, 150, 151 *and n.*, 158, 159, 160, 162, 164, 165, 166, 169, 170, 171, 183, 184, 185, 186, 187, 188, 189, 190, 191, 194, 195, 198, 200, 201, 202, 203, 204, 205, 206, 208, 209, 211, 212, 213, 214, 216, 221, 222, 226, 228, 229, 231
Communist party opposition, *see* Independent Communist Labor League
Communist philosophy, 64-65, 81-82, 85, 88-91, 92, 104, 120, 121, 122, 123, 126, 127, 132, 171, 226, 229
Congress of Industrial Organizations, 3, 20, 47, 48, 51, 54, 59, 67, 76, 77, 83-84, 85-86, 87, 93, 95, 98, 99, 100, 104, 107, 108, 109, 131, 136, 137, 143, 149, 151, 154, 170, 186, 192, 193, 194, 203, 204, 205, 208, 216, 220, 226; Michigan State Convention (Lansing, 1938), 83, 84; Michigan State Convention (Bay City, 1940), 134; Michigan State Convention (Jackson, 1941), 144; National Convention (Atlantic City, 1946), 203; National Convention (Boston, 1947), 213; *see also* UAW-CIO
Congress of the United States, 185
Conway, Jack, 211
Coolidge, Calvin, 25
Cornelius, Phil, 211
Coughlin, Father Charles, 35, 94
Crane, Henry Hitt, 179-80

Daily Worker (New York), 87, 159, 190, 191-92
Daladier, Édouard, 131
Danbury Hatters, 181
Davis, Bill, 31
Democratic Front, The (Browder), 90
Democratic party, 37, 87, 170, 226; National Convention (Philadelphia, 1948), 226
Detroit and Wayne County Industrial Union Council, 76, 144
Detroit Common Council, 72, 80
Detroit Free Press, 34, 182-83
Detroit News, 34, 45, 65, 90, 151, 159, 161
Detroit Times, 34, 161
DeVito, John, 214
Dies Committee, 87-88, 90
Dillon, Francis, 189
Disney, Walt, 147
Ditzel (delegate to UAW-CIO Convention), 73
Dodge Brothers Corporation, 19; Main plant (Detroit), 57, 68
Douglas, Helen Gahagan, 182, 226
Dowell, Elmer, 61, 70
Dubinsky, David, 191, 192

Edwards, George, 72, 80
Eisenhower, Milton, 180
Elston, Emanuel, 119
Emspak, Julius, 183
Engels, Friedrich, 65
Erdman, David, 160, 201

Farm Aid, 131
Farm Equipment and Metal Workers Union, CIO, 205, 206-207, 208, 220-223
Farrington, Frank, 201
Federal Screw plant (Detroit), 80
Ferguson, Russ, 113
Fisher Body Corporation, Pontiac plant, 111; Plant One (Flint), 72, 73; Plant Twenty-one (Detroit), 109; Plant Twenty-three (Detroit), 110; Plant Thirty-seven (Detroit), 111
Fitzgerald, Albert, 183
Ford, Henry, 18
Ford Motor Company, 19, 26, 27, 35, 36, 100, 115, 139, 140, 141-43, 217; Highland Park plant, 169; Memphis assembly plant, 31; River Rouge plant, 35, 142-43, 212; hunger strike massacre (1932), 35-36; Willow Run Bomber plant, 140
Fort Shelby Hotel (Detroit), 97
Fountain, Andrew (author's grandfather), 4, 5-6, 8-9
Fountain, Clayton W., appointed associate editor of the *United Automobile Worker*, 200-201; arrested, 80-81; attends UAW summer school, 70-71; birth, 3-4; birth of first child, 33; birth of second child, 35-36; and Caterpillar Tractor plant, 220-23; Chairman of Convention Education Committee (1939), 103-104; and consumer cooperatives, 158; and 1946 Convention, 187-98; and 1947 Convention, 208-213; delegate to Michigan CIO Convention, 83-85; to UAW National Convention, 68, 71-75; difficulties with Communist party, 88-92; discharged by Chevrolet, 53-55; early life, 9-12; Educational Director of local union, 62; employed at Briggs, 26-29; at Chevrolet, 38-43; by hospitalization plan committee, 152-55; at Packard, 19-24; experiences in South, 31-32; family background, 4-9; first contact with Communists, 46-48; first contact with labor problems, 6-7; first experience as member of working class, 13-14; jailed, 78-79; joins Communist party, 62-64; joins UAW-CIO, 50; laid off, 41-43; leaves Communist party, 94; life during depression, 33-37; looks for work in Detroit, 17-19; and Herb McCreedy, 106; marries Edith Maples, 129; marries Lee Taylor, 29; member of New America, 118-129; opinion of communism, 81-82; of Democratic Convention of 1948, 226-27; of labor's role, 227-32; of strikes, 116-17, 185-86; of unions, 104, 115; and pacifism, 131-33; reading tastes, 44-46; returns to Chevrolet, 60; returns to Detroit, 32-33; and Walter Reuther, 157-58; 210-213, 218-20; runs for president of local, 150-52; schooling, 10-12; staff member of *Local 235 News*, 130-32
Fountain, Dolores Jean (author's daughter), 33, 34, 55, 58, 95, 129
Fountain, Edith Maples (author's second wife), 128, 129, 218-19, 226
Fountain, Edward (author's father), 4, 7-8
Fountain, Lee Taylor (author's first wife), 26, 29, 32, 33, 34, 38, 49, 58-59, 95
Fountain, Lily Sly (author's mother), 8, 13
Fountain, Mary Ann (author's grandmother), 4
Fountain, Ronald (author's son), 35, 95, 129
Fountain, William (author's uncle), 9
Fowler, Curtis, pseudonym of Clayton Fountain, 64
Frankensteen, Richard T., 68, 74, 85, 86, 142, 144-47, 156, 157, 160, 161-62, 163, 164, 165, 166, 169, 170, 183, 193, 197
Furay, Mort, 77

GM Picket, 110-11

Ganley, Nat, 135, 166
Garrison, Lloyd K., 180, 181
Gebert, Bill, 69, 75, 85
General Motors Corporation, 38, 41, 42, 49, 50, 51, 52, 55, 56-57, 59, 60, 101, 102, 106, 107-15, 131, 151, 152, 153, 172-86, 193, 204, 217-18, 223-24, 228; Flint plant, 43, 50-51, 54, 57, 58, 108; Saginaw plant, 108; strike of 1937 (sitdown), 172; strike of 1939, 106, 107-15, 172, 180; strike of 1945–46, 172-86, 187, 188, 189, 190, 191, 192-93; Ternstedt plant (Detroit), 68; *see also* Chevrolet Motor Division
Germer, Adolph, 84, 98
Gosser, Richard, 205, 213, 215
Greathouse, Pat, 221
Green, William, 163, 189
Griswold Building (Detroit), 95

Hall, Ed, 68, 74, 85, 98
Hanna, John, 179
Harbaugh, Joe, 60
Harding, Warren G., 25
Hathaway, Clarence, 87, 88
Hawes, Elizabeth, 160
Haynes, George, 30-31
Health for Victory Conference (Detroit, 1942), 154
Hemingway, Ernest, 44
Henderson, Leon, 179
Henson, Francis, 96
Hill, Joe, 219
Hillman, Sidney, 87, 95, 100
Hirohito, Emperor of Japan, 115
Hitler, Adolph, 35, 115, 133, 143, 148, 229
Hofmann Building (Detroit), 49, 56, 77
Hollenden Hotel (Cleveland), 97
Hoover, Herbert, 24, 25, 35
Howat, Alexander, 201
Humphrey, Hubert, 226
Hupp Motor Company, 84
Hutcheson, Bill, 208

"I Saw Police Terror" (Fountain), 80
Incentive pay system, 158-64
Independent Communist Labor League (Lovestoneites), 63, 94, 96-97
Industrial Workers of the World, 17 *and n.*, 61
International Association of Machinists, 220-23
International Ladies' Garment Workers Union, AFL, 191
International Union, United Automobile, Aircraft, and Agricultural Implement Workers of America, CIO, *see* United Automobile Workers, CIO
"Internationale, The," 47, 71

Janeway, Elizabeth, 182
Jeffrey, Mildred, 202
Jeffries, Edward J., 169

Kelsey-Hayes Wheel Company (Detroit), 68, 155
Knudsen, William S., 59, 108
Kowalski, Joe, 202
Kraus, Dorothy, 145-46
Kraus, Henry, 145
Krechevsky, I., 119
Krolik, Day, 119
Ku Klux Klan, 113

Labor, Department of, 178
"Labor in the Community" (Fountain), 126-27
Lacey, Michael F., 151, 215
Lake Carriers' Association, 15-16
Lee, Ed, 202
Lenin, Nikolai, 46, 65, 120, 121, 122, 132
Leonard, Richard T., 84, 85, 148, 156, 161, 162, 163, 164, 165, 170, 183, 189, 190, 197, 200, 201, 204, 205, 207, 208, 209, 212, 213, 214, 215
Levinson, Eddie, 110-11, 163, 169, 180
Levitt, William, 160, 202
Lewis, John L., 48, 59, 67, 74, 84, 85, 86-87, 94, 95, 98, 100, 131, 135-36, 137, 138, 191, 192, 201, 208, 209
Liberal party (New York), 171
Lindahl, James, 134-35

Livingston, John W., 197, 213, 215, 217, 221, 222
Local 1, UAW-CIO (Buchanan Steel), 196
Local 7, UAW-CIO, 99
Local 12, UAW-CIO (Toledo), 166
Local 45, UAW-CIO (Fisher), 188, 209, 214
Local 51, UAW-CIO (Plymouth), 144
Local 155, UAW-CIO, 166
Local 157, UAW-CIO, 78, 110, 112
Local 174, UAW-CIO, 72, 80, 84, 155
Local 190, UAW-CIO (Packard), 71, 134, 170
Local 205, UAW-CIO (Detroit), 214
Local 208, UAW-CIO (Bohn Aluminum), 70, 208
Local 212, UAW-CIO (Briggs), 197, 214
Local 227, UAW-CIO (DeSoto), 84
Local 235, UAW-CIO (Chevrolet Gear and Axle), 50, 61, 62, 64, 66, 68, 76, 95, 97, 98, 99, 109, 111, 112, 113, 130, 137, 138, 149, 150, 151, 215; Education Committee, 62
Local 235 News, 131
Local 365, UAW-CIO (Brewster Aircraft), 170
Local 400, UAW-CIO (Ford), 220 *n.*
Local 599, UAW-CIO (Buick), 170
Local 600, UAW-CIO (Ford), 169, 213
Local 662, UAW-CIO (Delco Remy), 170
Local 669, UAW-CIO, 195, 196
Local 683, UAW-CIO, 144, 145
Loewe, D. E., Company, 181
London, Jack, 10
Longshoremen's and Warehousemen's Union, 170
Lovestone, Jay, 91-92, 96, 97
Lovestoneites, *see* Independent Communist Labor League
Lowndes, Clay, 202
Lundeen, Pete, 12

McCreedy, Herb, 106, 119, 128, 135
McGill, John, 170
McNutt, Paul, 162
MacLeish, Archibald, 7
Mannix, John, 154
Maples, Edith, *see* Fountain, Edith Maples
Marrin, Blaine, 112
Marshall Plan, 213
Marshall, Secretary George C., 213
Martin, Homer, 61, 67, 68-69, 72-74, 75, 83, 84, 85, 86, 87, 95-99, 100, 101, 103, 106, 107, 108, 115, 145, 189, 191, 220
Martinson, Mary, 119, 171
Martinson, Willard, 119, 171
Marxism, *see* Communist philosophy
Masaryk, Jan, 218
Matles, James, 183
Matthews, Norman, 224
Mazey, Emil, 197, 213, 214-15
Merrelli, George, 99, 151, 152
Merrill, Russell, 68
Merritt, Walter Gordon, 181
Michener, Lew, 145, 147
Michigan Commonwealth Federation, 170-71
Michigan Hospital Service, 152, 153, 154
Michigan Medical Service, 153
Midwest Daily Record (Chicago), 80, 81, 150
Mine, Mill and Smelter Workers (CIO), 203
Montgomery, Donald, 157, 158, 175, 177, 204, 211
Montgomery Ward & Company, 94, 170
Morse, Senator Wayne, 182
Mortimer, Wyndham, 68, 69, 74, 85, 145-46
Munger, William, 96
Murphy, Edward, 214
Murphy, Frank, 32, 35, 59, 87, 88
Murray, Philip, 87, 95, 100, 143, 192-193, 194, 202, 203, 207, 208, 213, 214
Mussolini, Benito, 115, 229

National Committee to Aid the Families of GM Strikers, 182

National Defense Mediation Board, 144
National Educational Committee for a New Party, 171
National Labor Relations Act, 56
National Labor Relations Board, 106, 107, 143, 178, 220
National Negro Congress, 75
National Planning Association, 209
National Recovery Administration, 37, 38, 43
Negroes, and discrimination, 166, 227; and race riots, 167-69; and unions, 165-66
New America group, 106, 118-19, 120-129, 130, 131, 133, 135, 170, 171; labor conference (Chicago, 1939), 128; National Congress (Lorain, Ohio), 1936, 121; National Congress (Chicago, 1940), 133; National Policy Council, 129
New Deal, 65, 131, 137
New Masses, The, 47
New Republic, The, 49, 56
New York Post, 110
New York Times, The, 183
Nietzsche, Friedrich, 44
North American Aviation Company, 144, 146

Oakes, Grant, 206
Office of Price Administration, 177, 179, 185
Office of War Mobilization and Reconversion, 176
Oliver, William H., 169
Opoka, Joe, 61
O'Shea, Art, 183
Overstreet, Harry A., 179

Packard Motor Car Company, 19, 20, 21, 24, 26, 30, 37, 71, 217
Peace Policy for the American People, A (New America publication), 133
Pearson, Drew, 209
Pecord, Ollie, 164
People's Front Illusion (Lovestone), 91
Père Marquette Hotel (Peoria), 221
Perkins, Frances, 135
Petrie (Chevrolet plant superintendent), 52-53, 61
Pickert, Heinrich, 109, 112
Political Action Committee (PAC), CIO, 149
Pressman, Lee, 203
Program for National Defense, A (New America publication), 133
Progressive Caucus (UAW-CIO), 68, 72
Progressive party, 171
Public Lighting Commission (Detroit), 32
Purchasing Power for Prosperity (UAW-CIO publication), 175-76

Reading, Richard, 80, 109
Reid, Paul, 119
Renters and Consumers League, 77, 81
Republican party, 88
"Reuther Plan," 141
Reuther, Roy, 68, 69, 83, 85
Reuther, Victor G., 68, 69, 83, 84, 85, 164, 199, 200, 201, 202, 222
Reuther, Walter P., 57, 68, 69, 70, 74, 83, 85, 100, 101, 103, 106, 108, 114, 124, 141, 142, 148, 151, 152, 156, 157, 158, 159, 160, 161, 162, 163, 164, 165, 166-68, 169, 170, 172, 173, 174, 175, 177-78, 179, 180, 181, 182, 183, 184, 185-86, 187-88, 189, 190, 191, 192, 193, 194, 195, 196, 197, 199-200, 201, 202, 203, 204, 205, 207, 208-15, 216, 218-20, 224-25, 229-30
Richter, Irving, 160, 200
Robinson, Reid, 203
Rochdale cooperatives, 158
Roman Catholic Church, 194
Roosevelt, Eleanor, 182
Roosevelt I Knew, The (Perkins), 135
Roosevelt, President Franklin Delano, 37, 48, 65, 87, 134, 135, 136, 137, 138, 141, 144
Ruch, Walter, 183

Safran Printing Company (Detroit), 96
Salvation Army, 31
Sawicki, Joseph, 61, 69-70, 98
Sayler, Allen, 200
Scarlett, Bishop William, 179
Schultz, Melvin, 166
Seaman Body Company (Milwaukee), 68
Sexton, Brendan, 202
Sherman Anti-Trust Act, 181
Sherman Hotel (Chicago), 155
Sifton, Paul, 175
Sly, Alex (author's grandfather), 8
Smith, Alfred E., 24
Smith, Bill, 54
Smith-Connally Act, 149, 179
Snyder, John, 184, 185
Socialist party, 63, 69, 121, 126, 170, 194
Spanish Loyalists, 46, 47, 75, 130-31
Stacy, Walter P., 181
Stalin, Joseph, 46, 120, 163
Stalinists, 96, 97
Starling, Thomas, 195
Stevenson, Bill, 209
Stone, Eve, 96
Strachan, Stuart, 72
Strachey, John, 132
Sugar, Maurice, 160, 200

Taft, Senator Robert A., 209
Taft-Hartley Act, 212, 213, 220, 228
Tappes, Shelton, 169
Taylor, George (author's father-in-law), 32, 36
Tennessee Valley Authority, 230, 231
Thomas, Roland J., 68, 74, 85-86, 87, 99-100, 101, 103, 104, 106, 108, 141, 148, 156, 157, 164, 167, 169, 183, 184, 187, 188, 189, 190, 191, 192, 193-94, 195, 196, 197, 200, 203, 204, 205, 206, 207, 208, 209, 212, 213, 215
Tobin, Daniel J., 135
Toledo Union Journal, 164
Travis, Bob, 68, 69
Trotsky, Leon, 92
Trotskyites, 63, 94, 126, 155, 170, 171
Truman, President Harry S., 173, 176, 180, 181, 184, 185, 193, 232
Tucker, Edna, 10

Unemployment Compensation Commission, 110
United Automobile Worker (UAW-CIO publication), 48, 50, 87, 145, 200, 201, 210-11, 224-25, 229-30
United Automobile Workers, AFL, 220-23
United Automobile Workers, CIO, 18, 48, 49, 50, 59, 60, 61, 62, 67, 75, 80, 83, 84, 85, 86, 90, 95, 96-99, 100, 101, 102, 106, 107, 108, 110, 111, 114-115, 117, 132, 134, 137, 138, 139, 142, 143, 144, 145, 147, 148, 150, 151 *and n*, 154, 155, 157, 158, 160-61, 162, 163, 165, 169, 170, 172, 173, 176, 177, 178, 179, 180, 181, 182, 183, 184, 185, 189, 191, 192, 193, 194, 195, 196, 198, 199, 200, 201, 203, 204, 205, 206-207, 208-15, 216-17, 220-23, 229-31; Constitution Committee, 74, 75, 165, 166; Education Committee, 75, 103; Fair Practices and Anti-Discrimination Department, 169; General Motors Department, 57, 157, 173; International Executive Board, 69, 70, 72, 75, 96, 160-62, 165, 166, 167, 182, 196, 197, 198, 199, 205, 206, 208, 210, 211, 215, 218, 229; Medical Research Institute, 154, 155; 1936 Convention (South Bend), 67, 189; 1937 Convention (Milwaukee), 68, 71-75, 99, 103, 189; 1939 Convention (Cleveland), 99, 101, 103, 107, 108, 119, 155; 1940 Convention (St. Louis), 135, 137, 139; 1941 Convention (Buffalo), 139, 145, 147; 1942 Convention (Chicago), 154, 155-56; 1943 Convention (Buffalo), 162, 166, 169, 189; 1944 Convention (Grand Rapids), 147, 169, 170; 1946 Convention (Atlantic City), 169, 181, 187-97, 199, 202; 1947 Convention (Atlantic City), 196, 202, 204, 205, 207, 208-15, 216; *see also* Locals

United Mine Workers of America, 48, 61, 67, 84, 201, 209
United Public Workers of America, 77
United Radio, Electrical and Machine Workers of America, CIO, 183-84, 188, 204
United Steel Workers of America, CIO, 207
Unity Caucus (UAW-CIO), 68, 69, 70, 71, 72, 73, 74, 75, 83, 84, 85
Urban, Ralph, 71

Van Wagoner, Murray (Pat), 143
Victory–and After (Browder), 160
Vinson, Fred M., 176

Wage Earner (Association of Catholic Trade Unionists publication), 217
Wallace, Henry A., 171
War Labor Board, 56-57, 170, 176
War Manpower Commission, 162
Ward, Harry, 118, 121
Washburn, Lester, 96
Wayne County Labor's Non-Partisan League, 151
Weinberg, Nat, 204
Weinstone, William, 69, 75, 85
Wells, Walter, 68, 74, 85, 86
White Motor Company, 68
Williams, Fred, 70
Willkie, Wendell L., 136, 137, 192, 208
Wilson, Charles E., 173-74
Wing, Hugh, 119
Winn, Frank, 49, 50, 56, 174, 175, 182, 199, 200, 201, 211, 219
Wisconsin Land & Lumber Company, 7
Wishart, James, 160, 200
Woll, Matthew, 192
Works Council, *see* Chevrolet Employees' Association
Works Progress Administration, 131
World War I, 17 *n.*, 30, 61
World War II, 129, 132, 133, 139, 172, 229
Wright, Thomas, 119

Young Communist League, 46, 64, 146